Praise for
Preparing Your Daughter for Every Woman's Battle

"*Preparing Your Daughter for Every Woman's Battle* is a book for every mom of a young daughter. If you read this book and integrate it into your relationship with your daughter while she is young, you will lay a firm foundation for the potentially stressful and stormy days of adolescence. Too many moms wait until the storms come to discuss these important matters with their children. If you want your daughter to pursue purity, then don't wait to read this book!"

—SHARON HERSH, author of *"Mom, Everyone Else Does!"*

"When has there been a more urgent time for this newest addition to the series? Shannon Ethridge answers the questions anxious mothers are asking, and in a thorough, straight-on way. I wish I had this book when my daughter was growing up."

—NANCY RUE, author of the Lily and the Sophie series

"Being in ZOEgirl has taught me to be very careful about the things I endorse or represent, but this book is one that I can stand behind completely. *Preparing Your Daughter* is the perfect tool for opening up the lines of communication between you and your child on some very tough topics: love, lust, singleness, marriage, and all that's in-between. Beyond that, it will help your daughter discover first and foremost God's unconditional love for her as well as increase the likelihood that she will embark on a healthy, whole, and enjoyable journey toward feminine maturity."

—CHRISSY CONWAY of ZOEgirl

Readers Rave About
Preparing Your Daughter for Every Woman's Battle

"I just wanted to tell you what a great response I've had to doing a *Preparing Your Daughter for Every Woman's Battle* class with moms and daughters. Many of them have commented they wish there had been something like your book when we were growing up. Thanks so much for writing this book. I'm really seeing how I'm not the only one in my community who feels this is such a strong and urgent need with our younger generation. God bless you!" —Melissa

"Thank you for your courage, strength, and love for Christ and for others. I am a Christian father who had been suffering for years with drug addictions, sexual immorality, and many internal issues. I have two wonderful, beautiful Christian daughters, ages thirteen and sixteen. I prayed to Jesus for help, strength, and guidance in raising them as a single parent. He answered me loud and clear when I heard a Christian radio talk show featuring your book. Christ touched me through your testimony. Thank you for your courage to share your life and wisdom. I am sharing all you have to offer with my daughters to strengthen them for their future. I want to give your books, DVDs, and tapes to every woman I know. You will never really know the blessing and answer to my prayers you have been. God bless!" —Robert

"I am twenty-nine and a mother of a ten-year-old girl. We are currently reading your book, and I really love it! It's been a great conversation (and confession) starter. It has helped me deal with my past sexual abuse, giving me understanding of the things I was still bringing into my relationship with my husband. I feel like I've been freed and empowered. I have the tools to guide my daughter and other young women. I appreciate the honesty with which you talk about your past. It reminds me of how God restores our lives so that we can glorify Him and at the same time help restore other lives." —R.M.

"*Thank you* for your message and your ministry! I heard you speak in Toronto, and I shed tears when I logged on to your Web site. To a divorced father of a ten-year-old daughter, this is the best, most valuable ministry I've ever encountered. I am planning to use your books and DVDs to help guide her into womanhood. I'm also going to share them with my girlfriend who has been raped and abused, as I sense these materials could be the answer to years of prayer for her. Thank you, thank you, thank you!" —Al

"I was reading your book with my twelve-year-old daughter and felt so convicted. How could I help my girls when I have struggled with sexual integrity my whole life? The fantasies, the flirting, the self-gratification, the desire to be the 'bad girl' were tormenting me, yet it felt so good at the same time. I was about to just give up and tell my wonderful husband of eleven years that I couldn't resist the temptation to have an affair any longer. (I was definitely mistaking intensity for intimacy.) I didn't understand why I was struggling with this problem/disease for all these years and couldn't find anything that really helped—until *Every Woman's Battle*. Now I am ready to fall in love with Jesus instead! Your book was right on time and almost like you wrote it just for me! I thank you from the bottom of my heart, for your book has saved my life, marriage, and family. I plan on using it in a study at our church so I can bring God's healing to other women, and I've already got so many moms reading *Preparing Your Daughter for Every Woman's Battle* that we're going to start a weekly study group with our girls. Hopefully we can give them the big dose of preventative medicine that many of us wish our moms could've given us!" —Kat

Foreword by Bethany Dillon

SHANNON ETHRIDGE

with Introduction by

STEPHEN ARTERBURN

Preparing Your Daughter for Every Woman's Battle

Creative Conversations about
Sexual and Emotional Integrity

WATERBROOK
PRESS

PREPARING YOUR DAUGHTER FOR EVERY WOMAN'S BATTLE

All Scripture quotations, unless otherwise indicated, are taken from the Holy Bible, New International Version®. NIV®. Copyright © 1973, 1978, 1984 by International Bible Society. Used by permission of Zondervan Publishing House. All rights reserved. Scripture quotations marked (MSG) are taken from The Message by Eugene H. Peterson. Copyright © 1993, 1994, 1995, 1996, 2000, 2001, 2002. Used by permission of NavPress Publishing Group. All rights reserved. Scripture quotations marked (NLT) are taken from the Holy Bible, New Living Translation, copyright © 1996. Used by permission of Tyndale House Publishers Inc., Wheaton, Illinois 60189. All rights reserved.

Details in some anecdotes and stories have been changed to protect the identities of the persons involved.

Trade Paperback ISBN 978-0-307-45858-2
eBook ISBN 978-0-307-55123-8

Copyright © 2005, 2010, by Shannon Ethridge

Published in the United States by WaterBrook, an imprint of the Crown Publishing Group, a division of Penguin Random House LLC, New York.

WATERBROOK® and its deer colophon are registered trademarks of Penguin Random House LLC.

Library of Congress Cataloging-in-Publication Data
Ethridge, Shannon.
    Preparing your daughter for every woman's battle / Shannon Ethridge.— 1st ed.
        p. cm.
    Includes bibliographical references.
    1. Sex—Religious aspects—Christianity. 2. Sex instruction for girls—Religious aspects—Christianity.
3. Child rearing—Religious aspects—Christianity. I. Title.
    BT708.E85 2005
    241'.66'08352—dc22

                                                                            2005002223

Printed in the United States of America
2016

10 9 8 7 6

SPECIAL SALES
Most WaterBrook Multnomah books are available at special quantity discounts when purchased in bulk by corporations, organizations, and special-interest groups. Custom imprinting or excerpting can also be done to fit special needs. For information, please e-mail specialmarketscms@penguinrandomhouse.com or call 1-800-603-7051.

To all of God's princesses,
especially the one who will someday
call herself Mrs. Matthew Thomas Ethridge.

contents

Growing up, I remember my mom saying to me that "monsters live in the dark." Whether it was being jealous of someone, or having a fear of something, or even being embarrassed about something I'd thought or done, she would say that to me. This has proven true over and over in my life! The more I bottle things up inside, and the more I try to hide what's really going on, the bigger the issue gets. It sounds so simple, doesn't it? But in the moment, whatever your monster is, all you know is (a) it's big, (b) it's scary, and (c) it's more than likely shameful—because it's in the dark. You can't imagine being freed from it and not living in fear of it anymore! Why? Because it means you'd have to acknowledge it, and the pit-feeling you get in your stomach when you think about that makes it feel even more impossible.

Both of my parents are social workers. Basically that means that we all talked a whole lot and explained our feelings until we were blue in the face. Even if you were trying to hide your feelings, either parent could read you like an open book. Everything was talked about—and I mean *everything*. So it's a given that "the talk" wasn't really taboo in our house. I remember the day I had the talk with Mom. She had a book called *God's Good Gift* (which was perfect for my eight-year-old heart), and we went through it together. I'd been coming home from school and sharing about dirty things the boys were saying about other girls, and I think that may have spurred her on in answering all the big questions before I even thought to ask them. And yes, as time went on, there were certain questions that didn't get answers right away—"I'll tell you when you're older, honey"—but for the most part, there wasn't a subject too awkward to bring up. Boy, did I ever have questions! It didn't take very long for this subject to pique my curiosity. And my mom, being the wise woman of God she is, didn't even flinch. She answered honestly.

Then, she would ask questions (I love this part) with no guilt-trip. My parents aren't perfect people; they're just like anyone else, but I am so grateful for their openness and candor when it came to the subject of sex.

I was on a girls-only cruise with Shannon Ethridge this past spring. A few Christian artists and authors were performing throughout the cruise, and I was so excited when I heard Shannon was coming! I've used her books as a resource in my own life and have had the honor of meeting her and getting to talk with her a few times. So, the night she was speaking at the main session, you better believe I was there! I loved every minute of her talk: She was honest, funny, relatable. But the thing I loved most was how the truth was spoken. She didn't tiptoe around topics that might be a bit uncomfortable for a group of ladies ranging in age from ten to sixty. Instead she approached the issue of sexual integrity with such clarity and courage that the concert hall suddenly felt like a living room. Things that can weigh like a ton of bricks on someone's heart and mind suddenly felt lighter; everyone's monster in the room finally had some light shed on it.

As a young woman, I'm grateful for Shannon's brave approach. Jesus handled uncomfortable and sometimes confrontational things the same way—in truth and love. I think we all need to hear that we're not the only ones struggling, that we aren't isolated cases of a mess-up, far beyond healing or redemption. The truth is liberating, but it takes someone to say it.

What could be a more powerful example of this than a mother speaking the truth to her daughter? I know there isn't for me. I needed someone I trusted to field my questions, and I needed to know that I was going to be loved no matter what I was dealing with. Whether you're a mother who sees some monsters in your daughter's closet and you want to be a voice of truth, or if you're thinking of some things tucked away in the shadows of your own heart, truth sets us free. When light is shed on something, it no longer holds power over us in its mystery.

I believe with all my heart that this book will be just that for you—a resource of needed honesty in your daughter's journey. I'm so grateful to have had a mom who provided that for me, and now as a married woman, I look back and see all the things I was spared from simply because I knew they wouldn't satisfy my soul.

What I love about Shannon, much like my own mother, is that while she's tackling the difficult subjects in a young woman's life, she is constantly pointing to the One who does satisfy our souls' every longing: Jesus. So don't wait. Dive into this book today, free yourself and your daughter from the monsters in the dark, and banish her fears forever!

—BETHANY DILLON

acknowledgments

Lord Jesus—thank you for helping me overcome my personal battles and for granting me such wonderful opportunities to lead others to victory.

Greg—thank you for being my devoted partner in preparing our children to have healthy relationships. Next to my salvation, our marriage is my greatest gift in life.

Erin and Matthew—my passion for writing this book stems from my hope for your incredible future. Thank you for inspiring me and cheering me on. I love being your mom so very much.

Friends, family, and colleagues at Teen Mania Ministries, Mercy Ships International, and Garden Valley Bible Church—thank you for your faithful prayers and support through the years. Mom and Pop, I especially appreciate the immeasurable time and energy you've invested in prayer on my behalf.

KVNE radio station and the Scroll Christian Bookstore in Tyler—I appreciate your enthusiasm for this series and all you've done to promote it throughout the East Texas area. Tricia Anderson, I love you, girl, and I look forward to recording many more "shows" with you! Dan Bolin, thank you for the valuable contributions you made to this book with your research and for sharing my vision for inspiring dads and daughters to connect more intimately. Corina Kojak, I also appreciate your helpful research assistance.

The Every Man team—Stephen Arterburn, Fred and Brenda Stoeker, Mike Yorkey, and Kenny Luck—I stand in awe of what God is doing through our collaborative efforts. I pray that each book in the series continues to transform lives and marriages for His glory.

The entire WaterBrook Press team—I can't thank you enough for your partnership in the Every Woman projects. Your belief in me and in these messages is appreciated far more than words could express. May God bless you richly for the hours you invest in His service. Alice Crider, I especially appreciate your creative contributions to this manuscript.

Liz Heaney—I can't imagine an editor more committed to excellence than you, girlfriend, and I consider it such a tremendous privilege to be one of "Liz's authors." The way you can slice and dice a rough manuscript with such finesse and turn it into a work of art amazes me. You've taught me well, and I thank you.

Pamela McClure and Jana Muntsinger—thank you for giving these books such a tremendous jump-start with your publicity efforts. Ben Laurro, I also appreciate your helping us spread the word to media outlets far and wide.

Moms and daughters who gave this book its first "trial run"—Coralie and Madeline in Australia; Mimi and Jasmine in Honduras; Beth and Chelsea, Veronica and Jessica in Pennsylvania; Lori and Mary in South Texas; and Holly and Hannah in East Texas. Thank you for being great guinea pigs.

Finally, I thank all the readers of the Every Man and Every Woman series for their thirst for righteousness and passionate pursuit of sexual integrity. Your encouraging responses give us great confidence to press on.

BOOK I

for parents

My good friend phoned me in tears. A few hours before, his fourteen-year-old daughter had just broken his heart. She was his pride and joy, and he had invested many hours away from his job to be there for her. He loved her with all his heart, but his heart was in tatters. Earlier that evening he had gone to pick her up from a birthday party. After clearing himself with the guard at the security gate, he followed the directions and pulled into the private driveway of his daughter's friend. The house was well lit and no blinds hung from the windows. As he got out, he could see the kids, including his daughter, run through the house from room to room. It looked like they were having great, innocent fun.

But as he walked up to the front door, he could see plainly what the kids were doing. They were playing some type of tag, and the bed was obviously home base. He watched as his daughter ran into the room and jumped on the bed, safe from whomever was "it." Then he watched the young boy she liked jump on the bed, followed by six others. They all laughed and poked at each other, then ran into the next room. But not all of the kids ran. His daughter and the boy stayed back on the bed after the others had left. He watched as his daughter lay back and allowed the boy to kiss her, mouth open and tongue engaged. Then he saw the boy's hand on her stomach, rubbing her, petting her as he kissed her with great force. And there she lay, allowing him to have her, looking very aware of what he was doing.

My friend raced to the front door and banged on it in desperation to break up the pair. All he could say was, "Let's go." The whole ride home he was speechless, not wanting to make something bad even worse.

He called me because he felt like a failure and did not know what to do. He had been planning to talk with her about how boys think and what they want to do and why, but he had put it off. He thought he had time to do it before his daughter started dating. He had no idea an innocent birthday party would be an opportunity for passionate kisses on a bed. I comforted him and guided him in confronting her and calling the boy's father. I reminded him that God had given him a gift of knowing the reality of his daughter's life rather than imagining her continued innocence. It might be easier to think of her as innocent, but it was not who she had become. Reality hit this father hard, but he had a chance to respond with love and strength and make the best of what had happened. Though he felt he had failed his daughter, he was determined to lead her in the way that she should go.

Most likely you have picked up this book to avoid what happened to my friend. You want to equip your daughter with truth and to motivate her to do the right thing when confronted with the opportunity to do otherwise. What you have in your hand is the best tool I've ever seen to do just that. I wish it had been around when my own daughter was nine or ten. When she was that age, we had devotions every morning before school. I did my best to prepare her for the coming adolescent years, but there was nothing I found that handled sex in a relevant, non-shaming, biblically sound manner. This book does. Shannon has taken her own experiences growing up and combined those with how she raised her own daughter to give all of us parents a great tool in equipping and protecting our little girls.

This book will help your daughter celebrate her coming adolescence and womanhood. It won't scare her or provoke her to eat too much or too little in an effort to avoid facing the realities ahead. It will guide her in making her own decisions and setting her own boundaries that will honor God, herself, and your family. It may save her life, and I know it will save her from great heartache and sorrow if she follows the path Shannon presents here.

You can be certain that your daughter is talking about sex with her friends by the time she is eleven years old. For some it is much earlier. If you are not talking to her about sex, it will cause a disconnection between the two of you. But if you start early, your interaction could form a strong bond as she looks to you and not to the street for truth. You do not want to wait until she is a teenager to begin to prepare her. You want to get ahead of the temptations and lay a foundation that is deep and solid. To paraphrase Proverbs 4:7-8, there is nothing more valuable than wisdom. So find it and give it to your daughter. It might cost you all you have, but above all help your daughter understand the realities of life. Help her appreciate

God's truth and embrace that truth, and she will honor you, your God, and your family." This book will give your daughter the wisdom she needs to make wise choices regarding her sexuality. You do not want to leave this to her school or even to Sunday school. You must lead the way to truth.

Children must learn to establish boundaries. They must come to see that their skin is a God-given boundary. Children need to honor that boundary and expect that others, too, will honor it—and they need to run away when others don't. This book will help you communicate that foundational truth to your daughter. It will help her see that she has the power to protect herself and give her the confidence to do so. It will help her appreciate that she is "fearfully and wonderfully made" and help explain some of the wonder that is within her.

There is one caution I want to give you before you begin: there is no guarantee your daughter will stay pure once you have read this to her and with her. She still has a mind of her own. There is no formula that always ends in successful parenting because we do not have control of our children. Having said that, I want to encourage you to do the best you can. Your investment of time and truth in her will help her find her purpose and live to fulfill it. May God richly bless you as you work to raise a wise and mature young woman.

—STEPHEN ARTERBURN

"pick me! pick me!"

Men and women who have lived wisely and well will shine brilliantly,
like the cloudless, star-strewn night skies. And those who put others
on the right path to life will glow like stars forever.

DANIEL 12:3, MSG

If you ever watched the sitcom *Welcome Back, Kotter,* a situation comedy from the seventies, you'll recall the nerdy Arnold Horshack. He was the short, curly headed "sweathog" who responded to Mr. Kotter's questions by impulsively waving his arm in the air yelling, "Ooh! Ooh! Pick me! Pick me!" If I remember correctly, Mr. Kotter would usually succumb to Arnold's plea and call on him to answer the question because he was such an eager student (and because no one else in the class seemed to know much!).

Wouldn't it be great if our kids always called on *us,* their parents, for answers to their questions about sexuality because they knew we were not only willing but *eager* to answer? And because they felt like no one else knew as much about the topic as Mom and Dad? Does your daughter see a "Pick me! Pick me!" attitude in you, or does she see an "I can't believe you asked that question!" attitude?

When your daughter is ready to talk about sex, who will she go to? Will she feel free to come to you?

RESEARCH PROVES YOU HOLD THE KEY

Many studies have been conducted on the value of parent-directed sex education. Consider these findings:

- Frequent sex-education talks between parent and child can greatly improve family communication and strengthen family bonds. When sexual issues can be discussed naturally and with openness and honesty, the anxiety and awkwardness that usually accompanies the topic can be reduced or perhaps even eliminated. When children can ask their parents anything about sexuality and use whatever words they need to use to convey their questions, it fosters an atmosphere of trust and respect, which can help parents and teens discuss other sensitive issues as well.[1]

- Both children and parents consistently report that they want parents to be the primary source of sexuality education. When parents are the main source of sex education, children are less likely to be sexually active, they positively identify with parents' traditional sexual values, their first sexual experiences occur at a later age, and the probability of promiscuity is lowered.[2]

- When parents talk to and affirm the value of their children, young people are more likely to develop positive, healthy attitudes about themselves. This is also true when the subject is sex. Research shows that positive communication between parents and their children can help young people establish individual values and make healthy decisions.[3]

While most parents *say* they want to be the ones their children come to, this rarely happens.

WHO'S AT THE TOP OF HER LIST?

Various studies have documented a significant difference between the frequency with which parents said they *should be* primary in providing this information and the frequency with which they reported they actually *were* the primary resources. In a survey of more than one hundred thousand parents, 96 percent felt that children should learn about sex from their parents. Yet when asked from whom they thought children actually received information about sex, only 24 percent of the respondents felt it was parents.[4]

Sadly, most kids don't place their parents very high on their lists of askable adults. If that's the case, then who is at the top of the list? Teens most often report that their primary source of sexual information is their peers. But this presents three major problems: (a) peers are notorious for being sources of sexual misinformation, (b) it is often very difficult to dispel the sexual myths that are pervasive among adolescents, and (c) peers will likely promote the adoption of sexual values that are contrary to parental values, thus promoting family conflict.[5]

So what can a parent do? How can we ensure that we are the ones our kids turn to when they have questions about sexual issues? Part of the answer lies, I believe, in understanding the reasons why kids don't come to their parents when they have questions about sex.

WHY KIDS DON'T TALK WITH THEIR PARENTS ABOUT SEX

Over the past decade, I've talked with kids about why this is so. Here are the three reasons I hear most often, along with my response about what parents can do to prevent their own kids from feeling this way.

1. It's Just Not Talked About in Our House

Obviously if we as parents don't bring up the topic, our kids are not about to. As adults, we set the pace and tone for what conversation topics are acceptable in our homes and what topics are taboo. If your daughter has never asked you any questions about sex, this could either mean that she has not thought about sex at all yet (which is unlikely) or that she doesn't feel comfortable bringing it up. Even if sex is considered an off-limits topic in her mind, you can still establish your home as a safe haven for such discussions by using the second section of this book with her (and *Preparing Your Son for Every Man's Battle* with your son).

2. I'd Never Ask My Parents About Sex Because They'd Freak Out and Suspect I Wanted to Do It or That I'm Already Having Sex When I'm Not

Freaking out over curious questions definitely disqualifies us from the "Pick me!" parent category. If we can accept that kids have a natural curiosity about sex and sexual issues, we can calmly discuss our daughters' questions without going into panic mode. When she brings up the subject, whether it's about her own questions or about what she's observed in someone else's life, don't be too quick to comment. Ask questions. Ask how she feels about what she's seen or heard. Once you've listened to her opinions, she'll be more open to receiving yours.

3. My Parents Don't Have Sex, so They Probably Don't Know Much More Than I Do

Do a double take at that statement if you need to, but believe it. Many young people tell me that their parents don't have sex. Of course, I chuckle under my breath and ask, "How do you think you got here?" Teens usually see the humor in this and go along by saying, "Well, okay, they've had sex three times because I do have a brother and a sister, but other than that, they *don't* have sex!" Then I get serious and ask, "What gives you that impression?" Most respond, "They don't even go on dates or hold hands or kiss! What makes you think they have sex?" Ouch.

We can learn a significant lesson from what our kids say about our marriages. Children associate sex with romance and affection, and if they are not seeing that in the living room or the kitchen between Mom and Dad, they can't imagine that anything would be going on in the bedroom. I recommend that you intentionally model tenderness and affection in healthy, appropriate ways in front of your daughter so she grows up knowing marriage is a relationship she can look forward to with hand-holding, kissing, sex, and all. (We'll talk about this in chapter 3 of book 2 for parents and daughters.)

In light of that last comment, you may wonder, *What gives kids these impressions?* I have a couple of theories.

How Did We Get Here?

First of all, remember that most kids learn about sex from their peers. This hasn't always been the case. Decades ago families were living all together in one-room cabins where kids were separated from their parents' sexual relationship only by a curtain or perhaps a makeshift wall. But today we have multiple walls and doors shielding our children from any knowledge whatsoever of our private activities. Kids also lived on farms where animals were having sex and giving birth right before their eyes. Most children knew all about sex and reproduction before they could learn to read and write.

Their other primary source of information about sex comes from the media, which glamorizes premarital sex and makes a mockery out of fidelity in marriage.

If kids grow up watching much television at all, they quickly get the impression that good sex is only to be had between young, beautiful, single people. Many shows portray married couples as bored or so consumed with work and kids that passionate moments are few and far between. I've had many young people tell me they aren't sure if they want to get married because they fear their sex lives will shrivel up to nothing, like most married couples' sex lives. Ouch again.

We've got to turn the tide, not just in our culture, but in our own children's minds. We must be the first ones to educate our children about sex, letting them know it's a pleasurable part of a healthy marriage, before anyone else instills values contrary to those we as Christian parents hold dear.

The Other Side of the Story

Unfortunately, some parents are hesitant or even afraid to discuss sexual issues with their children. Why? Here are the most common reasons I hear from parents, along with my responses:

My Child Is Too Young for This Discussion

Traditionally, many parents have attempted to seize an isolated opportunity to have "the talk" about "the birds and the bees" prior to their child's first dating experience. This talk is usually just a plumbing lesson about where babies came from so premarital pregnancy can be avoided. Then perhaps the same-sex parent would fulfill the expectation of giving a more in-depth talk about how to have sex just before the wedding night.

I propose that if this is still our approach to sex education with our children, we may as well be asking *them* questions, because they'll know almost as much about sex (if not more) than we do if we wait that long! Consider the following passage from a textbook titled *Human Sexuality:*

> Determining the appropriate age for discussions about sexuality can be
> problematic for many parents. One study found that when asked about the
> age at which children should learn about sexual topics, parents of young
> children inevitably suggest an age later than their own child's present age.

In other words, when it comes to sex, whatever age their child is, it's not old enough. Those parents who wait until their child reaches puberty to have the "big talk" about sex will probably find that they are repeating information that their child already knows.[6]

In case you didn't catch the author's recommendation, allow me to reiterate. As parents, we need to be talking with our children about sexuality even *before* puberty! Consider these statistics:

- Twenty percent of girls and 30 percent of boys have sex by age fifteen.[7]
- More than 50 percent of seventeen-year-olds have had intercourse.[8]
- Eighty percent of teens have had intercourse by age nineteen.[9]
- Almost one million teen pregnancies occur each year in the United States. Thirteen percent of all births in the United States are to teenage mothers, making the U.S. teen-pregnancy rate one of the highest in the developed world. About 78 percent of teenage pregnancies are unintended, and 22 percent are intentional.[10]
- Of the forty thousand new cases of HIV each year, half of those diagnosed are younger than twenty-five years of age.[11]

I realize these findings reflect the lifestyles of older teens, not prepubescent girls. However, I believe one of the biggest contributing problems to our teen pregnancy and sexually transmitted disease epidemic is that few abstinence programs address the early adolescent age group.[12] Most pregnancy-prevention programs target adolescents between the ages of thirteen and seventeen (grades eight to twelve). I believe that's too late, as many of these young people have already begun to engage in behaviors that endanger their health and put them at risk for adolescent pregnancy. Could these kids have made healthier choices if they had experienced quality sex education much earlier in life? I believe the answer is yes, most of them could have. It may be too late for them, but hopefully it's not too late for your daughter. Even if you're thinking you might be a little late getting started, don't panic. There's no time like the present to begin these creative conversations that you'll be reading together in the second section of the book.

Many experts recommend that sex-education programs begin between the ages of eight and fourteen, preferably at the younger ages on the continuum, in order to maximize the opportunity of reaching early adolescents when they are more open to parental influence. As parents, we need to embrace the research that supports the fact that communication about sexuality *will not* increase the chances that our children will engage in sex.[13]

I Don't Want to Rob My Child of Her Sexual Innocence with Too Much Information

Consider for a moment the huge difference between innocence and ignorance. One is a state of heart, the other a state of mind. Educating her mind about this wonderful gift that God has given her doesn't remove the innocence that is in her heart, nor will healthy knowledge tarnish her sexual purity. If anything, her heart will be all the more pure because she will have a better understanding of God's plan for her sexuality. Scripture says we are to be shrewd as snakes *and* innocent as doves (see Matthew 10:16), meaning we can be *both* knowledgeable *and* pure at the same time.

On the flip side, a lack of knowledge does not equate to innocence, but rather ignorance. I know many young people who are ignorant of sexual matters yet guilty of crossing many sexual boundaries. The Bible says it's a lack of knowledge that destroys people (see Hosea 4:6), and I believe that when it comes to sex, this is especially so.

Children deserve honest, age-appropriate answers as soon as they are old enough to begin asking questions such as:

- "Where do babies come from?"
- "How do they get in their mommy's tummy?
- "How do they come out?"
- "Why don't I have a penis like my baby brother?"

Talking About Sex with My Child May Awaken Her Sexual Desires

Keeping your daughter in the dark won't protect her from having sexual struggles of her own. If anything, ignorance and confusion will only exacerbate these issues. We must remember that humanity and sexuality are inseparable. While parents may choose to avoid specific details (sexual positions, frequency, and so on) we need to cover enough information to give our children a strong foundation of sexual understanding. I believe a lack of healthy information drives children to unhealthy sexual behaviors, such as inappropriate voyeurism, habitual masturbation, seduction, pornography, and promiscuity.

Be careful not to confuse being "sexual" with being "sexually active." Just because your daughter isn't sexually active doesn't mean she is not a sexual being. Sexual desires are eventually awakened in all human beings, whether or not anyone ever talks to them about sex. We aren't created with an "on" switch that gets flipped when we have our first conversation about sexual issues. We are born with an instinctual curiosity about our own bodies and the bodies of others, both male and female. That is why toddlers' hands frequently venture into their diapers and why "playing doctor" is a common childhood game. By nature children are curious and want answers to their unspoken questions about sexuality. If parents aren't providing these answers, our children may go searching for them in dangerous ways.

I've Tried, but My Child Doesn't Want to Talk with Me About Sex

Although children may not beg their parents to talk about this topic, nearly seven out of ten teens (69 percent) agree it would be easier for them to postpone sexual activity and avoid teen pregnancy if they were able to have more open, honest conversations about sex with their parents. The same percentage also say that they *are* ready to listen to things that parents thought they were *not* ready to hear.[14]

So even if you don't get direct questions from your daughter, don't mistakenly think that she isn't interested in what you have to say. Children may mask this interest out of embarrassment, perhaps even going to the extent of placing their hands over their ears and singing a silly song such as "Watermelon, cantaloupe! Watermelon, cantaloupe!" to drown out any parental attempt at candid conversation. What children are really saying by such overt behavior is, *I'm really embarrassed about this conversation because it just feels awkward to me!*

We can overcome this obstacle by making such conversations much more commonplace, allowing familiarity to develop and a sense of comfort to evolve slowly and naturally. You won't get this level of comfort by shutting up and assuming that it's just not the right time to talk about sexual issues yet. Any time a parent brings up the topic of sex after a long period of silence, it's likely going to feel awkward and therefore embarrassing. That's why frequent discussions are key to keeping the ice broken between parent and child about this sensitive topic.

My Child's School Has a Great Sex-Education Program;
I'll Just Let Them Handle It

Some parents rely on the schools to educate their children through a health or sex-education class because they don't feel comfortable talking about these issues. But it's important that parents view sex education in schools as merely supplemental to parental efforts. While many schools teach mechanics and safety, they likely over-look Christian sexual values. If your child's school has a program that educates both parents and children simultaneously, this is a preferred model over taking the sex education out of the family altogether, but your participation is still vital in such programs. In one study, adolescents who completed program-related assign-ments with their parents reported that they communicated more often with their parents about sexual issues, expressed stronger beliefs supporting abstinence, and had firmer intentions to remain abstinent than others who did not have parental involvement in the program.[15]

Other parents may rely on the church's youth pastor to instill Christian sexual values, but that's not very effective either. Why? Just think of the plethora of topics that your youth pastor is expected to cover with your church's teens—salvation, discipleship, evangelism, Old Testament history, New Testament principles, mis-sions, and stewardship, along with a boatload of other social issues such as drink-ing, smoking, drugs, and so on. How much time can actually be devoted to the topic of sexuality?

Also consider who your child spends more time with. How much time does she spend at church? Two or three hours each week at best. How much time does she spend in a health teacher's classroom? At the most one hour per day a few days each week for up to one year, and think of all the topics they have to cover in that short amount of time. But how much time does your child spend at home? The vast majority of it. And how much time do you have with your child? At least eighteen years. Are you getting the picture? As parents, we hold the key to giving our children the sex education they really need. Not peers. Not schools. Not churches. Parents.

I Don't Want to Answer My Child's Questions About My Own Sexual Choices
This is a valid concern for many parents. Who of us wants to confess our sexual struggles to our own children, especially if our lives are no examples for them to follow? If you have sexual skeletons in your closet, it may help to know that your daughter most likely isn't going to ask you blunt, personal questions. Most children have a sense of what's okay and not okay to ask a person, so don't feel that you can't begin talking to them about sexual issues until they are ready to hear all about your past failures.

With that said, I want to encourage you to examine your past failures in a different light. I think we can use these instances where we failed to guard our own minds, hearts, and bodies from sexual compromise to actually help our children. They don't need us to be "rocks" as much as they need us to be real. I'm not saying we shouldn't be strong and set good examples whenever possible, but when we communicate openly and honestly about the struggles we faced at their age, we are telling them, "I know where you're at, and I remember how it feels to be there!" We assure them that they are not alone in these struggles and that sexual temptations are common to all people, including moms, dads, and young daughters. Our daughters need to know we can give them the grace to be human, that God's mercy is unending, and that our love for them is unconditional. Finally, by being open about our experiences, we are setting the stage for them to feel comfortable coming to us with their questions, concerns, and personal struggles. Isn't that the goal?

A word of caution: keep in mind that personal confessions need to come at an appropriate season in your daughter's life and should only be revealed for her benefit. Several months ago a woman e-mailed me to ask, "Do you think it's okay if I want to confess to my daughter that I had an abortion when I was a teenager?" I asked her how old her daughter was and what was motivating her desire to bring this out into the open. If she had said, "She's eight and I just want to get it off my chest!" I would have encouraged this mom to refrain from such a confession because her motivation would have been selfish and her child would more than likely not have been mature enough to handle that kind of information. However, this mother responded, "My daughter is seventeen and dating a boy very seriously. I just want her to understand that unplanned pregnancy can happen to anyone so that she'll make wise choices and save sex until marriage." This mom was ready to humble herself for the sake of saving her daughter from future pain. I encouraged her to go with her conscience, and that if she felt confessing her abortion would ultimately benefit her daughter more than keeping it from her, such would be an honorable thing to do.

Just in case you are still wondering whether you should be talking with your eight- or nine-year-old about sex, let me tell you why my husband and I are so glad that we talked to our kids about sex at an early age.

OUR OWN SIGH OF RELIEF

A few months before Erin started kindergarten, I heard Dr. James Dobson say on the radio that before kids go off to public schools, they need to know the truth about where babies actually come from. I talked with my husband, Greg, and we both agreed that we wanted to put a filter in Erin's mind through which all sexual talk could be sifted and sorted into categories of *fact* or *fiction,* and *appropriate* or *inappropriate.* So we told her as much as we felt she could handle at her age.

Within the first few weeks of school, Erin told me that a little boy pulled down his pants on the playground and was showing his penis to everyone. I asked, "Honey, what did you do when Jack did that?" She replied, "Mommy, I turned away. Everyone else was looking, but I knew what Jack was doing was wrong, so I didn't look." *Whew!* Even though I would not have punished her for looking out of curiosity, I was glad Erin chose to look away even when I wasn't there to govern her behavior.

Less than a year later, another more serious situation came up. Erin came home from first grade, obviously bothered by something. Later that evening we were reading in the book of Genesis and came across the story of how Lot's daughters lay with their father to get pregnant by him. After I finished that story and explained why it is wrong for relatives to be sexual with one another, Erin asked if she could tell me a secret. She said that during recess, a friend whispered in her ear, "Sometimes I go in the closet with my cousin, and he makes me put his weenie in my mouth." My heart sank, but I knew I couldn't ignore the situation. I asked, "Erin, if we invite your friend over, would it be okay with you if I talked to her about this?" Erin said she wished that I would.

A few days later, Molly came over. I struck up a conversation about how I was a youth pastor and that sometimes young people have secrets they need to share with adults. I assured her that if she had a secret, I was someone she could talk to about it. Erin told Molly she had let me in on her secret. At first, of course, she was embarrassed. But I explained that what her eleven-year-old cousin was forcing her to do was wrong, and that her mother would really want to know. Molly replied, "Oh, I could *never* tell my mama! But Mrs. Ethridge...*you* could." Days later I was explaining to this mother that her nephew was sexually abusing her daughter. She was horrified but admitted she had been suspicious. With a difficult family meeting at her house with her sister and nephew, the situation was remedied.

How would Erin have responded to that situation had we not had those private, personal conversations about sexual purity? Would she have told me about what was happening to Molly? Probably not. Would she have thought this was normal if someone tried to convince her to commit a similar act? I don't know. Could it still be happening to Molly years later had Erin not shared the secret? Perhaps. What a relief that my daughter knows she can talk to me about things such as this.

I tell you this story not to shock you, but to encourage you. Be the first one to talk to your daughter so you can write your sexual values on her heart. If you've already missed that opportunity for whatever reason, ask questions to find out what she has already learned and help her sort fact from fiction.

Let's be "askable" parents with "Pick me!" attitudes. We can be the generation of parents who move from anxiety to authenticity so our children can learn how to be the best stewards of God's gift of sexuality.

filling her sponge

Train a child in the way [she] should go,
and when [she] is old [she] will not turn from it.

PROVERBS 22:6

When we were growing up, most of our parents didn't know what to say about sexuality, so they usually said nothing. Or if they did say something, it was a clever one-liner that made us cringe and groan while our eyes rolled back in our head and we made some gagging gesture. Some of those well-meaning attempts at sex education were comments that sounded something like these:

- Boys only want one thing.
- Good girls aren't easy.
- We're not ready to be grandparents any time soon.
- Keep your legs crossed and your panties on.
- A boy won't buy the cow if he gets the milk for free.
- Just don't let him score a home run with you.
- What would the neighbors think if you came up pregnant?
- If you are going to have sex anyway, at least use a condom.
- You tell him, "No ring, no ring-a-ding-ding!"
- If you do have sex, I don't think I want to know about it.

None of these comments gives your daughter the information she needs about sexuality. Nor will they help prepare her to be victorious in the battle for emotional and sexual integrity. For that, she needs a comprehensive sex education. By addressing a wide variety of sexual issues with her, you will help ensure she gets the right information and formulates healthy attitudes about her sexuality.

Think of your daughter's brain as a sponge. When she is young and impressionable, she is thirsty for any information she can get, especially about her body and sexuality. Her brain will soak up knowledge from any available source. Because young people often soak up information from peers, television, movies, music, and the Internet, your daughter's sponge will get filled somehow, some way. So the more correct information you place in her brain about sexual issues, the more saturated her mind will become with healthy attitudes about God's gift of sexuality. Studies show that the greater the number of sexual topics discussed by parents, the less likely the children are to have had sexual experience or to have been promiscuous.[1] In other words, our conversations need not be just about sex, but about the much broader topic of sexuality.

This chapter briefly introduces the topics you should cover when talking with your daughter about sex, but don't let this list overwhelm you. These issues will be covered more thoroughly in upcoming chapters and in book 2. Let's start with the basics and work our way through to the more complex issues.

Sexual Vocabulary

When our children are old enough to speak, we begin teaching them vocabulary words about their bodies. We tell them things like, "This is your nose; these are your ears; here's your elbow; this is your belly button; that's your peepee...or weewee...or private part." What's wrong with this picture? When we can't even bring ourselves to teach our kids the correct biological term for their reproductive organs, we're instilling awkwardness and shame regarding the subject of sexuality.

While it is important for your daughter to realize that vaginas are indeed private parts, you can teach her that by saying, "This is your vagina, but it's a private part. We don't talk about it with anyone except Mommy or Daddy." Of course, now that your daughter is a preteen, she's certainly not going to feel comfortable talking with you or her doctor about her weewee. She's growing up, and she needs grown up words to communicate.

Incidentally, young people tell me another reason they don't talk about sex with their parents: "They would punish me if I used 'those words' around them," referring to vulgar slang terms (which I'm sure I don't need to list here) because these are the only words they know. Don't let your daughter's vocabulary consist of nothing but inappropriate or offensive slang. We'll talk about proper sexual terminology in the first three chapters of book 2.

GENITAL DIFFERENCES

It didn't take long after bringing my newborn son home from the hospital for my three-year-old daughter to notice a big difference. "Mommy! I don't have a penis!" Erin declared with great concern. Of course, as my son grew older, he was also just as curious as to what was actually "down there where Mommy's penis should be." It's in those moments that human-sexuality encyclopedias have come in handy in our home. Greg and I have referred to Roger Sonnenberg's *Human Sexuality: A Christian Perspective* (Concordia, 1998) many times. We occasionally go through such books with our kids just for a refresher course in male and female anatomy.

Our sexual organs are complex, and I still learn new things as we read different books together. It's fascinating to understand the wonder of how God designed our bodies; children need to know that our reproductive anatomy is nothing short of a miracle. The first two chapters of book 2 will help you teach your daughter about her own body, while chapter 3 will help you talk with her about the male body and how God designed male and female spouses to "fit" together.

MENSTRUATION

Believe it or not, some young women have told me they had no idea what was happening to them when they first got their periods. Some thought they were bleeding because of a terminal illness! Another told me that she had no idea what was happening when one of the other fifth-grade girls in her camp cabin started her period. In the absence of correct information, she thought something was wrong with the girl who was bleeding and feared she might "catch" it. What a scary thing for a young girl to not understand that her menstrual cycle is a normal, healthy event in her life! Chapter 2 of book 2 will help you prepare your daughter for when her biological clock begins ticking.

CONCEPTION AND BIRTH

Children can't hide their curiosity about where babies come from and how they get out of their mommy's tummies. During your daughter's early years, give her brief, nondescriptive, age-appropriate explanations as long as they are true. (A friend tells me that her mother kept up the "swallowed watermelon seed" myth until she was in her teens. My friend says she still doesn't eat watermelon!) But by age eight or nine, a girl is likely ready for a much more detailed explanation of the miracle of how God formed her. She is ready to hear that she came from her father's sperm inside her mother's womb, and that hopefully she'll experience the joy some day of bringing her own beautiful baby into the world through God's gift of sex. Again, the first three chapters of book 2 will help you explain this miracle fully.

Sex Play with Peers

What mom isn't taken aback when she walks into her daughter's bedroom with milk and cookies for a playtime break only to find her and the neighboring child examining each other's naked bodies? Or what dad doesn't cringe when he overhears his daughter and slumber-party guest discussing things little girls shouldn't be discussing? Some parents confess they worry about the nature of their daughter's relationship with a male or female peer that seems a little friendlier than normal. All of these are valid concerns, and as parents we need to educate our children so they understand that sexuality is a topic they can openly discuss with their parents, but it is not something to discuss outside of the family or to experiment with in the company of others.

However, if you discover that your child is engaging in sexual play with her peers, don't respond with shock and horror. Children commonly engage in sexual play out of innocent curiosity. As a matter of fact, researchers include the following activities as "normal behaviors" among prepubescent children:[2]

- genital or reproduction conversation with peers or similar-age siblings
- "show me yours and I'll show you mine" behavior with peers or similar-age siblings
- playing doctor
- imitating seduction (for example, kissing or flirting)
- dirty words or jokes within cultural or peer group norms

We'll talk more about how to respond to such discoveries in chapter 7 of book 1, and then provide fodder for discussion with your daughter in chapter 7 of book 2.

MASTURBATION

While touching their genitals may be a normal, healthy part of our children's physical development in their earliest years, there comes an age of accountability when children must learn to exercise sexual self-control. It is my opinion that young people need to understand that while masturbation is far from an unpardonable sin, it can serve to fuel the sexual fires that come later in life. Chapter 7 of book 2 will paint that picture.

SEXUAL ABUSE

Every beautiful thing that God created for our good, Satan also attempts to use for our harm. Our sexuality is no different, and it's a sad reality that we have to explain the evil cruelty of sexual abuse to children. However, we need to be very careful in how we do this so we don't create an unnecessary paranoia in our daughters. But if we don't warn them, they'll be less likely to tell us about any abuse because they may not understand that abuse is wrong or that they are not to blame. Sadly, it's not just neighborhood pedophiles our children need to be cautious of; they often experience sexual abuse at the hands of someone near and dear to them. In *Treating Sexual Disorders,* Randolph Charlton candidly explains:

> Kids get ogled and kissed inappropriately by relatives and in-laws—all without any ways to describe what is happening. It is a studied exercise in cultural denial: if we don't really speak of it, perhaps it doesn't exist. And if it doesn't exist, then we're all safe (presumably) from its abuses.[3]

When we educate our daughters about the sanctity and privacy of their bodies, we are giving them the tool they need to discern when others may be attempting to lure them into unhealthy sexual behaviors. Chapter 4 of book 2 will help you teach your daughter how to exercise her right to be treated with dignity and respect.

HOMOSEXUALITY

With all of the prime-time television programs showcasing homosexuality, parents must be vocal about this topic if they want their children to respect God's design of heterosexuality. Younger generations have moved beyond tolerance of homosexuality; many girls are experimenting with lesbianism and bisexuality. Some are rejecting opposite-sex relationships altogether and embracing a homosexual lifestyle. At a recent sexuality seminar that I led for junior-high girls, three of the ten anonymously written questions submitted were:

- What's so bad about being bisexual?
- Why can't a girl experiment sexually with a same-sex friend?
- Why is lesbianism wrong if you are still a virgin?

You'll find help for talking with your daughter about such questions in chapter 7 of book 2.

PORNOGRAPHY AND PUBLIC NUDITY

What will your daughter do the first time she comes across a pornographic magazine or Web site? Or if someone exposes his body to her inappropriately? Does she know where you stand on issues such as pornography, cybersex, and public nudity? Her peers will more than likely expose her to such things eventually. With your warning and encouragement, hopefully she'll guard her eyes and mind from such inappropriate sexual images. Chapter 7 of book 2 also provides help for talking about secretive activities such as these.

BIRTH CONTROL

Finally, our daughters should be aware that although various forms of birth control are readily available and even promoted by such organizations as Planned Parenthood, they are not foolproof nor do most of them provide protection against sexually transmitted diseases. We don't want our daughters growing up thinking birth control is a license to have consequence-free sex. There's a lot more at stake with premarital sex than getting pregnant, so make sure your daughter knows birth control is only ideal for monogamous, married couples who want to avoid pregnancy, but can deal with "accidents" should they occur. We'll briefly discuss birth control in this context in chapter 3 of book 2.

EQUIPPING HER TO WIN THE BATTLE

In addition to talking with your daughter about the above ten topics, you will also need to equip her with the tools she will need to become a whole, healthy, and godly young woman who will reap the benefits of living with sexual integrity. For that reason, book 2 will help you cover these additional topics with your daughter, about how she can

- guard her mind, heart, and mouth in this sex-saturated world (chapters 8–10), as well as how she can make sure her wardrobe remains appropriate as her body blossoms (chapter 11);
- be a good influence on her friends rather than following the crowd (chapter 12), discern whether boys are treating her with respect (chapter 13), and enjoy healthy relationships with her family members (chapter 14);
- accept Christ's forgiveness if she strays (chapter 15) and prioritize her life to please God (chapter 16).

To uncover any other topics that you should discuss with your daughter, find out what's happening in her world.

DIVE INTO HER WORLD

You can dive into her world by talking with her teachers. If parents ask, teachers are usually willing to share some of the things they are seeing or hearing as it relates to sexual development. For example, the teachers at my daughter's junior high school told me some sixth-grade girls were stuffing their bras and that a few eighth-grade girls had been overheard bragging about how they are bisexual because they think it makes them more attractive to guys. It was obvious I needed to talk with my twelve-year-old about body image and lesbian experimentation because of what was going on at her school.

You can also look for teachable moments. When you and your daughter overhear on the news about someone's undergoing a sex-change operation or a politician's sexual affair being exposed or a child pornography ring being busted, don't ignore it and hope she didn't catch on. Such situations are perfect discussion starters. Ask, "What do you think about that?" You may be amazed at how openly your daughter responds if she knows you won't criticize or judge her responses.

A SATURATED SPONGE

What if the provocative messages that the world tries to feed your daughter about premarital sex could roll right off her mind like water off a duck's back? Wouldn't it be great if her brain was so completely saturated with nothing but healthy messages about sexuality that the unhealthy messages couldn't possibly find room to settle in her brain?

While we can't hope to hide our daughters from every worldly sexual message, we *can* fill their sponges with so much positive information that they are unaffected by the negative. When your daughter is filled with insights about God's gift of sexuality, her attitudes will more than likely spill over into the world she lives in, changing it and her friends' lives for the better.

the cutting edge
of adolescence

Wisdom is supreme; therefore get wisdom.

Though it cost all you have, get understanding.

Esteem her, and she will exalt you;

embrace her, and she will honor you.

PROVERBS 4:7-8

While puberty brings obvious physical changes, it also brings some subtle mental, emotional, spiritual, and social changes for our daughters. We may wonder, *What is she thinking? Why is she feeling this way? What can I do to help her cope? What does she need to survive puberty and succeed in life?*

The mental, emotional, spiritual, and social stresses felt between childhood and adolescence can be tremendously painful and confusing for a preteen girl. Most can't identify the source of their stress or understand why they feel so frazzled, so their sometimes-destructive coping mechanisms kick into high gear. Many shut themselves up in their rooms for hours at a time, listening to blaring music to drown out the thoughts in their heads. Some search for comfort in the cookie jar, use their parents and siblings as emotional punching bags, or go to bed in tears for no apparent reason. Others reach for affirmation from their peers through the phone or in cyberspace. All of these strange new behaviors are their ways of coping with the cutting edge of adolescence.

Consider this passage from *Reviving Ophelia: Saving the Selves of Adolescent Girls,* by Mary Pipher, PhD:

Something dramatic happens to girls in early adolescence. Just as planes and ships disappear mysteriously into the Bermuda Triangle, so do the selves of girls go down in droves. They crash and burn in a social and developmental Bermuda Triangle. In early adolescence, studies show that girls' IQ scores drop and their math and science scores plummet. They lose their resiliency and optimism and become less curious and inclined to take risks. They lose their assertive, energetic and "tomboyish" personalities and become more deferential, self-critical, and depressed. They report great unhappiness with their own bodies....

The story of Ophelia, from Shakespeare's *Hamlet,* shows the destructive forces that affect young women. As a girl, Ophelia is happy and free, but with adolescence she loses herself. When she falls in love with Hamlet, she lives only for his approval. She has no inner direction. Rather she struggles to meet the demands of Hamlet and her father. Her value is determined utterly by their approval. Ophelia is torn apart by her efforts to please. When Hamlet spurns her because she is an obedient daughter, she goes mad with grief. Dressed in elegant clothes that weigh her down, she drowns in a stream filled with flowers.... Girls know they are losing themselves.... Wholeness is shattered by the chaos of adolescence.[1]

This passage confirms what I hear mothers lamenting about so often—what happened to the self-confident little girl I once knew? What's happened to my daughter that's caused her to become so self-conscious and insecure? Why is she suddenly so moody and unpredictable? To help you better understand what is going on with your daughter, let's look at some developmental and societal pressures that pubescent girls experience.

CUTTING THE PARENTAL CORD

When our daughters are little and attached to our hips or wrapped around our legs, it is difficult to imagine that within a few short years they will want to separate themselves from us, their parents. But little girls do grow up, and part of that process is cutting the cord that binds them to Mom and Dad. Although this separation can worry us when it first begins to happen (usually because *we* aren't ready for her to grow up just yet), it's actually a good thing. We want our daughters to grow up to become confident, capable, and independent women (which we'll talk more about toward the end of this chapter), and that requires practice. Unfortunately Mom and Dad are usually the ones who get practiced on first.

Since Erin was born, she's always been a "mama's girl." She wanted to go everywhere I went and do anything I wanted to do. Just before she turned twelve, I took her with me on a business trip to Colorado Springs. She went to all of my meetings and was excited to meet people she had only heard about. She and I sat and talked forever in restaurants as if we couldn't possibly run out of things to say. We walked through department stores hand-in-hand, enjoying each other's company and making each other laugh hysterically. On the return flight, with her face beaming, she declared, "Mom, we've got to do this more often!"

Just a few months later, Erin was in the car when Greg dropped me off at the airport for another out-of-town trip. Reminiscing over the Colorado trip we'd taken together, I asked her, "Will you miss me?" and puckered up for the usual good-bye kiss. Her lips barely brushed mine as she replied, "No. You're only gone for two days."

What happened to, "I wish I could go with you again!… How long until you get home?… Will you call me from your hotel to tuck me in tonight?" I felt a little hurt, but then I realized that Erin's friend was in the car and Erin certainly didn't want to look like a "mama's girl" in front of her friend. Erin's entering a season where looking "cool" in front of her peers is far more important than publicly expressing affection to her mom. I reminded myself that this is a natural part of her growing up process and that I needed to give her the freedom to go back and forth between being "Mommy's little girl" and the young, independent woman she is becoming.

You can help your daughter through this confusing time by cutting her a little slack. Give her the freedom to gravitate back and forth between friends and family as she feels the need to. Delight in the moments when she's running to be by your side, but also delight as you see her walking away from you toward her own friends and the independent life she'll someday lead. Knowing that Mom and Dad are cheering her on in her pursuit of healthy friendships will give your daughter the confidence to enjoy strong relationships with both family and friends.

CUTTING EACH OTHER DOWN

The saying goes, "Sticks and stones may break bones, but names can never hurt me!" But you and I both know that's not true. Sometimes a swift kick or hard punch would be much easier to recover from than some of the hurtful words kids can sling at each other and the horrific labels they often place on their peers. Along with budding personalities, sharp wits, and keen senses of humor comes the tendency for preteens to try to build themselves up by cutting others down. Adolescents can be merciless to one another, displaying zero tact and concern for others' feelings.

In her book *"Mom, I Hate My Life!"* Sharon Hersh says:

Statistics and stories confirm that the world our girls are growing up in is often a cold, cruel place. Bullying, sexual harassment, and profane utterances are daily realities in teenage life. Boys don't just call girls "fat" or "ugly" anymore; they mimic the words of their musical icons and label girls "bitch" and "slut." Girls aren't much nicer to one another. Research from the 1990s suggests that an incident of bullying takes place once every seven minutes in school and that by the eighth grade, 81 percent of girls have experienced sexual harassment. When you add these startling statistics to more familiar stories of gossip, breakups, and jealousy, you have a relational climate that easily explains our daughters' tumultuous climate.[2]

What can you do when your daughter becomes the brunt of such behavior? Acknowledge that it hurts when others talk bad about us, but remind her of all the wonderful qualities you see in her, even if her friends fail to see them. Also, don't be afraid to step into the middle of the ring to referee if necessary, especially if her peers aren't fighting fair. My dad stood up for me once, and he never had to do it again.

Kerry and Rhonda had written several mean notes to me, saying I was a pathetic loser and that I shouldn't sit anywhere near them on the bus anymore. They folded the notes like little doghouses and wrote on the outside, "This is where you belong, bitch!" My dad called each of them on the phone and calmly said, "Hon, I don't know which of you wrote those notes to Shannon, but if she's done something to hurt you, I hope you'll tell me, and I'll take care of it. But what you've done has hurt her, and I don't appreciate it. If it happens again, I'll be calling your parents. Okay?" I could hear their startled, quivering voices on the other end of the line saying, "Yes sir!" The next day they apologized, and I was never the brunt of their cruel antics again. In hindsight, I can see that this incident taught me never to treat anyone else like that and to discourage my friends from excluding other girls. I knew how painful that felt.

MAKING THE CUT

Do you remember wanting to be part of the "in" crowd but feeling as if you were on the outside looking in? Was there ever a slumber party or get-together that all the popular girls were invited to, but not you? Do you remember what it felt like to wonder if you would be welcomed to sit at the table with your friends in the cafeteria, or if you would be eating all alone or, worse, at the geeks' or losers' table? Surely we can all remember how important it was to feel as if we made the cut with at least one group of cool kids. This is how your daughter feels—or will be feeling

Questions Young Adolescents Worry About[3]

1. Are all of these changes supposed to be happening?
2. Is there something wrong with me?
3. Do I have a disease or an abnormality?
4. Am I going to be different from other people?
5. Does this pain in my breasts mean I have cancer?
6. Will I be able to have intercourse, or will there be something wrong with me?
7. Will the boys laugh at me? Will the girls reject me?
8. Will God punish me for the sexual thoughts that I have?
9. Wouldn't it be awful if I became a homosexual ?
10. Could I get pregnant without having sexual relations?
11. Do some people fail to mature sexually?
12. Will my modesty be sacrificed (that is, in a doctor's office or locker room)?

very soon if she's like most middle-school or junior-high students. She likely has a deep desire to fit in and be popular.

She and her peers are jockeying for positions such as head cheerleader, all-star athlete, all-region choir member, first-chair band member, the starring cast member in the school play, and so on. They are vying not only for official ranking but also for social recognition, such as "most popular" girl in school. Some girls so deeply crave popularity that they will seek attention at any cost, even if they wind up being popular for all the wrong reasons, such as being known as a flirt, a tease, or "easy." If a girl isn't able to establish the identity she desires for herself, these years can be spent wallowing in what feels like an identity crisis. Making the cut somehow, some way—whether socially, athletically, or academically—is a huge part of a young girl's world.

If your daughter struggles with fears about whether she's liked by her peers, remind her that popularity is a figment of other people's imaginations and that it changes with the tide. Also help her understand that popularity is a huge responsibility, because everyone looks to you to define who and what is "in." Share some personal stories from your preteen and teen years about the effects that popularity can have on people who give in to peer pressure just to become or remain popular with the crowd. Some of the most popular girls in my junior high were often the ones who got pregnant or involved in alcohol and drug abuse by the time we graduated high school. Teach your daughter to be true to herself and to take pride in being liked for who she really is rather than doing what everyone else is doing (we'll talk more about this in chapter 12 of book 2). Encourage her to hang out with friends that share her interests and values, even if they are not the most popular girls in school.

CUTTING CALORIES

You may not think she notices, but she'd have to be blind not to. The magazine cover models, the television celebrities, and the popular girls in school are usually pencil thin. Girls get the message early in life that "thin is in," so if they're going to be "in," they've got to be thin, even if it means not getting adequate nutrition for their bodies to function properly. Consider the following statistics:

- Models today weigh 23 percent less than the average woman. Twenty years ago, when we were growing up, models weighed only 8 percent less.[4]
- Eating disorders are the third most common illness among adolescent girls in the United States.[5]
- Seventeen percent of girls ages eight and nine and about one-third of girls ten to twelve think they are fat and need to diet.[6]
- Half of all girls will obsess about the flatness of their stomachs and the size of their thighs by the time they reach middle school, and almost 40 percent will already have tried dieting.[7]

In addition, one of the most influential factors for girls who struggle with an eating disorder is their mother's relationship with food and body image.[8] In other words, Mom, if you want your daughter to have a healthy body image, don't let her see you looking in the mirror and declaring, "I'm too fat!" Instead, model healthy eating habits and being comfortable in your own body. This will go a long way toward dispelling the media's message that a flat tummy will lead to eternal bliss.

If either you or your daughter is truly at an unhealthy weight, make it easier to eat right by keeping the pantry stocked with good choices. By eating appropriate amounts of the right foods and exercising for a stronger, healthier body, you'll both settle into a weight that's just right for you. In addition, teach her not to focus on the number on the scale or the desire to be skinny, but instead to focus on being healthy and enjoying the strong, useful body that God gave her.

CUTTING HER SPIRITUAL TEETH

Most denominations offer some sort of confirmation class, baptism class, or foundations of the faith class to kids between the ages of ten and twelve for a reason. This is the prime age at which our minds begin to conceive what Jesus did for us on the cross when He purchased our salvation. It's also the time when kids develop a much stronger conscience. This is due to metacognition, the sophisticated intellectual process that enables children to monitor their own thinking, memory, knowledge, goals, and actions. *Metacognition* is best described as "the ability to think about how you think." The ability to monitor thinking usually begins around age six and develops more completely between the ages of seven and ten.[9]

As your daughter begins to monitor her thinking, she will also begin to feel a pang of conviction when she recognizes that her thinking or behavior is not in line with what God or her parents desire of her. Younger children don't usually consider themselves in trouble until they get caught. During puberty, however, they no longer have to get caught to feel troubled or guilty about their thoughts or actions. This new level of personal monitoring and spiritual conviction can create a great deal of internal stress as adolescents wrestle with questions such as these: *If God knows what I'm thinking, how can He possibly still love me? Does the fact that I'm tempted to do wrong make me a bad person? If my parents knew what I really think sometimes, wouldn't they be terribly disappointed in me?* They may start asking deep theological questions that can throw a curve ball to even the most experienced parent or youth pastor.

You can help your daughter through this season of her development by challenging her to begin digging into God's Word for answers to life's questions. Be willing to search the Scriptures with her when she's struggling, and spark her interest in God's Word by giving her some devotional books for teens. Since being with like-minded friends will enhance her spiritual development, get her involved in some sort of youth group or Bible study. Such activities will feed her spiritually, help her find answers to her theological questions, and encourage her to spread her spiritual wings and soar above the trials and temptations of this world.

CUTTING TO COPE

A growing issue plaguing adolescent girls is self-injury or cutting, not as a suicide attempt, but as a way of surviving some emotional pain they are unable to identify, verbalize, or cope with. Using such things as razors, knives, scissors, pen caps, or broken glass, many girls have carved words such as *ugly* or *fat* or some grotesque image into their forearms or thighs to express their self-contempt. They express hidden emotions through slashing or puncturing themselves, then hide those scars beneath long sleeves.

Often girls who self-injure have suffered sexual or physical abuse during childhood, have been fatherless for a time in their lives, suffer with an eating disorder, or simply have low self-esteem and feel as if they don't fit in. According to Jose Cano, professional counselor on staff with Teen Mania Ministries, some girls often turn to cutting as an outlet for their pent-up aggression. While boys can channel their anger and aggression through sports, girls often don't feel as if they have any other target for their anger besides inflicting harm upon themselves. Cano further explains, "In some cases they cut so that they can feel *something*. They are in emotional pain but suppress it to the point they eventually feel numb until they experience the sharp sensation of self-injury. This gives them a sense of relief that they must still be alive because they can feel the physical pain in spite of the emotional numbness they live with from day to day. Others feel they can distract or express their intense emotional pain by inflicting a different sort of pain."[10] As bizarre as this form of self-abuse may sound to you, it's been done since biblical times. In Mark 5, Jesus encounters a demon-possessed man who cuts himself with stones.

In *Bodily Harm,* Karen Conterio and Wendy Lader claim, "The syndrome is more prevalent than most people think, and yet it is grossly underreported and misdiagnosed.... A particularly alarming aspect of the rising tide of self-injury is that the behavior is making its appearance earlier and earlier in the childhood and adolescent years."[11]

When young girls insist on wearing long sleeves in warm weather, tend to collect sharp objects, or frequently "doodle" on their arms or legs with sharp objects without penetrating the skin, parents need to take notice as these could be warning signs that a girl is cutting herself. If you see warning signs or suspect that your daughter may be struggling to cope with intense emotional pain, I recommend you talk openly with her about what she's experiencing and involve a professional counselor as soon as possible. The help and healing a self-injurer needs goes beyond any simple Band-Aid or advice we can offer.

Cutting Off Her Nose to Spite Her Face

Adolescent girls sometimes intentionally "dumb down" academically for the sake of fitting in. In fourth or fifth grade, girls often pride themselves on making the best grade in the class. But by middle school, these same girls will lie about their grades or stop trying to do well in school, so their friends won't think they're geeks or nerds. Girls often do this so as not to stand out as "brains" (preferring recognition for beauty rather than brains) or to keep from intimidating cute boys.

Such was the case for Cady, the main character in the movie *Mean Girls* (which is *not* one I'd recommend your young daughter watch). Although Cady was a whiz at math, she pretended to need tutoring from the cutest boy in the class, even though he was nowhere near as mathematically inclined as she was. She even faked wrong answers on tests to prove to him that she really needed his help (and attention).

Many young girls say they would prefer to be seen as cute and sassy or as a damsel in distress over being seen as smart. Perhaps that's why girls often color or streak their hair blonde in spite of the "dumb blonde" stigma. Blondes have more fun, and sometimes girls are tempted to have fun with friends and flunk tests instead of studying hard and succeeding.

Thirty Developmental Assets that Kids Need to Succeed[12]

1. family support
2. parents as social resources
3. parent communication
4. other adult resources
5. other adult communication
6. parent involvement in school
7. positive school climate
8. parental standards
9. parental discipline
10. parental monitoring
11. time at home
12. positive peer influence
13. music
14. extracurricular activities
15. community activities
16. involvement with a faith community
17. achievement motivation
18. educational aspiration
19. school performance
20. homework
21. helping people
22. global concern
23. empathy
24. sexual restraint
25. assertiveness skills
26. decision-making skills
27. friendship-making skills
28. planning skills
29. self-esteem
30. hope

One of the best ways parents can offset this tendency in young girls is by helping them see beyond the awkward season they are currently in. Your daughter needs to know that adolescence is a time to practice our independence and aim for a much more fulfilling life down the road. So talk with her about where she's at now, but also brainstorm with her about what her life will be like when she successfully completes her high-school education, selects a college where she can learn even more and make lifelong friends, and enters a career field that stimulates and challenges her to use the gifts and talents God has placed in her for His glory. Encourage her to set future goals and help her work toward them, looking ahead, far past the new zit on her nose or the fact that she didn't make the cheerleading squad.

Dr. Sylvia Rimm wrote a small book filled with ideas on how you can help your daughter not just survive puberty but also maximize this season of preparation for her future. It's called *See Jane Win: The Rimm Report on How 1,000 Girls Became Successful Women.* She makes suggestions such as setting high educational expectations for your daughter (including encouraging math skills), supporting your daughter's involvement in extracurricular activities, and assuring your daughter that popularity is not important in the long run, even if it feels important to her right now.[13] Dr. Rimm also wrote a short follow-up book packed with wisdom called *See Jane Win for Girls: A Smart Girl's Guide to Success.* Consider encouraging your daughter to read it.

CHEER HER ON

In addition to setting high standards for her academic and professional pursuits, you can also help your daughter survive these preteen years by displaying extraordinary amounts of patience and understanding when it comes to the emotional rollercoaster rides she'll be experiencing. During this challenging yet critical time in her life, she needs your unconditional love, understanding, and acceptance. This kind of emotional support combined with solid parental advice, academic encouragement, and spiritual guidance is a surefire recipe for turning a struggling, insecure pubescent girl into a confident, competent young woman. Even while on the cutting edge of adolescence, your daughter can learn not only to survive, but to thrive!

mom's modeling career

Guide older women into lives of reverence so they end up
as neither gossips nor drunks, but models of goodness.
By looking at them, the younger women will know
how to love their husbands and children,
be virtuous and pure, keep a good house, be good wives.

TITUS 2:3-5, MSG

While only a handful of women ever grace the runways as supermodels, we moms have not missed our chance to be super models for this next generation. We have a far more important stage to walk across than any on Madison Avenue. Our daughters are watching our every move and taking mental notes on how to transition from girlhood to womanhood. Because our lowest standard will more than likely be her highest, it is important for us to ask ourselves, "What kind of model am I?"

In this chapter, we'll examine seven appropriate behaviors that moms need to be modeling to daughters, as well as what to do about minimizing the negative influences of other models, such as close relatives or family friends.

1. MODELING MODESTY

When I was a youth pastor, I was frequently flabbergasted not just by what the girls were wearing when they came to church, but by what their moms were wearing when they dropped their daughters off. I often wondered, *How can I possibly encourage modesty in these young women when their moms' voices and actions speak so much louder than mine?*

Marla, a junior-high principal, recently echoed this same sentiment. She nabbed a seventh grader walking down the hall in a low-cut, high-rise, skintight T-shirt and insisted that she put on some sort of jacket while on school premises. The student didn't have one, so she was escorted into the lost-and-found area to find something to cover her the rest of the day. Not finding anything to her liking, she asked if she could call her mom to bring a jacket from home. When her mother arrived, Marla was shocked to hear her explain, "I didn't buy that top for her. I bought it for *me,* and she borrowed it out of my closet this morning after I had already left for work. It won't happen again." Marla thought, *Yeah, right! If you think you can dress like that and expect her not to, you're out of your mind.* Marla's thinking is right on target. Our daughters will *do as we do,* not as we *say.*

Moms, if you want your daughter to dress modestly, you need to dress modestly. We'll be looking at some specific guidelines for modest attire in chapter 11 of book 2. As you read through them with your daughter, put your own clothes to the test. Consider what fashions may need to be cleaned out of your own closet for you to be a modest role model for your daughter.

2. MODELING MEDIA CHOICES

One of the most confusing nights of my life was when I was ten years old. As a summertime ritual, my family watched television together until we all went to bed. But one night a movie came on at 8:00 p.m. with a disclaimer that the subject matter was not suitable for young viewers. Rather than change the channel so we could watch something else as a family, my parents sent me to bed incredibly early for a summer evening. It wasn't even dark yet. My brother (who was six years older) was allowed to stay up, and I was bewildered that he got to watch the movie and I didn't. I wish I could say that I was wondering, *Why is it okay for them to watch if it's not okay for me?* But I wasn't. I was straining to listen to the television in the next room, trying to figure out what was going on and thinking, *When I get older, I'll certainly watch too!*

I share this story because I want you to understand the mind-set of a young child who witnesses her parents and older siblings watching things she is not allowed to watch. She is not thinking, *I shouldn't watch this—thanks for helping me guard my mind!* She is thinking, *Why can't I watch too?* And as soon as she is able, whether she grows older or just has an opportunity when there is no parental censorship, she more than likely will view such movies. Over the years, the graphic nature of the media has increased, and the disclaimers about graphic content have just about vanished.

To offset the negative influence this can have on our children, we must build censors into their spirits that can help them discern when something is appropriate and when it crosses the line and therefore shouldn't be watched. What's the best way to do this in your daughter? By intentionally modeling such behavior. If something inappropriate comes on television, don't send her to another room while you take it in. Let her see you change the channel, and let her know why you are choosing to guard your mind as well as hers. Do the same with radio stations and magazine subscriptions and any other forms of media, and you'll greatly increase the chances that your daughter will censor her own media choices as well, even when you are not around.

3. MODELING A HEALTHY BODY IMAGE

On a recent episode of one of the many makeover shows on television, a woman struggled with her decision to have the bump removed from the bridge of her nose. Both of her teenage daughters had inherited the same facial feature, and she didn't want to communicate to them that they needed nose jobs too. In spite of her plastic surgeon's recommendations and the fact that the surgery was completely free, this mom opted to leave her nose just the way it was and wear her bump proudly, hoping her daughters would do the same. I applauded this mom's courage and desire to be that kind of role model.

What about you? What things about your body would you change if you could wave a magic wand? Have you asked God to grant you the serenity to accept the things you cannot change and the courage to change the things you can? I'm referring to proper self-care here, not radical plastic surgery! Does your daughter see you as someone who is more concerned about your inner beauty than any outer beauty that will eventually fade?

Remember, if we want our daughters to love themselves and appreciate the bodies God wrapped them up in, we can't just *tell* them how to do so. We must *show* them how. Nix frequent complaints about your disappointments with your physical appearance. When you exercise, let your daughter hear you thank God for a healthy, strong body. If you are unable to exercise for whatever reason, let her hear you thank God for some other personal attribute, such as your discerning mind or your compassionate heart. Let her know that you appreciate God's handiwork in your own life, and she'll be far more likely to see herself as a masterpiece as well.

4. Modeling Passion and Intimacy in Marriage

You may have read in one of my previous books that my past includes sexually promiscuous years. Because of that, people often assume I come from a broken home or that perhaps my mother was a "loose" woman who set a bad example for me. Nothing could be further from the truth. My mom modeled modesty in her wardrobe and propriety in her relationships with men. However, I never saw much romance or passion between her and my dad. My mom's life seemed so boring: making dinner...cleaning house...attending PTA meetings... Where was the excitement? Where was the passion? Where was the fun?

When your daughter begins looking ahead to serious relationships someday, you can bet that she's not fantasizing about doing her husband's laundry, paying bills, or scrubbing bathtubs. She'll be daydreaming about romance! In a few short years, she'll be imagining warm embraces in her man's arms, writing sweet notes to tuck into his wallet, or kissing him good-bye when he leaves for work in the morning. But will this man be her husband? Or just her boyfriend or live-in lover?

Recall our earlier discussion about how young people often disassociate passion from marriage because their parents' relationship seems boring and undesirable compared to what they see in the media between unmarried couples. We moms must model passion and intimacy in our own marriages if we want our daughters to look forward to marriage.

Let your daughter walk into the living room to find you and your husband embracing on the couch. Sneak up from behind and plant a kiss on his cheek when your kids are looking. Ask her to be an accomplice and distract her dad while you hide a love note in his jacket pocket. Draw a heart on the bathroom mirror in lipstick and leave it there until your daughter sees it. Show her that marriage is a passion-filled, romantic relationship she can look forward to.

Do You Need a Course Correction?

Following a book interview in Tempe, Arizona, I had some free time and went for a walk in a neighborhood of nondescript houses. At a fork I turned left, but after a few blocks of the same, something inside told me to head back and go right. I was so glad I did! Within a couple blocks I came to a magnificent oasis! Green rolling hills, tall shade trees, and a ten-acre lake with paddle boats, fishing, joggers, and ducks waddling around picnic blankets. It was like a glimpse of heaven.

What a shame it would be if I'd missed it. I was so glad I heard a voice saying, *Correct your course! Go back!* Back during my seven-year itch, I went hunting and ended up on a desert road, luckily correcting my course from superficial intensity to genuine intimacy before too long. Twenty years later, I'm still at the oasis of genuine love I found in Greg.

If you need a course correction before your daughter starts mimicking your behaviors, don't hesitate. Compromise and infidelity are a desert road. Read *Every Woman's Battle* and check out www.shannonethridge .com to connect with women on the same journey to a marital oasis.

5. MODELING SATISFACTION IN SINGLENESS AND SEXUAL PROPRIETY

In order for your daughter to grow up into a young woman of sexual integrity, she needs *you,* Mom. Your presence. Your instruction. Your understanding. Your strength. Your love. She needs your full attention. One of the biggest parenting mistakes a divorced, single mom can make is to sacrifice her children's emotional and spiritual well-being on the altar of wanting to remarry.

If you are a single mom, a desire to remarry is normal and valid. However, your first priority needs to be your children. Now is not the time to expend all of your energy trying to meet a man. A parent who makes dating and remarriage her top priority puts her children at risk.

When single parents begin dating, they often get caught up in the euphoria of a new relationship and the wonderful feelings that come along with it. Sometimes they are so enamored with a new love that they inadvertently begin to neglect the emotional needs of their children. Sometimes new relationships move so quickly that children have little or no time to process their own feelings or to learn to trust the new person. Though you may think you're inviting in somebody who will improve your life, your daughter may feel abandoned. If she feels you are choosing your new love over her, she may feel betrayed and lose respect for you.

One benefit of making your daughter a priority over your love life is that you enhance the likelihood that she will grow up feeling valued and loved. You will gain her respect and consequently earn the right to speak words of wisdom at opportune times. You will also be showing her that women do not have to have a man in order to live a completely satisfying and joyful life. If a daughter gets the message that her single mother is desperate to get married again, she is more likely to grow up believing that she, too, will need to find a man if she wants to be happy. With this notion planted in a young girl's head, seeds of desperation, premature relational commitments, and codependency can bloom quickly in her life.

Of course, it's possible that God might bring someone into your life (even though you aren't looking). If so, remember that your kids still need to be your first priority. And also remember that your daughter is watching every move you make. Don't rush the relationship and become too serious too quickly. This will not only help you tend to your daughter's needs but will also help her learn to pace herself and guard her own heart.

6. MODELING HEALTHY FRIENDSHIPS

Maybe you've heard a young woman declare, "All my best friends are guys! I can't stand girls! They're such backstabbers!" I know I have many times. I also get several e-mails each month from women crying over how they accidentally "fell" into an affair with a close male friend. That's why I believe it's important for us to demonstrate to our daughters how to have healthy friendships with both women and men.

We can do this by putting far more stock in our female friendships rather than in our male friendships. Only female friends can truly understand a woman's innermost struggles and desires. I don't believe any married woman should have a male best friend other than her husband, and any male friends she has should be friends with both her and her husband.

If your daughter witnesses your spending time alone with a man other than your husband, what does that teach her about emotional faithfulness in marriage? She needs to understand that when you got married, your male friendships took a backseat to your relationship with your husband.

7. Modeling a Passionate Relationship with Christ

I believe one of the best lines of defense against inappropriate sexual activity is to have a close walk with the Lord. Intimacy with Jesus Christ makes all other relationships pale in comparison, and our daughters need to know that with God there is a level of satisfaction that can't be experienced in earthly relationships. When she's feeling a natural hunger for attention and affection, does she know that spending time with the Lord can fulfill this longing far better than calling some boy on the phone? We need to model such passion in our own personal walk with God so our daughters will know that God can satisfy their souls.

By attending worship services on a regular basis, you will show your daughter that spending time in God's presence is a vital part of the Christian life. But because all genuine love relationships are carried on in private as well as in public, make sure she understands the importance of connecting personally and privately with Christ every day of the week, rather than just on Sunday mornings.

Also strive to read the Bible, God's love letter to you, often. When you come across a new insight or something of particular interest, make it a point to share that with your daughter. Let her witness your excitement over how the Lord is speaking to you, and she will develop a hunger to hear directly from the Lord as well. On occasion I will read a passage out of my journal to Erin, and then we'll talk about what we sense God doing in our lives as a family. We frequently pray together about the things that are on her heart, and I encourage her to make daily quiet times with God a priority. Sometimes we'll search the Scriptures for a passage that addresses a particular struggle she is going through, such as fear, timidity, or loneliness. The more our daughters can look to God's Word for comfort, the less they'll be tempted to go looking for comfort in unhealthy relationships.

Of course, moms are not the only examples of womanhood in our daughters' lives. What do we do when someone they look up to sets a really poor example of sexual integrity?

THE OTHER MODELS ON HER STAGE

When I was a preteen, I frequently spent time with a single female relative who was in her late teens. I looked up to her a great deal as I felt she exemplified all the fun and excitement my parents seemed to lack. When she became pregnant, I was old enough to know that everyone was raising their eyebrows and wondering how this could have happened, myself included. What a teachable moment that could have been for my parents, but they didn't seize it. Instead, they swept the incident under the rug without explanation, leaving me confused and wondering if the situation was acceptable since no one was telling me otherwise.

My friend (I'll call her Dawn) handled a similar situation much more wisely than did my folks. Dawn recently confided in me that her neighbor (I'll call her Lynn), who had a daughter the same age as Dawn's daughter (Kim), had kicked her husband out of the house and moved her lover in who was also still married to someone else. Then Lynn became pregnant by this new man before either of their divorces were final. No doubt the situation caused a great deal of confusion for both Dawn's and Lynn's daughters, who were close friends.

Rather than leaving Kim to her own imaginations and conclusions, Dawn felt she had to tell her ten-year-old daughter what was going on. She didn't want Kim to get the impression that Lynn's choices were good ones. On the other hand, she didn't want her to think that she was condemning Lynn either. Dawn says:

> I approached the conversation by asking Kim what she thought about the sudden changes taking place in Lynn's house. Kim responded, "It's really weird. I don't think it's right. I feel sorry for her husband because now he can't see his kids as often, and that's got to be hard on everybody."
>
> I replied, "You are right. Lynn may think that she's happier with this other man, but she's making a lot of other people miserable. God intends for married people to stay married and to remain faithful to each other.

What Lynn did is a big mistake and a sin, but God still loves her in spite of that sin, and I believe He wants us to keep loving her too. He doesn't want us to ever make the same mistakes that she is making, but He doesn't want us to throw any stones at her, either."

Together we read about the woman caught in adultery in John 8 and talked about what that must feel like for other people to stand around you in judgment and want to condemn you. We also talked about what it must have felt like for that woman to watch all of her accusers drop their rocks and walk away and to hear Jesus say that He doesn't condemn her either.

While many of us would be tempted to wring Lynn's neck and make sure our daughters know how vehemently opposed we are to what was happening, Dawn was able to model not just a sense of propriety, but also a beautiful picture of God's love and mercy. What about you? Are you willing to demonstrate God's love and mercy to those who aren't such great role models for your daughter? As tempting as it might be to throw stones at bad role models, don't. Far better to pray for these women and other role models like them. We can't change anyone, but we can pray that the Holy Spirit initiates the changes He wants to make in a person's life. If you demonstrate compassion and spiritual concern for others, your daughter will also learn to treat people as Jesus did.

SHE'S LOOKING TO YOU

Have you ever caught yourself doing or saying something, only to stop and declare, "Oh no, I'm turning into my mother!" It's true. The older we get, the more our personalities and mannerisms resemble dear ol' mom. The same will be true of your daughter. Regardless of who else she looks up to and attempts to imitate, you are ultimately the most influential person in her life. As you embrace modesty, make wise media choices, demonstrate self-acceptance, exemplify a healthy marriage or satisfaction in singleness, foster friendships with other women, and pursue a passion-filled relationship with Christ, you are teaching your daughter how to show love inwardly (toward herself), outwardly (toward others), and upwardly (toward our Creator).

dads and daughters

What marvelous love the Father has extended to us! Just look at it—
we're called children of God!

1 John 3:1, MSG

Note: This chapter is especially for dads,
but I encourage moms to read it too!

Before the struggle to remain faithful to my husband…before the heartache of living a sexually promiscuous life…before the confusion of being inappropriately pursued by my uncles or the pain of being date-raped…there was a much more powerful battle going on in my subconscious mind…the battle for my daddy's attention.

I suspect it started when I was very young. I remember how I loved being the baby of the family, spending more time in Daddy's lap than my brother and sister combined. I remember waking up in my parents' bed long after Dad had left for work and curling up on the couch with him for an afternoon nap when he came home.

But the last time I remember climbing into my parents' bed was when I was four. My dad was lying down and sobbing uncontrollably, while my mother was passed out on the couch with lots of friends and family gathered around and fanning her. As I made my way through the crowd toward my parents' bedroom, the atmosphere in our house felt heavy, making it hard to breathe. All I knew was that my eight-year-old sister had been rushed to the emergency room the day before after vomiting repeatedly and complaining of a bad headache.

As I climbed in bed next to my dad, he verbalized the words that no parent ever wants to hear, let alone have to tell one of their children. "Donna died. Sissy's gone, and she's not coming back." I remember lying there, trying to let the meaning of those words sink in, but my four-year-old mind just couldn't do it. After a few minutes of listening to my dad cry and feeling helpless to console him, I wandered off into my brother's bedroom. I was surprised to find him crying on his bed as well. After all, my brother never cried, at least not that I had ever seen. I didn't know what to say or what to do, so I didn't do anything. I hid behind a chalkboard, stood as still as I could, and tried to just disappear.

After my sister's sudden death (caused by an aneurysm), my father became somewhat of a recluse. He no longer attended church with us because he said it reminded him too much of Donna's funeral. I can only remember going out to eat with my dad one time while I was growing up, to Burger King for a Whopper Jr. He preferred his meals at home rather than out in public. As a matter of fact, he didn't like to be out in public at all from what I could tell.

He hid out in his shop from the time he got off work until it was time for bed. He was always too busy with some project to come to any of my junior-high choir or senior-high pep-squad performances. The only time I remember his leaving the house other than to go to work was to make an occasional trip to Roper, Harris, and Dunn, the local auto-parts store. He was a master mechanic by trade and a tireless tinkerer in his off-hours. It wasn't until I had my own car in need of repair that I recognized his incredible gift of being able to fix anything. But by the time I was sixteen and driving, my bitterness toward him had grown so fierce that we barely talked. I'm pretty sure I even told my mother I hated him. I told myself I wasn't bothered that he didn't have time for me, but based on how avidly I sought attention and affection from every other male on the planet, it must have bothered me tremendously.

How did I go from snuggling with Daddy on the couch to rebelling against him altogether? Josh McDowell said it best, "Rules without relationship lead to rebellion."[1] Dad had plenty of rules, such as, "Don't talk back" and "Don't talk while I'm trying to watch television." There were also many unspoken rules, such as "Don't make Dad mad" and especially "Don't talk about Donna." We all knew the rules and tried to walk a straight line, but we suffered greatly in the relationship-building department.

It wasn't until I was in my twenties and had my own children that my relationship with my father, by the grace of God, went through a dramatic transformation. I began to understand that it is usually hurting people who hurt people, and I suspected that as deeply as I felt my dad had hurt me, he was likely hurting even more. I couldn't imagine what it had been like to have a child die, but I suspected there had to be far more to his deep-seated anger and fear of intimacy than just losing my sister. I set out on a mission to try to understand him and to understand myself, since my mother repeatedly told me that the reason my dad and I butted heads was because we are just alike. I boldly wrote him a letter, telling him I didn't feel as if I really *knew* him but that I desperately wanted to. He responded with an invitation for a family camping trip, where he took me by the hand and led me on a walk so we could talk privately. It felt so odd. I felt tempted to let go of his hand to ease my awkwardness. The last time I remembered holding his hand was when I was too little to cross the street by myself and I wrapped my entire hand around his index finger. But I told myself this kind of intimacy with my father was what I'd been craving all those years. I couldn't reject it now.

For over an hour, Dad told me stories about his incredibly painful childhood, the divorces and remarriages that his parents went through, the abuse he suffered at the hands of his stepmother and his mother's boyfriends, and the sting of rejection as he was passed around like a hot potato from parent to parent, then on to grandparents and uncles. In his early teens, he often didn't know where his next meal would come from. "I was determined to be a better father and provider than what I had," he explained. I had to acknowledge that he certainly was reliable in that sense. I never doubted he would come home or that he'd bring home a steady paycheck. He continued, "I know now that you needed things from me that I just didn't know how to give, but it wasn't because I didn't love you. I just never had anyone show me how to give them." In light of his tearful explanation, I suddenly found it easy to give my dad the grace to be human.

I'm so thankful for the love that I've learned to have for my dad, but I do regret the many years that we wasted ignoring and hurting each other. Those were years when I was experiencing what every growing girl feels—a deep yearning for the time, attention, affection, and approval of the most special man in her life, Daddy.

MOVING BEYOND THE BASICS

Like my dad, many fathers assume they are doing great jobs as dads because they work hard to keep the roof over their daughters' heads, provide them with clothes and food, and keep them relatively safe. Being a daughter's protector and provider comes naturally for most men. However, those are just the basics. In order to help a young woman reach her full potential, Dad needs to meet her emotional needs as well—her need to feel a sense of belonging, to be loved unconditionally, and to be valued for who she is. Some fathers assume that their role is to work hard so that *Mom* can be free to tend to their daughter's emotional needs. After all, it's really Mom she needs, right? Not so. Studies show that an emotionally present father plays many vital roles, of which we'll focus on two in particular—how he shapes his daughter's sexuality and how he shapes her spirituality. Let's look at what's so special about Dad.

SHAPING HER SEXUALITY

If you take a one dollar bill and a hundred dollar bill, close your eyes, and try to "feel" the difference. Chances are you can't. The paper used to print currency is the same, regardless of the denomination of the bill. The imprint on that paper determines its value.

The same is true of your daughter. All of us are made with the same genetic material, but it is our imprint that will determine how valuable we believe ourselves to be. What imprint am I referring to? Your daughter's sexual imprint— whether she feels valued by the opposite sex and loveable as a female. And who will create that imprint in her mind, heart, and soul? The first man she falls in love with—*Daddy.*

Screenwriter and playwright Richard Wesley wrote of this "imprinting" so eloquently in an article titled "My Daughters, My Heart" in *Essence* magazine:

I am, as all fathers are, a daughter's "first boyfriend." That means that every man who comes into her life will be measured, for better or for worse, against me. And how a father treats his daughter—the lessons, both direct and indirect, that he has taught her—will determine her attitudes and behavior toward men.... A daughter learns what to expect of men and of sexuality from her father. If a man has cherished his daughter, she will probably choose men who cherish her.[2]

Long before any boyfriend comes along and tries to "love" her (whatever his teenage definition of "love" may be), an emotionally present father communicates to his daughter that she is worthy of love, simply by being who she is. He does this, in part, by not expecting his daughter to do anything in exchange for his love (least of all to give her body or perform sexual favors). He grants his love freely as a gift from a man whose only hope is that his daughter will learn to reciprocate with a love that is just as innocent, pure, and unshakable.

But if a girl does not receive such a special first love from her father, she suffers greatly as a result. Monique Robinson is one of the multitude of women who can attest to this suffering. Her father saw her once as a newborn but never returned. In her book *Longing for Daddy*, she writes:

Growing up without a father or a father figure generates a dire need for love, attention, affirmation, and affection from a man. The indelible mark of a healthy father's love was not placed on our hearts and minds in our tender formative years, leaving us with an insatiable longing to be loved.[3]

Girls who don't grow up with the benefit of an attentive father tend to have very fluid boundaries, not just as teens but also later in life. In his book *Father Hunger*, Robert McGee explains:

Many women hunger so for a father's love that they easily fall for men who seem to be everything they had hoped for as little girls needing a daddy. Perhaps a male supervisor with whom a woman spends long hours at work may seem to be an irresistible magnet. Others become infatuated with the pastor at church who seems so loving and kind. Often these women are married with children of their own, but the attraction can be very insidious and powerful.[4]

Without a doubt, a loving dad plays a significant role in satiating a daughter's need for male attention. Dad, you may love your daughter with all your heart, but if she doesn't recognize or feel your love herself, she is much more likely to go searching for male attention wherever she can find it.

Studies consistently show that a father's approval has a positive effect on his daughter's self-esteem and sexuality. By being attentive to his daughter, a father will enhance the likelihood that she will become a high achiever and develop firm boundaries in opposite-sex relationships. Dr. Linda Neilsen reports, "Regardless of their age, daughters who have meaningful, comfortable relationships with their fathers are generally more self-confident and independent, have better relationships with men, are less depressed, have fewer eating disorders and drug and alcohol problems, and achieve more in school and work."[5]

Here are a few examples of what dads can do to help their daughters be more comfortable with their sexuality and have a high self-esteem:

- Never stop hugging your daughter, especially after she has developed breasts and hips! My fifteen years' experience in youth ministry indicates that when dad suddenly becomes "hands off" with his adolescent daughter, the boys are more welcomed by her to become "hands on." Just because she looks more like a grown woman than a little girl doesn't mean she doesn't still need physical affection, especially from a male who will not take advantage of her.

  William says, "As my daughters entered their teen years, I made an even greater effort to be appropriately physical with them. I went out of my way to hug them, arm wrestle with them, tickle their feet, and rub their shoulders. I believe it went a long way toward helping them avoid unhealthy relationships with guys who just wanted to use them."

- If your daughter is still a lapsitter, I encourage both moms and dads to savor this season as long as possible. The question has been posed, "Is it inappropriate for a teenage girl to sit on her father's lap once she develops breasts? Wouldn't that arouse him?" Scott, father of three daughters, says, "Absolutely not. A father doesn't look at his daughters that way. All of my girls have always sat on my lap. The oldest is twenty-one, and I'm not about to tell her that she can't do it anymore. She'll probably stop when she's married, but if she needs to sit in a man's lap for attention and affection, I want it to be mine until her husband can take over."

Of course, Dad, if having your adolescent daughter sit on your lap makes you feel incredibly uncomfortable for whatever reason, I recommend that you casually adjust her position to where you are comfortable (perhaps sliding her to the side of you and putting your arms around her shoulders). But be careful not to send signals of rejection when she attempts to have physical contact with you.

- Make a concerted effort to invite her on a special "Daughter Date Night" once in a while. Treat her exactly the way you'd want her to be treated on a real date someday. Call her on the phone from the office and schedule ahead of time. Let her pick the restaurant and/or activity. Open doors for her and give her your jacket if she's cold. Engage her in conversation about what's going on at school or things that she's interested in. Occasionally smile at her and mention one of the special things you love about her. Treating her like a princess now will teach her to hold out for a prince in the future rather than settling for just any toad who'll spend time with her.

In addition to needing a healthy sense of self and affirmation of her sexuality, a growing girl also has a deep-seated need for a strong spiritual foundation. Once again, Dad plays a key role.

SHAPING HER SPIRITUALITY

Fathers can nurture their daughters' healthy spiritual development by modeling the love, care, and compassion the heavenly Father has for His children. As a lay counselor to college-age students, I have observed that young women who describe their relationships with their biological dads as close and intimate often describe their spiritual lives as deeply rewarding and intensely passionate.

On the other hand, women who grew up without a father in their home or who describe their father as "emotionally unavailable" often struggle with the idea of "intimacy with Christ" as if it's a foreign concept. These women often feel as if God "doesn't really care about me," is "untrustworthy and unreliable," or perhaps "is not even really there." I believe this mental and emotional correlation between the earthly father and the heavenly Father indicates that the role of a father is to model the relationship God desires to have with us. A close father-daughter relationship seems to help daughters have a closer relationship with God. A distant father-daughter relationship seems to increase the likelihood she will have a distant relationship with God and a rebellious heart that resists submission to a heavenly Father.

Here are a few practical ways you can lay a strong foundation of healthy spirituality in your daughter's life:

- Pray, not just *for* her, but *with* her. Communicating our hearts to our heavenly Father is one of the most personal, intimate, and beneficial things we can do while here on earth. Listening for God's still, small voice in response to our prayers is one of the most important things we can do to grow stronger in our faith and commitment to Christ. I believe that the time Greg spends by our daughter's bed every night praying with her is the most precious gift Erin could receive from her daddy.

- Challenge her to read and memorize God's Word. This will help her understand more about God's lavish love for her. When girls believe God truly loves them, provides for them, and has a plan for their lives, they gain the confidence to go out and conquer the world in the name of Jesus. Both Greg and I have attempted to train our daughter to be an independent young disciple of Christ. At thirteen, Erin has already found the courage to raise her own support and go on three mission trips to Honduras, Costa Rica, and Panama, thanks to the scriptures she memorized and internalized: "For God did not give us a spirit of timidity, but a spirit of power, of love and of self-discipline" (2 Timothy 1:7) and "I can do everything through him who gives me strength" (Philippians 4:13).

- Model forgiveness. By all means, hold your daughter accountable for her actions. But when she repents, let her know all is forgiven. Avoid bringing up her past sins in future conversations, and make every reasonable attempt at reestablishing trust in her. In doing this, she will know that the nature of our heavenly Father is also to forgive and to trust us to do better in spite of how we've let Him down in the past. As problematic as our relationship was, my dad was very strong in modeling forgiveness. I believe that's contributed greatly to my ability to overcome much of my past sexual sin rather than remaining entrenched in it. He saw who I could be if I tried rather than who I had chosen to be in the past. His forgiveness taught me I could also forgive myself.

When a girl grows up with a strong spiritual foundation coupled with a healthy view of her sexuality and high self-esteem, she is going to be one tremendous blessing to her parents, her friends, her future husband and children, and to the body of Christ. And what more could a dad ask for in a daughter?

Before we close this chapter on dads and daughters, I want to offer a couple of thoughts especially for moms who are reading this as well.

A Note to Married Moms

I share yet another embarrassing personal story with you for the sake of revealing a lesson I've had to learn the hard way. As our daughter entered her prepubescent years and began emotionally clinging to her father a little more than she did to me, I wasn't sure how to react. I began to notice that Greg spent quite a bit of quality time with Erin each night when he tucked her in, and I tried to convince myself this was a good thing. However, sometimes he would come to bed and pass out before saying much to me at all beyond, "Good night. I love you." I began to feel slighted. Actually, a more accurate term would be *jealous*. I was glad my daughter was getting to experience the very thing I missed so much growing up, but the selfish side of me wanted to say, "Hey! What about me? Why don't you spend that kind of time talking to me each night?"

As a matter of fact, the selfish side eventually won out and I spoke up. As soon as the words came out of my mouth, I felt ashamed for being jealous of my own daughter and the special relationship she shares with her daddy. Fortunately, my husband was very tender and compassionate, and he has tried to be as sensitive to my needs for emotional connection at the end of the day as he is to our daughter's. He knew I didn't want him to stop what he was doing with Erin, but that I didn't want him to underestimate my need for quality time with him as well.

As moms, we must guard our hearts against any jealousy we may feel toward our growing daughters and their dads, especially if we didn't have healthy relationships with our own fathers. While balances should certainly be maintained and the marriage relationship always kept a priority over any other family relationship, we must encourage our husbands to spend that quality time with our daughters if we want them to grow up with healthy attitudes toward themselves and their sexuality. This is a gift your husband can give not just to your daughter but to you as well and to your family's future generations.

A NOTE TO SINGLE MOMS

Perhaps you have read this chapter with a heavy heart because your daughter doesn't have a father who lavishes love, attention, and affection on her. Maybe death or divorce has robbed you of a husband and your daughter of her dad. Perhaps she only sees her dad every other weekend, or maybe she's never known her real father because he slipped out of the picture before they could get to know each other. Regardless of why your daughter has only one parent in her life on a daily basis, know that the power of one parent's love can go a long way in healing a multitude of wounds.

Build the strongest relationship possible under these circumstances. Be present. Be her biggest fan at her sporting events. Show her you believe in her. Be available to her as much as possible. You may be busy and exhausted from your full-time job, but look for opportunities to spend time with her. She may decide she needs to talk to you when you're ready to fall into bed at night. Stay awake and listen. She'll translate your interest as love, and your investment in her will bear fruit in time.

While the temptation can be overwhelming to focus on your own issues and desires to find a loving mate, keep your focus on meeting your daughter's emotional needs. Frequently remind your daughter that God is our everlasting Father (see Deuteronomy 10:18 and Psalms 10:17-18; 68:5; 146:9). He promises to take care of us, and because He is sovereign, He can do that better than any earthly dad can. Help your daughter build a strong sense of who she is in Him.

Also encourage her to forgive her earthly father for his actions that contributed to the divorce. In doing so, she (and you) may find some healing. Help her recognize the positive attributes she inherited from him—even if it's only the color of her eyes. You don't have to paint an unrealistic picture or convince her to trust an unsafe person, but try to find something commendable she can appreciate about her dad. After all, whether distant or close, he is part of who she is.

If your daughter desires an earthly father figure in her life, pray that God would provide healthy male relationships through a grandfather, uncle, pastor, family friend, youth leader, and/or teacher. However, be wisely vigilant over such relationships as you do have the responsibility of guarding her from any type of abuse. It would be appropriate that such a father figure might attend her basketball games, send her a card or small gift on her birthday, or give her a pat on the back and encouraging compliment in the presence of others. However, I caution you against allowing the two of them to spend time alone together out of eyesight or earshot of anyone else. Healthy surrogate relationships don't have to be private to be powerful influences in your daughter's life. By keeping everything out in the open, you'll be keeping your daughter safe from even more relational pain than she's already experienced.

Remember, having only one parent isn't necessarily what stunts a young woman's emotional and spiritual growth. Feeling unloved does. I know girls from two-parent families whose lives have taken major nosedives into sexual immorality once they went through puberty and became teenagers. I also know many young women who did not have fathers or whose dads were not emotionally available, but because they had tremendous moms who attempted to meet their emotional needs at every turn, they have become incredibly well-adjusted young women who embrace sexual propriety and enjoy healthy relationships.

A PRIZE WORTH PURSUING

Shaping a daughter's sexuality and spirituality is no small task. If you are successful in making her feel valuable and unconditionally loved, she stands a much better chance of embracing sexual purity, rejecting unhealthy relationships, and learning to love her heavenly Father. These aspects of her personality will determine the quality of her life and will positively influence the quality of your family relationships for many generations to come.

Let us remember that our daughters ultimately belong to God and have been entrusted to our stewardship and care. As parents, we are charged with molding them into godly young women. We must meet the many basic physiological needs our daughters have, but we can't stop there. Dads, I encourage you to go the distance in striving to meet your daughter's vital emotional needs as well. Only then can she know beyond a shadow of a doubt that she is worthy of the pure love, attention, and affection that she naturally craves.

Of course, she's not the only one who benefits from a strong father-daughter relationship. When Dad helps mold and shape his daughter into a happy, healthy young woman, he has the opportunity to experience for himself a deeply committed love relationship like no other. In the words of Joe Kelly, "For a dad, a daughter's love is often the most unconditional love he ever experiences."[6]

Indeed, the unconditional love of a daughter for her father is certainly a prize worth pursuing with every ounce of energy that can be mustered. Because females equate loving feelings with deep communication, and because deep communication is often the very thing many males struggle with, I encourage you to keep reading, Dad, as we examine more about how to communicate your love to your daughter.

speaking her language

If I speak in the tongues of men and of angels, but have not love,
I am only a resounding gong or a clanging cymbal.

1 CORINTHIANS 13:1

In the summer of 2002, our family embarked on a one-month mission trip to Honduras. Our group carefully planned our ministry activities, which targeted an all-girls orphanage, an audience right up my alley. For weeks I envisioned getting to know these girls and showing them the love of Jesus Christ. I had high hopes and dreamy expectations of the emotional connections we'd make and the spiritual bonds we would form during our monthlong stay.

While we certainly had an excellent experience, my hopes and expectations soon proved to be unrealistic. Why? Because I found the language barrier to be just that, a very frustrating barrier. Fortunately, when I taught, I had an interpreter by my side, bridging the language gap. But during our free times, our interpersonal communication with the girls was limited to smiles, hugs, painting toenails, and playing Uno. We couldn't just talk and get to know one another as I had hoped. As passionately as I felt about ministering to the girls on a personal level, I could not. They simply couldn't understand my love for them because they could not understand the language I was speaking.

Something similar often happens within families over time. We may all speak English or some other common language, but we don't always speak the same *love language*. This usually isn't an issue when our children are very young. It's easy to show attention and affection to those sweet little babies we bring home from the hospital or to those toddlers who really know how to steal the show and tug on our heartstrings. But those cute little girls grow up to become "tweeners" (in between being a child and a teenager) who are far more interested in their friends than their families. Then they become teenagers who are often more interested in boys than anyone else on the planet. Eventually they become adult women who don't seem to need Mom and Dad much anymore. As our daughters go through these transitions, sometimes we wonder what happened to our little girls, and we wonder if and how we can reestablish that loving connection between their hearts and ours.

At times we may try to communicate our love to our growing girls, but the message seems to get lost in translation. This has happened to me several times, not just in my relationship with my daughter, but with others in our family. It was during the first year of our marriage when I began to recognize that not everyone speaks the same love language. For the first several months, I made it a habit to mail sweet cards to Greg's office, but then one day I realized he had never once sent me a card. I felt neglected and taken for granted, so one day my disappointment came oozing out in the form of gushing tears. As I cried and complained about how I didn't feel his love for me because he had never sent me a card, Greg tried to explain that he shows his love for me by mowing the grass every week and washing my car.

My response was, "But those are your jobs! You live here too!"

He replied, "Well, honey, your cards don't mean much more to me than my car washes mean to you."

Stunned, I couldn't believe he hadn't felt loved by my weekly postal sentiments. Neither could he believe I did not feel his love when he worked so hard to do chores around the house for me. Obviously, we weren't communicating.

Then we found Dr. Gary Chapman's book *The Five Love Languages,* which categorizes the unique ways we express affection:

- Gifts
- Acts of Service
- Quality Time
- Words of Affirmation
- Physical Touch

Reading this book was like discovering a bilingual dictionary of terms. We discovered that my primary love language was *gifts,* my secondary love language was *words of affirmation,* and my last was *acts of service,* and that Greg's primary love language was *acts of service,* his secondary was *physical touch,* and his last was *gifts.*

In other words, our love languages were exact opposites. If we wanted to communicate our love for each other in ways that would be recognized and received, then we had to speak the other person's love language. Greg had to learn to be more of a gift giver, and I had to learn to be more of a servant.

Add two kids to the mix, and now you have a multilingual family. Until our children are old enough for us to discern what their love languages are, we tend to speak our own to them. When our kids were young, I never came home from Toys "R" Us empty-handed. I frequented souvenir shops on every out-of-town trip. I would sometimes bring an after-school snack in the car with me when I picked them up from school, just so I'd have something to present to them when they got in the car.

With my son, this worked well. Obviously gifts was Matthew's love language too, because every time I came home from a trip he'd ask, "What did you bring me?" He delighted in anything he could hold in his hand—a Hot Wheels car, a book, or even just a stick of gum. He needed something tangible to let him know I loved him and had thought of him while I was away. Over time, I noticed that Matthew's expressions of affection toward me were usually something he had made at school and pulled from his backpack as soon as he got in the car, or fresh flowers he had plucked from the yard. He is a gift giver at heart, just like me.

Erin, on the other hand, never seemed all that thrilled with any gift. Oh, she appreciated it, but it wasn't what she really wanted from us. What she really wanted became clear one day when Greg was going to drive into town to pick up dinner and return some videos. Everyone else was busy, so he was heading out the door by himself. He asked Erin if she'd like to go with him. Her beautiful face lit up, and her eyes just sparkled as she looked at her daddy. She stopped what she was doing and headed out the door proudly as if her Prince Charming had just asked her out on a date. If you haven't guessed it by now, her love language is *quality time*.

Matthew's secondary love language is physical touch. When I would tuck him in at night when he was little, he'd always say, "Nuggle wif me two minutes, okay Mommy?" He had to snuggle before he could go to sleep. He still climbs into bed with me every morning for a two-minute snuggle under the covers before he starts his day. When we take a walk, he wants to be right up next to me and our legs or arms often clumsily get tangled up.

On the other hand, Erin's least favorite love language is physical touch. She doesn't snuggle up with Mom every morning like she used to when she was younger. Now she wants me to help her with her hair, or help her decide what to wear, or help her pack her lunch, or give her a "freebie" on her bed-making chore. Obviously, acts of service rank right up there on her love language list, just second to quality time. Erin also doesn't much value words of affirmation because, as she says, when people compliment her, she gets embarrassed and doesn't know what to say. Matthew loves words of affirmation and thrives on the compliments of others. Different children, different love languages.

As parents, we can learn to decipher our children's love languages and speak them fluently. In light of all we've talked about so far, we can't underestimate the power that speaking a daughter's love language will have on her ability to remain sexually pure in the face of future temptations.

In order to discover your daughter's primary love language, I suggest you follow the steps outlined in Gary Chapman and Ross Campbell's follow-up book, *The Five Love Languages of Children:*[1]

1. Observe how your child expresses love to you.
2. Observe how your child expresses love to others.
3. Listen to what your child requests most often.
4. Notice what your child most frequently complains about.
5. Give your child a choice between two options, for example, "Would you prefer to shop for new clothes (gifts) or go for a walk together (quality time)?"

Let's take a look at each of the love languages and consider practical ways we can satisfy our daughters' emotional needs to feel loved and cherished by Mom and Dad.

Gifts

- Send flowers or balloons to the school on her birthday or some other special occasion, or better yet, just to say, "I love you!"
- Tuck a card or handwritten note into her backpack wishing her success on a big test.
- Bring home her favorite snack from the grocery store or take her shopping.

- Give her a disposable camera and a cute picture frame or photo album next time she goes to a slumber party, a school field trip, or a church-group trip.

Acts of Service

- Surprise her by making her bed while she's getting ready for her day.
- Pack her favorite lunch and include a personal note or funny drawing on her napkin.
- Help her organize her closet and dresser drawers.
- Sit down with her while she's doing homework or a school project just to see how you can help her finish faster.

Quality Time

- Attend her sporting events, drama performances, or whatever extra-curricular activity she's involved in.
- Invite her to come along on errands or road trips where the two of you can enjoy time alone together.
- Invite her to go on a long walk with you where you are free to talk without interruptions or distractions.

Words of Affirmation

- Compliment her appearance when you notice she's taken special care to groom herself. Better yet, tell her how beautiful she is even when she's not all spruced up.
- Tell her how much you appreciate how hard she works in school, or how often she helps around the house, or whatever ways she strives to please you.
- Ask about her day at school. Find out what she's learning in her classes. Praise good grades on daily work as well as on report cards.

Physical Touch

- Give her lots of hugs and kisses on the cheek or the top of her head.
- Frequently pat her on the back or give her a gentle shoulder squeeze to let her know you just like being with her.

- Offer to give a back, neck, shoulder, or foot massage at the end of a long day using yummy-smelling lotion.
- Snuggle on the couch with her while you're watching a movie.

Over the years, I've heard some heartwarming stories from parents who went the extra mile to speak a child's love language. Dan told me he takes his daughter to McDonald's every Saturday morning for breakfast. He uses their meal blessing to grab her by the hand and verbalize to God all the things he loves about her so she'll hear how special she is to her dad. His daughter's love language is quality time and words of affirmation.

Kay told me her kids all seem to enjoy physical touch, so she took a class in body massage and bought a massage table for their den. Her kids frequently ask for one of her special massages, and this gives her the opportunity to meet some of their physical touch needs in healthy, bonding ways.

When Mark was called overseas as a reservist, he knew his absence would be especially hard on his ten-year-old daughter, Moriah, whose love language was gifts. In addition to sending frequent letters home, Mark made arrangements with their neighborhood florist to deliver a small vase of flowers each month to Moriah in the late afternoon once she was home from school. He asked that they prepare a different arrangement each time, but that somehow it would always include a white daisy. That was Moriah's favorite flower, and they frequently played the "he loves me, he loves me not" game with the wild daisies that grew in their backyard. He told me, "I always counted the petals ahead of time so I'd know for sure she'd end up with 'he loves me.'"

Another couple told me that once each month they take their kids on a special date night, and they alternate—mom with son, dad with daughter one month, the other month vice versa. That way they get one-on-one quality time with each of their children, and it's something their kids look forward to as much as they do.

By the way, we'll be looking at these love languages again in chapter 14 of book 2 from the perspective of how your daughter can learn to speak her other family members' love languages and foster healthy relationships. With attention and affection being exchanged both ways between daughter and parents, everyone is more likely to feel that sense of emotional connection that is so very important in families and foundational to your daughter's future.

Even though we've already talked about words of affirmation as a distinct love language, let's examine the art of conversation even closer, keeping in mind that, by nature, girls usually spell love T-A-L-K.

STRENGTHENING PARENT-DAUGHTER COMMUNICATION

While it's important for girls to be able to communicate with both parents, I want to focus on father-daughter communication for a moment. As mentioned in the previous chapter, the relationship a girl has with her dad affects her emotional, sexual, and spiritual development. With so much at stake, why do dads often find it so hard to come up with anything to say to their daughters? Besides having little in common with girls and having very different interests, I believe it's also due to the differences between male and female communication styles. Consider the results of Dr. Rhonda Kelly's research on the differences in how and why males and females communicate:[2]

Dr. Debra Tannen summarizes these communication differences by saying, "Men use communication to maintain independence, while women talk to maintain intimacy."[3]

Dad, at this age your princess longs for intimacy far more than she longs for independence (that longing will come later as an older teen). In order to help her experience your love for her, it's essential that you make a concerted effort to adjust your communication style to connect with her more intimately.

But it's not just dads who struggle with how to talk to their preteen daughters.

Female Communication Patterns	Male Communication Patterns
Little girls talk to be liked.	Little boys talk to boast.
Little girls make requests.	Little boys make demands.
Little girls speak to create harmony.	Little boys speak to prolong conflict.
Little girls talk more indirectly.	Little boys talk directly.
Little girls talk more with words.	Little boys use more actions.

Sometimes moms also find it hard to think of much else to say beyond, "So, how was school?" This is certainly the case for me. When I've spent the day teaching classes, editing manuscripts, and responding to e-mails, it's hard to remember what it was like to stress over getting your locker open. A parent's world is far removed from their kids' world. So how can we get creative and make a strong communication connection with our daughters, even when we lead such different lives?

Remember that effective communication isn't just about what *we* need to tell *her* about our world. It's really more about what we can get *her* to tell *us* about her world. A wonderful way of showing genuine interest in your daughter's life is to ask questions—about her struggles, her likes, her dislikes, her dreams, her fears, and all of the other things that swirl around in her mind from day to day. According to Chap Clark and Dee Clark, authors of *Daughters and Dads,* "Most parents are terrible at drawing out their kids' thoughts. The questions they use are usually so obvious and directive that a child doesn't have to stop and think to answer them."[4]

John Hicks echoes that sentiment. He writes, "The great philosophers of history are regarded as wise, not because they knew all the right answers but because they could ask the right questions.... Good questions will give you entrance into another person's world."[5] Isn't that the goal of every parent? To gain entrance into a daughter's world? To find the key to the door of her heart, ask questions that require more than *yes, no,* or *fine* in response.

According to my own thirteen-year-old daughter, here are some good questions you can use to connect more intimately with your daughter.

- What was the best thing that happened today? What was the worst?
- Have you read anything in your Bible lately that particularly interested you?
- The next opportunity we have to spend time together, what would you like to do?
- What kinds of tests do you have coming up? How can I help you study for them?
- What do you enjoy thinking about most these days? What thoughts cause you the most stress?
- What's your favorite restaurant? Your favorite food there? Do you think we can duplicate the recipe at home?

- Where are your favorite places to shop? Why?
- What do you want to be when you grow up? Why?
- What do you like most about yourself? What do you like least? Why?
- Has anything happened at school (or home) lately that you want to talk about?
- Where would you like to go on a future family vacation? Why?
- What's your favorite television show? Why?
- Who is your favorite musical artist these days? Favorite song? How does it go?
- Which friend do you most enjoy spending time with lately? Why?
- What do you think your life will be like a year from now? five years from now? ten?
- Who is your favorite teacher? What do you like most about him/her?
- What's the best part of being your age? The worst part?
- What are three things you want to do in your lifetime?
- What person, living or dead, do you admire most? Why?
- What's the funniest thing you've ever seen or heard?

Asking these kinds of questions and interacting about her responses will go a long way toward creating that bond of intimacy between the two of you that can be so healthy and fulfilling to you both. Dad, your efforts will also teach her the art of conversing with someone of the opposite sex, a very beneficial characteristic for a young woman to possess. According to Robert Wolgemuth, author of *She Calls Me Daddy*, "Properly teaching the skills of conversation is the most critical thing a dad must do in building his little girl. The ability of you and your daughter to effectively exchange words—and the feelings they're usually connected to—will provide the bridge between you that will last the rest of your life."[6]

IMAGINE THE POSSIBILITIES

My husband and I discovered the hard way that we had to learn to speak each other's love languages before we could experience the intimacy we both longed to have in our marriage. But with our children, we have tremendous hope that our efforts to speak their language will result in their full knowledge of our fierce love.

What about your daughter? What kind of impact might it have on her life to know how much you treasure her? That you don't just tolerate, provide for, or discipline her, but that you truly cherish her? Just imagine the possibilities of how the unquestionable knowledge of your love could equip her to become all that God created her to be. As you identify her unique love language, learn to speak that language fluently, and ask her questions that demonstrate your genuine interest in her life, you *can* give your daughter the incomparable gift of knowing she is sincerely loved.

disheartening discoveries

If we had forgotten the name of our God
or spread out our hands to a foreign god,
would not God have discovered it,
since he knows the secrets of the heart?

PSALM 44:20-21

Parenting reveals one exciting discovery after another about a child. I remember being in awe of every little thing my baby girl learned how to do—when I found her in her crib on her back two minutes after I placed her on her tummy, when she took her first step toward her daddy on our hardwood kitchen floor, and when she figured out how to scoop SpaghettiOs into her mouth with her Barney spoon. I found her later achievements even more exciting as she became aware of what she could do if she really put her mind to it, such as learning to tie her own shoes, reading *Goodnight Moon* all by herself, and riding her Barbie bicycle without training wheels.

As parents, we celebrate every new discovery. But as children grow older, we sometimes learn that they have discovered things that are not exactly causes for celebration. Such was the case when Erin was only six. I assumed I had protected her from pornography because we block certain cable television channels and have a filter on our home computer. We even live in the middle of the country, where my kids aren't exposed to all of the sexually graphic billboards you often see in larger cities. So you'd think my kids would be safe, right? Wrong.

One day Erin and I were walking along our roadside picking up trash. Tall grass disguised tons of aluminum cans and candy wrappers that people thoughtlessly tossed out of car windows. Erin was walking several feet in front of me, then suddenly yelled in a panicky voice, "Oh, Mommy, I think you need to look at what I found!"

Assuming that maybe she had stumbled upon a beer can or cigarette package at worst, I was shocked to see what she was holding in her hands. Two fistfuls of separated magazine pages, which upon closer examination turned out to be pages from a pornographic magazine.

I'll never forget the confused and sickened expression on my daughter's face. She looked up at me with her big brown eyes and asked, "Mommy, what *are* those people doing? Why did they let someone take their picture?" I was saddened to have to explain pornography to my first grader, but I knew she deserved answers to her questions. I told her that some people don't respect the fact that God created sex as a way for mommies and daddies to make babies and to be an expression of love between a married couple. I said that some people use sex outside of marriage just to feel good, or to get attention, or even to make money since those people were probably paid to pose for those pictures. I was glad Erin found that hard to believe. It confirmed that she considered sex as more sacred and holy than that.

Years later, my heart broke when she said to me, "Mom, remember those magazine pages I found by the road when we were picking up trash? I've never been able to get those pictures out of my mind." I wish I could get those images out of her head, but there's no magic potion I can have her drink or fairy dust I can sprinkle over her to work that miracle. That's one of the frightening things about pornography—even when you aren't looking at it anymore, the images often continue to flash on the screen of your mind.

I was angry that she stumbled upon pornography at such a young age. But I am glad she stumbled upon it in my presence. I was able to help her understand that what the people in those pictures were doing was not right, and that it is not right for us as Christians to look at those kinds of pictures, either.

Of course, our daughter's exposure to pornography is only one of many possible disheartening discoveries we may make as parents.

DISCOVERING THEIR SEXUAL ORGANS

Alisa found her eight-year-old daughter, Celia, in the bathroom one day with a hand mirror between her legs, obviously curious about her own vagina. Standing at the door somewhat shocked, Alisa asked her daughter what she was doing. When Celia said she wasn't doing anything, Alisa asked her to put her panties back on and come sit down with her. Alisa tells what happened next:

I held her in my arms and said, "Honey, you are not in trouble! It's okay to be curious about your body, but let's talk about it. Why were you doing that?"

She tearfully replied, "I don't like the way it smells, and I wondered if it smells that way all of the time."

"Well, any part of our body that we don't wash regularly is going to have a bad smell. Do you know how I always make sure you wash underneath your armpits and behind your ears and in between your toes?"

"Uh-huh."

"You could also use a washcloth to clean your bottom and your vagina if you need to. I did that for you when you were in diapers, but now you are big enough to do that for yourself."

"But, Mom, sometimes when I touch myself there it feels good. Why?"

"Celia, remember how I told you a couple of years ago where babies come from and how they come out of their mommy's vagina when they are ready to be born? Remember how I told you that the way they get in there is because their mom and dad come together in private and a 'seed' goes from inside the daddy's penis to inside the mommy's vagina?"

"Uh-huh."

"Well, God made that part of your body in a very special way. It's not just for making babies, but it's also to give you pleasure and make you feel good whenever you and your husband touch each other. But Mommy feels it is important for you to save that feeling for when you are married instead of touching yourself now. Do you think you can do that?"

"But it's okay to touch it if I want to make the smell go away?"

"Yes, honey, it's okay to clean it when you are in the bathtub or to wipe it when you go to the bathroom, or even scratch it if it itches, as long as you do that in private. Okay?"

"So I'm not in trouble?"

"No, sweetie, but if you have questions about your body, you can ask me anything. If I don't know the answer, we'll get out an encyclopedia and look it up to find the answer. Okay?"

Celia grinned a little and nodded her head, then wrapped her arms around me for a tight squeeze.

Bravo, Alisa! What an honest, loving, and courageous response to a daughter's natural curiosities. This sort of dialogue truly sets the stage for continued conversations in the future, and that is definitely a primary goal. Remember, askable parents don't want to just have one big "sex talk" with their kids but rather a series of age-appropriate conversations throughout their formative years.

DISCOVERING OTHERS' SEXUAL ORGANS

Sometimes our daughters' natural curiosities aren't just about their own bodies but about others' bodies as well, especially that of the opposite sex. Paula found this to be true with her nine-year-old daughter and her daughter's playmate, Jason. The two had played together since they were both three years old. Six years later, it hadn't occurred to Paula that it may be time to start monitoring their playtime a little more closely.

Carly and Jason were playing in the basement while Paula was working in the yard. She took a peek through a dirty window in the basement to make sure all was well, but all was *not* well. Her daughter was on top of the pool table, crouched on all fours with her naked bottom in the air. Jason appeared to be examining her with a flashlight. Dropping her gardening tools, Paula ran inside the house and hollered down that they needed to run to the grocery store, so Jason went home and Carly and her mom hopped in the car. Paula told me:

Before I opened my mouth, a graphic memory from my own childhood flooded my mind. I remembered the shock and embarrassment I had felt when my mother discovered Donny and me playing doctor. I also remembered that my motives for playing were purely innocent.

I wanted to give my daughter the same benefit of the doubt, so I said,

"Carly, I wasn't spying on you, but when I was working in the flower bed I just happened to see you and Jason 'playing' through the little window at the top of the basement wall. Now do you want to tell me the full story?"

"It was Jason's idea, Mom! I promise! I told him we shouldn't do it, but he said I was just chicken."

"So you did it to prove you weren't chicken?"

"I guess so."

"How do you feel now?"

"Stupid... I'm sorry, Mom. I won't do it again, I promise!"

"I hope not. But what about Jason? Do you think he realizes how wrong it is to tease a girl into doing something she doesn't want to do? Especially something like taking down her pants? Don't you think I should I talk to his mother?"

"I dunno."

"Can I tell you a story? A real one that happened to me when I was even younger than you?"

"Sure."

"When I was little, I played the same 'doctor' game with a friend who was a boy. My mom caught us in the act. She walked Donny home and asked *him* to tell his mother what we had done. It took him forever to get the words out and he cried the whole time, but Donny did grow up to be a fine young man who respected women. By the time we graduated high school, he had a reputation as a guy who was committed to sexual purity. Had he never gotten that wake-up call when he was younger to help him understand the importance of controlling your sexual curiosities, do you think he would have grown up to be that kind of person?"

Carly agreed that Jason needed to know what was appropriate and what was inappropriate when it came to how he treated girls, so she agreed that Paula should talk with his mom.

You may find it hard to imagine ever telling another mother something like this about her child, but turn the tables for a moment. What if you were Carly's mom, but it had been Jason's mom who caught them in the act? Would you want to know? Of course you would, so you could talk with your daughter about it. A friend of mine says that this is her biggest prayer for her preteen daughters: *Lord, if she does something wrong, please let her get caught! If not by me, by someone who will either tell me or at least guide her appropriately!*

WHAT WOULD YOU DO IF...?

Let's consider a few more disheartening scenarios. Regardless of how remote these possibilities may seem right now, it's important that we consider the possibilities and rehearse appropriate responses to them:

- What if you found out through a neighbor that your daughter was hanging out with a group of guys and girls when she specifically told you she was going to a girlfriend's house to study?

- What if you were to pick up the phone to accidentally overhear a conversation between your daughter and a friend about "how far" they had gone with boys?

- What if you found a note to a friend in your daughter's pocket when you were doing her laundry that mentioned how she dreamed about being kissed by a particular boy and that she was thinking of writing him a note, too.

- What if a teacher at your daughter's junior high school informed you that she and a slightly older boy were found snuggled up together outside the cafeteria during lunch?

- What if your daughter seems to gravitate toward a coach at her school or an older man in your church because he compliments her frequently and gives her special treatment, but you suspect he has less than honorable motives?

- What if you found out your daughter has a reputation for being a major flirt and somewhat of a tease because of how she interacts with young men at school or in the youth group?

- What if you discovered that your daughter's sexual behavior has crossed the line, moving beyond innocent self-gratification or child sexual play to more intentional sexual activities?

If any of these scenarios actually occurred, what would you do? Would you freak out and get on a soapbox? Or would you be tempted to ignore it, hoping it would never happen again? Could you keep a level head, help your daughter process what is really going on, and effectively guide her back onto a healthy track? If your preference is to do the latter, here are some practical tips for you:

- *Be sensitive to her feelings.* If your daughter gets caught involved in any sort of sexual act, whether by herself or with a partner, she will be vulnerable to feelings of guilt and shame. While guilt can serve as conviction that something was inappropriate, shame is an unhealthy emotion that makes the person feel as if *she* is bad. Be sure to separate the action (which you disapprove of) from the person (which you love dearly).

- *Discern what's really going on.* Is she acting out of innocence or ignorance (not realizing that what she is doing is wrong), or is she rebelling against what she knows to be right? Is this a conversation you've had before, or have you just assumed she would know better? Is this a case of curious child sexual play or an attempt to gratify herself sexually? Is this a situation of sexual abuse, or do you suspect there has been some sort of sexual abuse in the past that would lead her to act out in such a way?

- *Ask questions.* Give your daughter the benefit of the doubt, but don't let her snow you either. Ask her questions like these: Can you describe to me exactly what happened? Whose idea was this? Where do you think the idea came from? Did you think twice before doing it? Do you remember what you were thinking at the time? Do you know you can tell me anything and I'll still love you? Do you know I want to help you handle things like this?

- *Affirm her sexuality.* Let your daughter know it's perfectly normal to be curious about her own body, others' bodies, or sex in general, but that marriage will be the season of her life when she is free to explore those curiosities without harmful consequences. Encourage her to channel her curiosities appropriately by coming to you with her questions or concerns.

- *Explain why you feel her actions were inappropriate.* Children do not understand "because I said so." Be clear about how you see the situation so your daughter's view can become clearer as well. If you can incorporate some biblical principles into the discussion, do so patiently and lovingly, being careful not to use Scripture as a whip to beat her with. The truth spoken without love isn't really truth, and love spoken without truth isn't really love. Combine the two and speak the truth in love as God's Word speaks to us.

- *Consider who else is involved.* If she has an accomplice, is he or she acting out of innocence? Is the accomplice older and taking advantage of your daughter or just being a bad peer influence? Does that person need to be confronted or have his or her parents made aware of the situation?

- *Discern if intervention is necessary.* Is the matter serious enough to warrant intervention by a professional counselor? Or a pastor? Or the police? Be willing to get your daughter the help she needs to process the situation appropriately. Professionals can help her develop a strategy for moving on with her life without a load of emotional baggage or debilitating shame.

- *Commit the matter to prayer.* Know that God desires your daughter to live a sexually pure life even more than you do. Pray for a hedge of protection around not just her body but her heart and mind as well.

Even if you have never made any of these disheartening discoveries, you'll want to be on the lookout for warning signs that your daughter may be headed down the wrong path.

Don't Ignore the Warning Signs

If asked, my parents would probably say their most devastating discovery was my asking for birth-control pills at fifteen because I was already sexually active. However, looking back, I can see some earlier behaviors I wish my parents had recognized as warning signs.

Even as a fourth grader, I was excessively boy crazy. By the sixth grade, I frequently had private telephone conversations with boys, sometimes calling my brother's friends who were seniors in high school. In junior high, I was caught several times lying to my parents about where I was going and who I would be with. In the years that followed, I was sometimes late getting home from dates because we fell asleep (no one asked what we were doing lying down together in the first place!). I remember walking in once from a date with my shirt obviously on wrong side out, but nothing was said. I'm not sure the birth-control bomb I dropped on my parents at fifteen was completely unexpected. Had they heeded the earlier warning signs, could things have turned out differently? We'll never know.

I urge you not to ignore the little red flags your daughter may wave on her journey toward sexual maturity, even during her puberty years. If you address those smaller issues as they arise (such as acting boy crazy or insisting on private phone conversations with boys, which we'll discuss more in chapter 5 of book 2), you will be way ahead in preventing big red-flag issues later.

Of course, some red-flag issues may arise that call for a very different approach than what we've discussed. If your daughter were to ever become addicted to drugs or some other illegal behavior, unconditional love often must come in the form of "tough love" where you have to give an ultimatum in order to foster change. For example, "As long as you live under this roof, there will be no illegal activities or else you'll be asked to leave," sounds tough, but it is the most loving response to a crisis situation where genuine change is a life-or-death issue. With less life-threatening issues such as flirting or boy-craziness, consistent conversations and firm boundaries can prevent little red flags from growing into large red flags down the road.

REDEEMING LOVE

If you are like most parents, your daughter can do nothing to make you love her less. Even if she struggles repeatedly with the same issues, don't give up on her. Whether the situation calls for a compassionate, "I understand your struggle" stance, or a tough, "things have to change" stance, shower her with the unconditional love that can ultimately redeem even the most prodigal of daughters.

Regardless of how disappointed my parents were to know of my inappropriate relational pursuits, they never stopped praying for me, believing in me, or loving me. Every time I ran out of my parents' house and into the arms of yet another hormonal boy spouting empty promises, the door was always open for me to come back home. Even though they couldn't find the words to communicate with me openly about the terrible mistakes I was making, they communicated their unconditional love in so many different ways. Of course they couldn't affirm my inappropriate actions, but they always tried to affirm me as their daughter and as a child of God. This love gave me the freedom to go running back to the safety and security of my parents' home when my irresponsible relational pursuits left me lonely.

No matter how many disheartening discoveries may be waiting around the corner as your daughter blossoms into a mature young woman, shower her with your unconditional love so she can know she always has a home in your heart and in the heart of Jesus Christ.

minding her media exposure

> Finally, [sisters], whatever is true, whatever is noble, whatever is right,
> whatever is pure, whatever is lovely, whatever is admirable—if anything
> is excellent or praiseworthy—think about such things.
>
> PHILIPPIANS 4:8

All of us have tendencies to become products of our environment, and children are no exception. Their minds become molded to the shape of the world they live in. This is a real concern for parents in light of how sexually saturated our world has become.

In just a few decades, we've moved from television programs such as *I Love Lucy* and *The Dick Van Dyke Show,* where even married couples slept in separate beds, to prime-time reruns of *Sex in the City,* where unmarried couples sleep together whenever and wherever the mood strikes. Sexual content has become so prevalent that we can no longer simply block the "bad shows," making them off-limits to our preteen daughters. Sex seems to pervade the television screen, regardless of what stations or shows we select. Consider the following statistics found at the National Coalition for the Protection of Children and Families' Web site (www .nationalcoalition.org):

- Seventy-five percent of prime-time television in the 1999–2000 season included sexual content.[1]
- Sixty-four percent of all shows include sexual content, and only 15 percent mention waiting, protection, and consequences.[2]
- The Center for Media and Public Affairs' new study found that sexual content is featured once every four minutes on network television, with 98 percent of all sexual content having no subsequent physical

consequences, 85 percent of sexual behavior having no lasting emotional impact, and nearly 75 percent of participants in sexual activity being unmarried.[3]

- Sexual content on prime-time television more than tripled in the past ten years.[4]
- The average American adolescent will view nearly fourteen thousand sexual references per year.[5]

Sadly, sex is now prime-time entertainment, and we can't be naive enough to think for a minute that it hasn't primed our daughters for future sexual compromise. Consider these sobering statistics about the sexual behavior of youth in America:

- In grades seven through twelve, 23.4 percent of first sexual relationships are one-night stands.[6]
- Thirty-three percent of guys and 23 percent of girls feel some or a lot of pressure to have sex.[7]
- Twenty-one percent of ninth graders have slept with four or more partners.[8]
- One in twelve children is no longer a virgin by his or her thirteenth birthday.[9]
- Fifty-five percent of teens ages thirteen to nineteen admitted to engaging in oral sex.[10]
- Twenty-six percent of teens think it is embarrassing to admit they are virgins.[11]
- Over 40 percent of fifteen-year-olds are sexually active.[12]

Unfortunately, television is only part of the problem. One of the biggest stumbling blocks to a girl's passion for purity may be the Internet, which can usher over 372 million pages of pornography into your child's line of sight with simple clicks of the mouse. Incidentally, please don't assume that girls are not prone to sexual temptations over the Internet like boys are. The median age for a girl's first exposure to pornography is only slightly older (twelve to fourteen years old) than for boys (eleven to thirteen years old).[13] Therefore we need to be just as concerned about our daughters' Internet activities as we are our sons'. If you have a hard time imagining what a negative influence Internet pornography is having on your daughter's generation, consider these statistics from Internet Filter Review (www .internetfilterreview.com):

- The largest consumer of Internet pornography is the twelve-to-seventeen age group.
- Thirty-five percent of all e-mail downloads (1.5 billion daily) are pornographic material circulating from peer to peer.
- Eighty-nine percent of sexual solicitations of young people are made in Internet chat rooms.
- Eighty percent of fifteen- to seventeen-year-olds have had multiple hard-core pornography exposures.
- Ninety percent of eight- to sixteen-year-olds have viewed porn online (most while doing homework).
- Twenty-nine percent of seven- to seventeen-year-olds would freely give out their home address over the Internet.

Because males are so visually stimulated, they may be more drawn to hard-core porn than females, but girls are more drawn to the Internet chat rooms and interactive sites where they can converse in cyberspace with their virtual buddies. This should cause parents tremendous concern. Nearly 1.4 million Americans are stalked online each year (four out of five are women).[14]

Obviously we can't completely shield our daughters from the media. Whenever they sit down in front of a television, go to a movie, surf a Web site, pick up a magazine, or turn on a radio, they are at risk for exposure to sex-saturated media messages. Is there anything we can do? You bet there is!

WHAT'S A PARENT TO DO?

If parents start early enough, they can teach their daughters to filter the avalanche of media messages they'll encounter to discern appropriate messages from not-so-appropriate messages. Let me give you an example of how I've done this with Erin.

When our daughter asked to go see *The Lizzie McGuire Movie* because her friends were all talking about it, I decided I'd take her and watch it closely so I could discuss the movie with her afterward. At first glance, parents may have thought this to be a harmless PG-rated movie. After all, it contains no foul language or graphic sexual scenes. But the movie does contain a more subtly inappropriate message, one that can be just as damaging to a girl's sense of values and even dangerous to her physical safety.

In the movie, Lizzie goes to Paris, France, on a school field trip. Soon she's lying to her chaperone and running off to meet a cute boy she knows nothing about. I kept thinking, *How many girls have been allowed to watch this movie with no parental guidance?* (After all, a PG rating does mean that children should have parental guidance as they watch.) *Does a young audience realize that what Lizzie is doing could prove to be mortally dangerous? Is running away with a stranger in pursuit of an exciting romantic fling something we want our daughters to view as a desirable fantasy rather than an impulsive antic that could get a girl raped or killed?*

Of course, Erin knew exactly what I was thinking as we walked out of the theater, so she got on the soapbox before I did. "I don't know what my friends saw in that movie! She was lying to everyone and expecting her friend to lie for her and running off to be alone with a boy she didn't even know! If a girl really did that, she'd get in *soooo* much trouble!" I was relieved to hear that Erin recognized the inappropriate theme running through the movie rather than getting caught up in the glitz and glamour of Lizzie's fantasy field trip to France.

Alice often uses the media to teach her daughter Hannah useful discernment skills. She's found that because she asks her daughter intelligent questions and expects intelligent answers in return, her daughter has become more confident in her problem-solving skills and in expressing her own opinion. Alice does something similar with music. She says:

> My daughter and I like country music. She likes to sing along with the female vocalists; I like the harmony of the tunes. And I like to use the lyrics to teach her the principles of healthy relationships versus codependency. "Would a woman actually *die* if her man left her? What is our true source of life? Do you think you have to do whatever somebody else wants [with your body] in order for that person to love you? Does God expect us to compromise for Him?"

Hannah knows she can never give a wrong answer and that she can ask me questions too. Her answers often lead to new questions and open a new discussion. My goal is to get her in the habit of questioning all kinds of messages so she'll continue to use discernment as she grows older and begins making her own choices. And while she's young, my goal is to keep her talking to me!

Isn't that the goal of every mom and dad? To keep them talking to us about whatever they are facing, especially sexual issues? Of course it is.

KEEPING SEXUAL MEDIA MESSAGES AT BAY

In addition to asking your daughter questions about the movies and television shows she watches and the music she listens to, you can minimize her exposure to negative messages by implementing the following filters:

- Keep televisions and computers in common areas of your home (such as the living room or family den) rather than allowing them in your daughter's

Here are a few questions you can ask your daughter following a movie with subtle, inappropriate themes, whether you attend with her or not:

- Did you like the movie? Why or why not?
- Did you notice any inappropriate scenes or themes?
- What did you think of the lead character before the inappropriate scene?
- What did you think of that character after that scene?
- Can you tell me what Hollywood's agenda was by slipping in that scene?
- What was the message, and at whom were they aiming the message?
- If you were to make up more of the story to tack on to the end of the movie, would you say the characters "lived happily ever after"? Why or why not?
- What can you learn from the experiences of the characters in this movie?

private bedroom. Simply being in a public place allows for some measure of accountability.

- You may want to establish a rule we have in our house for our ten- and thirteen-year-olds. Mom or Dad are the only ones who can open e-mail in-boxes to see what is waiting there. This gives us the opportunity to delete the "Do you want a bigger penis?" and "Check out my new web-cam!" types of spam e-mails before our children happen to open them.

- Put a filter on your computer that will screen out inappropriate Web sites and e-mails. When it comes to your daughter's innocence and safety, it's well worth the minimal investment to keep those pop-ups and porno-graphic pages at bay.

- As radical as it may sound, *turn off the television!* Try an experiment we've done in our family. Unplug all the televisions in the house and declare a thirty-day television fast. We've found that the first few days are challeng-ing, but once you get used to the increased productivity around the house and more interactive family times, you almost dread the end of the thirty days. When you plug the television back in, restrict how many hours each day you allow it to be on. When it is on, watch shows *with* your kids so you know what they are being exposed to and can provide guidance, seiz-ing every teachable moment.

- Let your daughter know that if there's a popular television show she wants to watch, you will view an episode with an open mind and then let her know your opinion. But also tell her that one of your primary roles and responsibilities as a parent is to help her mind her media exposure, and if you decide something's inappropriate, she needs to accept that as loving protection rather than overprotection. Assure her that while you want to protect her from graphic, sexual media messages, you don't want to keep her completely in the dark and ignorant about how to properly respond to sensual media messages, either.

- Attend PG-rated movies with your daughter so she can receive the parental guidance that needs to accompany the movie's message. Screen PG-13 movies completely before you decide whether you will take your child to see it. If you are unsure, a good way to decide is to ask yourself whether you would mind if your pastor or her Sunday-school teacher knew you allowed her to watch it. If you would mind, then don't let her view it. And if you wouldn't want her talking about the movie in front of other adults, don't put her in the position where she'd be expected to avoid telling the truth about whether she's seen a certain movie.

• Steer your daughter toward contemporary Christian music artists who promote sexual purity. ZOEgirl, Rebecca St. James, Bethany Dillon, Joy Williams, and Jump5 are a few of my daughter's favorites. This will help her not be tempted to listen to music by artists that model sexual compromise—Britney Spears, Christina Aguilera, Shania Twain, and so on.

Family-Friendly Filters and Reviews

• Cybersitter (www.cybersitter.com), BSafe (www.bsafeonline.com), and Net Nanny (www.netnanny.com) are great tools that will allow you to monitor your kids' Internet activity.

• A DVD player from RCA allows parents to filter movie content deemed objectionable in several categories including violence, language, sex, and nudity (Gary Gentile, "DVD players filter movies for content," *Cincinnati Enquirer,* 19 April 2004).

• ClearPlay created a new seventy-dollar DVD player (available at Wal-Mart) that has built-in filters designed to skip over violence and nudity and to mute salty language in one hundred movies; more than six hundred titles are available for download (Mike Snider, "Hollywood Riled Up over ClearPlay," *USA Today,* 6 May 2004).

• If you aren't sure whether something is appropriate for your children, Focus on the Family provides reviews of movies, videos/DVDs, music, and television shows at www.pluggedinonline.com

- For a great alternative to often-inappropriate magazines such as *Teen People, Young Miss,* or *CosmoGirl,* check out magazines that will encourage your daughter in her pursuit of modesty and sexual propriety. Focus on the Family's *Brio* magazine for girls is ideal and candidly addresses many issues young women face today. I also recommend *Revolve,* a New Testament in cool girl-magazine form, complete with articles and fun questionnaires (Thomas Nelson Publishers).

By limiting your daughter's exposure to sexual messages in the media and providing some great alternative music and magazines, you'll help her guard her mind. If she can learn to guard her mind during these formative years, she'll have the skills to successfully guard her heart and body in the bigger battles she'll face down the road.

Teachable Moments

When Bristol Palin was in the media with her new baby, I realized again the value of teachable moments. I asked my own seventeen-year-old daughter, Erin, "What do you think of Bristol's situation?" She admitted, "Babies are great, but there's no way I'm ready for one. I want to finish college first and be married and financially stable." Me too, Erin. Me too.

In this sex-saturated world, it's more important than ever to instill sexual values and healthy confidence in our daughters. Use teachable moments in news, media, and advertising to prepare them.

shopping sensibly

I also want women to dress modestly, with decency and propriety, not
with braided hair or gold or pearls or expensive clothes, but with good
deeds, appropriate for women who profess to worship God.

1 TIMOTHY 2:9-10

The "guards" were heavily armed and ready to protect the bank from any "bad
guys" that might wander in. Matthew (four years old at the time) stood on one
side of the entrance to the bank lobby with a toy bow and arrow in ready position.
On the other side of the door stood his friend Cameron, also four, with an impres-
sive plastic sword drawn from its sheath. As I stood in line at the teller window, I
noticed that all the bank patrons, relieved that they were in such capable hands,
were looking on appreciatively at these self-appointed guards.

Then *she* walked in, a long-legged young woman in high heels, a formfitting
miniskirt, and spaghetti-strap top. The young guards glanced at each other with
eyes wide. The rest of the onlookers turned their heads back and forth between
the little boys and the young woman as if watching a tennis match, eyeballing the
woman, then the boys, then the woman again. As this scantily-clad bombshell
strutted across the bank lobby, made an ATM transaction, and then strutted back
out through the armed doors, I sensed that everyone in the lobby was holding their
breath and wondering, *What could those boys be thinking right now?*

As soon as the door closed and the woman was out of earshot, Cameron satisfied everyone's curiosity as he leaned over to Matthew and loudly exclaimed, "The
Bible *warns* about women like *that!*"

Of course, the entire bank erupted in laughter! That incident happened years
ago, but it's no laughing matter that today we often see young women dressed more
like stereotypical hookers than modest young women.

Here are two of the most valuable principles we can teach our daughters when it comes to how they dress:

You teach people how to treat you.

and

Whatever bait you use determines the type of fish you'll catch.

If a young woman dresses seductively, guys are likely going to treat her as if she wants to be seduced. She's going to get attention from lustful guys, not godly ones who want to guard themselves against sexual compromise. If we want our girls to be treated with the dignity and respect they deserve, we'll teach them to dress modestly. If we want to protect them from boys who are more interested in their bodies than in their minds, hearts, or spirits, we'll teach them to shop for clothes that present a passion for purity rather than a plea for attention.

As mentioned earlier, chapter 11 in the next section offers guidelines for how your daughter can evaluate her wardrobe to ensure that it reflects the Christian-girl image she is striving for. But I want to challenge you, the parent, to consider what you can do to help your daughter become a smart shopper who values modesty and responsible stewardship.

WHO'S IN CHARGE?

On occasion when I speak to parents about encouraging our daughters to dress modestly, some will retort with statements like these:

- *Wearing the latest fashions doesn't make my daughter less sexually pure.* If we look at sexual purity in strictly a physical sense, then granted, a girl is no less a virgin if she wears immodest clothes. But as followers of Christ, we are to pursue not just physical purity, but mental, emotional, and spiritual purity as well. Do you want your daughter dressing in such a way that boys flirt with her and try desperately to get her attention? Do you want older guys noticing her? I believe that when parents let their twelve-year-old dress like she's twenty, they are not protecting her from vulnerability to unhealthy, premature relationships.

- *I don't want to spend my hard-earned money on clothes that are going to just hang in the closet.* If this is our mind-set as parents, we need to reconsider what we value most. Will we sell out our daughter's sense of modesty and her reputation so that she'll get more mileage out of what's hanging in her closet? While inappropriate clothes may get worn more often by an attention-seeking preteen, eventually a parent's hard-earned money may have to go toward professional counseling to get her out of the relational messes she'll find herself in if she continues to dress provocatively.

- *I can't control what clothes she wears.* Funny how some parents say this about their preteen daughters, yet in truth, these same parents facilitate their daughters' bad choices by driving them to certain stores, whipping out the credit card to buy the clothes, and standing at the door when their daughters leave for school in the morning, wearing those clothes. Regardless of how powerless we may feel, we *do* have control over our daughters' wardrobes as long as they're living under our roofs. We simply have to be secure enough in our role as parents to exercise that control.

  If you feel that your preteen daughter is calling the shots when it comes to what she wears, you may need to seek counsel for how to regain the parental control you've abdicated to her. Remember, the battles will only get more significant, and if she's accustomed to getting her way, you will certainly travel some bumpy roads ahead.

- *But my daughter wants to wear what all of her friends are wearing.* One of the most significant ways we can help our daughters is to teach them to *lead* rather than *follow,* especially when it comes to fashions. Think about it. If your daughter looks to others to determine what she should wear, she will be more likely to look to others to tell her what to do in other areas of her life. She will be more likely to follow the crowd into sexual compromise. Teach her to blaze her own trail through life—one that will steer clear of the many pitfalls to sexual compromise.

- *She doesn't even have breasts and hips yet, so I don't think she's turning any guys' heads by what she wears.* News flash: your daughter may not have a rounded figure just yet, but guess what? That's only temporary. Better to prepare her for modesty in the near future by expecting it today, during her tweener years.

In addition to teaching a sense of modesty, we can also teach our daughters to value practicality and quality, as well as how to be responsible stewards of resources.

TAKING CHARGE OF YOUR INVESTMENTS

It alarmed me when my daughter developed a hearty appetite for shopping when she was only eight years old. Anytime we went into a store, Erin felt she had to pick something out for herself, regardless of whether she needed anything or not. If I told her I didn't have the money for the purchase, she'd sometimes say, "But Mom, you can charge it on your credit card!" She had no concept that at the end of the month her father and I would have to pay the entire bill or we would start accruing interest on those purchases. Greg and I knew we were heading for trouble and that we needed to teach our daughter how to spend money wisely.

So when Erin turned nine, we started an annual tradition for back-to-school clothes shopping trips. We buy the basic updates she needs (new socks, underwear, and bigger shoes if necessary), but she has to make nonessential new clothes purchases from the cash we give her for these shopping excursions. We determine the amount of money she gets each year by multiplying her age times ten dollars, so when Erin was nine, she received ninety dollars. She could spend that money however she wanted, as long as her choices were modest. She could either buy one pair of jeans for forty-five dollars and one sweater for forty-five dollars from an upscale store and be done with her shopping trip, or she could shop in stores where clearance sales and bargain racks abound. Fortunately Erin proved to be no dummy when it came to math. She figured out quickly that she could get lots more bang for her buck by steering clear of brand names and posh department stores. That year she purchased two pairs of jeans, a dress with a jacket that could be worn with other things, two casual shirts, a sweater, and a pair of capri overalls with her ninety dollars. She was proud of her new clothes and her shopping savvy.

A pastor and his wife recently told me how they teach their children to appreciate the limited value of a dollar. As soon as their children are old enough to have a checking account, the parents begin depositing a set dollar amount each month.

The kids are expected to tithe 10 percent off the top, and anytime they need something, it comes out of their own account. When they walk into Wal-Mart, they each grab a cart and go their separate ways. Mom purchases the family groceries and household items, but personal items such as makeup, toothpaste, hair-styling products, clothes, and school supplies come out of the child's own checking account. While Greg and I have not implemented this plan with our children yet, we do plan on asking the bank about the minimum age requirement on a checking account! What a great way to teach kids valuable skills, such as comparison shopping, budgeting, and accounting.

Make sure your daughter understands that money doesn't grow on trees. Teach her to discern her *wants* from her *needs*. As parents, we always want to provide for our kids' genuine needs, but when it comes to their wants, we must teach them moderation.

THE POWER OF RESPONSIBLE CONSUMERISM

We also need to teach our girls responsible stewardship and consumerism. The money we have to spend doesn't really belong to us, but to God. He owns everything. Therefore tithing isn't a matter of how much of our money we are going to give to God, but how much of God's money we are going to keep for ourselves. I believe God blesses us financially so we can be a blessing to others. Tithing and charitable giving should not be options but regular acts of worship. The more money we spend on ourselves and our selfish desires (things we don't really need), the less we have to help those who truly are in need.

Because all of our money belongs to God and He entrusts it to us, I feel we have a responsibility to channel our resources in directions that honor Him. One day I had an incredible opportunity to teach my daughter this concept. We were shopping, and Erin found a T-shirt that she liked. It wasn't overpriced and was relatively modest, but I suggested we continue looking to see what else we could find. As we made our way toward the back of the store, we saw young girls looking through racks of shirts and bins of miscellaneous items, so we thought we might find some cool stuff there. Upon closer examination, I discovered that many of the shirts broadcast sexually graphic messages and the bins were filled with gag gifts such as "boob pasta" and "gummy penises." I wondered where the parents of these girls were, and if they knew their kids were rummaging through such things.

Trying to keep my cool, I walked back toward the front of the store, and Erin followed right behind. I asked her, "How much do you like this shirt you are wanting to buy?"

She replied, "Mom, I don't want the shirt that badly. I can find something better at a store we can feel good about. Come on, put the shirt back, and let's go." I breathed a prayer of gratitude that she and I were on the same page.

Unfortunately, many people don't make the connection between how we spend our money and the explosion of irresponsible sexual messages in retail stores. For example, many kids (and parents) know how offensive Abercrombie & Fitch catalogs and graphic window displays are, yet they are still regular patrons of the store. They say it's okay because they don't buy the really seductive clothing. However, they are fueling a business that is contributing to the moral decay in our country. If Christian consumers don't send the message loud and clear that they want clothes and companies that support their values, no one else will.

For years Calvin Klein has targeted young adults and teens with sexually provocative black-and-white advertisements. The company manufactures clothes, yet their models rarely have any on. They blatantly use sex to sell their products. I coach consumers of all ages, "I don't care how great their clothes look on you or how good their cologne smells, don't pour your dollars into Calvin Klein's pocket so he and his company can continue putting borderline-pornographic advertisements in kids' faces."

Again, we teach people how to treat us, and retailers are no different. If we reward them with our business, they are going to assume we like being bombarded with sexually inappropriate advertisements. We can turn the tide by channeling our dollars away from rather than into companies that use sex to sell their products.

LESSONS THAT LAST A LIFETIME

As a parent, you may feel it's not worth the fight to try to control where your daughter shops, what clothes she buys, and what she leaves the house wearing. It seems so much easier just to give her the freedom to make her own choices and hope for the best.

The same could be said for many other parts of her life. It would be easier just to leave her alone and let her do her own thing rather than getting her out of bed, taking her back and forth to school every day, helping her with her homework, and attending teacher conferences. Why do you make her education a priority? Not just because it's the law, but also because you want the very best for her and you know a good education will take her where she dreams of going in life. It may seem easier to let your daughter do whatever she wants on Sunday rather than dragging her to Sunday school and church every weekend. Why do you make church activities a priority? Because you want her to develop a strong spiritual life and enjoy an intimate walk with the Lord.

Are values of modesty and responsible stewardship any less desirable? Of course not. Since you are reading this book, I know you want to develop the strongest character possible in your daughter. You want her to have a sense of pride in how she presents herself to others, to enjoy the respect of peers and adults, and to attract like-minded friends and a healthy, future romantic relationship.

Every struggle you may experience along the way toward instilling these values is worth the fight. Every ounce of energy you pour into encouraging these concepts is a worthy investment. These lessons on modesty and responsible stewardship will guide your daughter not just through puberty and her upcoming teenage years but also throughout her lifetime.

setting high standards

Righteousness goes before [her]
and prepares the way for [her] steps.

PSALM 85:13

I find all televised Olympic events fascinating to watch, but my favorite event has always been pole vaulting. I can still remember being a little girl in the 1970s and watching Dwight Stone in his Mickey Mouse tank top as he launched himself up and over the bar time and time again. It seemed as if the bar couldn't be moved high enough to make Dwight trip up. He simply adjusted his trajectory and soared higher and higher to accomplish the goal.

Compare pole vaulting with the more amateur game of limbo. With limbo, the horizontal pole is moved lower and lower as participants strive to see just how low they can go to clear the bar without touching it. In pole vaulting, the goal is to strive to reach higher and make it over the top, while in limbo, the goal is to stoop lower and remain under the bar. Why all this talk of pole vaulting and limbo? I want to create some word pictures in your mind as I ask you these questions: Where are you setting the bar for your daughter? Have you established high standards and lofty goals for her to strive toward, or are you playing limbo and lowering the bar of expectation with each passing year?

As I mentioned earlier, parents often ask me, "How can I expect my daughter to do something I didn't do?" What they are really saying is, "I'm afraid to set the standard any higher than what I accomplished, because I don't want her to fail." These parents can't see that by lowering the bar, they are setting their daughter up to fail in her upcoming battles for sexual and emotional integrity. In response, I sometimes turn the question back to the parent by asking (with a compassionate voice, of course), "If you robbed a bank when you were a teenager, would you tell your daughter it's okay for her to rob a bank too? Or would you set a higher standard for her than what you lived up to at her age?"

The same principle applies to sexual mistakes. If we lower the bar, our daughters are automatically going to lower their standards as well. If we raise the bar, they'll at least try to live up to the expectations we establish and perhaps even go above and beyond the standards we set. I'm all about giving our kids the grace to be human and forgiving them when they fall short, but I also believe we need to raise the bar and expect them to reach for victory when it comes to living a life of sexual integrity.

So let's talk about how we can raise the bar, using the questions parents often ask me. I realize you may not be asking some of these questions—yet. However, I've included them because I think it's better to prevent problems than to react to them. When parents tell me they are butting heads with their thirteen- and fourteen-year-old daughters about when they'll be allowed to date, whether they can invite a boy over, or why they can't be trusted to have a private phone conversation, my heart bleeds for them. If we wait to lay out the rules and regulations until the time when our daughters *desire* these things, we may face a fierce power struggle. With that said, let's discuss some questions you need to think about.

SHOULD I ALLOW MY PRETEEN DAUGHTER TO CALL BOYS?

Most young girls might think, *What's the big deal? It's just a phone call!* But it's a very big deal when young women go out of their way to pursue a boy's attention. Just ask any mother how it makes her feel when the phone rings and a giggly girl on the other line asks to speak to her son.

This is likely one of the first struggles your daughter will face in her battle for emotional integrity. Will she indulge her desire for attention from the opposite sex, or will she make self-control and propriety her goals? The wise parent will talk to a preteen daughter *now* about how pursuing a boy's attention puts him in an awkward position and can make her look foolish or desperate.

Of course, a girl may need to call a boy about a homework assignment, youth-group activity, or some related matter. Still, I recommend you insist she ask your permission to call beforehand, and if you feel her motives are pure, tell her she can make the call from a phone in a common area, such as the kitchen or living room. If she insists on taking a cordless phone into her room so she can talk to a boy in private, there's probably cause for concern at this young age. In that case, it's time to establish some clear telephone boundaries and consequences for disobedience (such as withdrawing phone privileges for a period of time).

SHOULD I ALLOW MY PRETEEN DAUGHTER TO ACCEPT CALLS FROM BOYS?

If and when a boy calls, enforce the rules mentioned above. Require that telephone conversations remain public for built-in accountability. Just as you wouldn't allow your daughter to be alone in her room behind a closed door with a boy, allowing private telephone conversations at this age can quickly lead to inappropriate behavior. Just because a boy and girl are separated by distance while on the phone doesn't prevent them from engaging in steamy conversations, which can lead to inappropriate physical behavior during future face-to-face encounters.

I also suggest you give her a reasonable time limit on phone calls with boys. Five to ten minutes is more than enough to say what needs to be said and lets her know she can't hang on the phone with a boy for hours at a time.

By all means, if you feel such boy-girl phone conversations would be outside the realm of a healthy, age-appropriate friendship for your daughter, trust your parental instinct and discourage such conversations until your daughter is older, wiser, and more discerning. Because preteens and teens are generally far bolder over the telephone than in person, ask that she do her guy-girl socializing while at school or church, but limit her telephone conversations to female friends.

IS IT APPROPRIATE TO ALLOW MY PRETEEN DAUGHTER TO HAVE A BOYFRIEND?

Encourage your daughter to have boys who are friends but to save the "boyfriend" status for much further down the road, when she's actually allowed to date or court.

While it's normal and healthy for girls to have friends who are boys, I believe it's unhealthy for a preteen girl to have a boyfriend. I was disturbed when I noticed some of my daughter's friends talking about their "boyfriends" as early as the third grade. I wanted to discourage Erin from any ideas (even unformed) of pursuing a boyfriend, so one day I asked her, "What do you think about a nine-year-old girl having a boyfriend?" She responded, "I think it's silly! She can't get married for at least ten more years, and I don't think they'll like each other for that long!"

I was thankful for her response and wanted to encourage her to keep this mind-set, so I talked with her about when she might be ready to consider having a boyfriend. Together, we decided that her senior year of high school would be the earliest she would even consider dating a boy. Because Erin was part of this agreement, I feel she'll strive to accomplish that goal of remaining free of relational entanglements during her early teen years.

This Hurts My Heart...

"Student auctions off virginity for offers of more than £2.5 million"
A student who was auctioning her virginity to pay for a master's degree in family and marriage therapy saw bidding hit £2.5million ($3.7 million). Natalie Dylan, then twenty-two, claimed that her offer of a one-night stand persuaded ten thousand men to bid for sex with her. In September 2008, when her auction came to light, she had received bids up to £162,000 ($243,000), but after that, interest in her rocketed.

Natalie said she was persuaded to make the offer by her sister's experience of paying for her degree by living as a prostitute for three weeks. Natalie said she didn't think what she was doing was particularly significant. "I know that a lot of people will condemn me because it's so taboo, but I really don't have a problem with that.... I'm not being taken advantage of in any way. Me and the person I do it with will both profit greatly from the deal." She added, "It's shocking that men will pay so much for someone's virginity, which isn't even prized so highly anymore."

When virginity has become a commodity, instilling sexual standards becomes paramount. Healthy sex happens only in the context of a healthy marriage! If your daughter is old enough to understand this, consider summarizing Natalie's situation and ask, "What do you think this will do to her sexual confidence when she gets married? How will her husband see her character? What advice would you give her?"

SHOULD I ALLOW HER TO HAVE A CHAPERONED DATE AT HER AGE?

If the date is your daughter's idea, let her know you are supportive of her having healthy friendships with boys, but that she can't go out on chaperoned dates until she is older. It's one thing when a junior or senior girl makes such a request; it's another if your daughter is twelve or thirteen (or even younger!).

Unfortunately, I've heard of parents actually encouraging their preteens to invite opposite-sex friends over for dinner or to attend a football game or other event with their families. I believe this is unwise. We don't need to push our kids toward opposite-sex relationships. They'll gravitate in that direction in due time. Also remember that kids don't take steps backward in their pursuit of romantic relationships. Once you encourage or allow your daughter to "couple up" with a particular boy, even if it's under the protective umbrella of family fun, you are setting the stage for her to want to be alone with him much sooner than she might otherwise.

AT WHAT AGE SHOULD I ALLOW HER TO DATE OR HAVE A BOYFRIEND?

While parents should certainly enforce a minimum-age requirement (in my opinion, girls younger than sixteen or seventeen are too young to date or have boyfriends), I don't think it's wise to tell our daughters they can date when they turn some magical age. Instead, they need to demonstrate certain qualities over time in order to earn the privilege of dating. I've seen sixteen- and seventeen-year-olds demonstrate enough maturity to handle dating or courtship, but I've also seen adults in their twenties and even thirties who have no business dating because of their immaturity, self-centeredness, and lack of respect for the sanctity of serious relationships.

Consider this analogy: Even when your daughter gets old enough to drive a car, that doesn't mean she'll be ready to drive. She will need to have plenty of practice behind the wheel and to be able to demonstrate responsibility and good judgment before you will allow her to drive a car by herself. You want to make sure she's ready for this responsibility because you love her and care about her physical safety.

The same holds true with dating. Even when your daughter reaches what you consider the minimum age for dating, that doesn't mean she's ready. She needs to demonstrate a certain maturity level in her family relationships because it's in our families that we get "practice time" in properly conducting loving relationships. She also needs to show emotional and spiritual readiness by demonstrating:

- respectful submission to parental authority
- an understanding of and joyful obedience to biblical commandments
- investing time in developing a more intimate relationship with God
- ability to maintain good grades and a desire to remain focused on her education
- willingness to fully participate in family activities (including chores, conversations, and trips) so that strong emotional ties are maintained in spite of new romantic relationships being introduced

Add to this list to make it your own and feel free to discuss your expectations with your daughter whenever she inquires about when she'll be allowed to date. Let her know that as long as she's living in your house, she must demonstrate certain qualities in order to earn the privilege to date. Also consider requiring that your daughter read my book *Every Young Woman's Battle*, as it spells out clear boundaries for dating relationships and offers specific help for how young women can guard their minds, hearts, and bodies from sexual and emotional compromise.

WHAT'S THE DIFFERENCE BETWEEN COURTSHIP AND DATING, AND WHICH DO YOU RECOMMEND?

While your preteen daughter is not mature enough to date or be courted, you can expect that will change in a few years. In light of that, it would be good for you to decide *now* how you want her to approach getting to know the opposite sex.

Dating and courtship introduce different levels of intended commitment on the front end of the relationship. Dating has a casual, "We'll just go out and have a good time and see how things go" approach to a guy-girl relationship. Courting, on the other hand, has a more marriage-minded approach: "If we begin seeing each other, it's because we know each other well enough to believe we have real potential for a permanent relationship, so we'll see each other exclusively until we discern if we're truly compatible and want to commit to marrying." I can't say that one method is necessarily better than the other, because I've seen both dating and courting done very maturely and responsibly, and I've also seen both done in very immature and irresponsible ways.

A young woman is dating recklessly when she spends time with any guy who asks because she doesn't want to be stuck at home on a Friday or Saturday night. Without firm boundaries, such a girl can wander into sexual temptations out of boredom or poor judgment.

A young woman courts irresponsibly when she gallops into an exclusive relationship before she really gets to know the guy well enough to discern his true character. Just because one chooses courting over dating doesn't guarantee sexual integrity. I've known many couples who decided to court rather than date, but the relationship turned sexual prior to marriage in spite of their best intentions.

Some girls have a tendency to try to force serious relationships a little too soon. One fine young man recently complained to me that he didn't know how to respond to a girl when she informed him on their first outing, "I believe in courtship rather than dating. Can you tell me your intentions? Can we define the relationship?" It may not have been what the girl wanted to hear, but he responded, "I don't have *any* intentions yet. Can't we just spend some time getting to know each other as friends before we attempt to define the relationship?"

Rather than allowing our daughters to date recklessly or court irresponsibly, we need to teach them that romantic relationships are for the purpose of selecting a future marriage partner. A young woman who approaches dating this way is much less likely to date just to pass the time or because everyone else is dating. She will hopefully choose to be friends with a guy for at least a year before considering whether to date him or court at all; she will get to know him even more through time spent together (preferably in group and social settings to avoid isolation and the temptations that come with that); and she will see only someone she considers to be a good potential marriage partner.

No matter what label you place on your daughter's pursuit of a potential mate—dating or courtship—encourage her to enjoy healthy relationships that honor God; to maintain firm boundaries; to guard her mind, heart, and body from inappropriate behavior; and to know that time is her friend when considering who to marry.

Should There Be a Limit on Age Spreads When It Comes to Dating?

Absolutely. There is a "tight connection" between teen girls' sexual behavior and dating older boys.[1] Also, the majority of teen girls who get pregnant out of wedlock are impregnated by much older guys.

Until your daughter finishes high school, I recommend a "one year older or one year younger" rule. For instance, allow your seventeen-year-old to only date someone who is sixteen, seventeen, or eighteen. Two years means a big difference in sexual development during adolescence. Be sure to discuss this standard with your daughter long before her season of dating begins. This may seem so far off in the future that you aren't concerned about it, but wouldn't it be better to have this rule firmly established already if a fourteen- or fifteen-year-old boy begins calling your twelve-year-old daughter?

If you ever discover that your daughter has lied about a boy's age just so she can date him, that's reason enough to suspend her freedom to date for a period of time until she earns your trust once again. Remember, as long as she's still in high school, dating should be seen as a privilege to be earned rather than a right to be expected.

What About Sleepovers at Other Houses?

Spending the night with a girlfriend can be an especially fun treat for your daughter, but when an older brother also sleeps under the same roof, you may want to think twice before allowing this. The attention a cool older brother can lavish on his sister's friend is usually more of an emotional temptation than you want your daughter to have to handle at her age. I also don't recommend sleepovers if only the inviter's dad—and not mom—is going to be present. In such cases, you might request that the overnighter be at your house (assuming there are no older male children in your home). Or ask that overnighters be scheduled when older brothers are going to be away for the night. Explain your position up front to the other parents, and let the family know it's not a personal distrust issue because of their son (or yours) but rather a blanket policy you've established in your family to protect your children (both your daughters and your sons). Also give your daughter a similar explanation to help her understand your position without feeling like you don't trust her or the older boys. You can say something like, "I don't feel good about boys and girls who aren't related to each other being together overnight. It just wouldn't be appropriate."

The only exception to the "no coed overnighter" rule I would consider is when a daughter reaches the age that she is old enough to go on overnight retreats with her coed youth group (which is usually at least thirteen years of age). Most such retreat experiences are wonderful opportunities for youth to create spiritual milestones. Granted, counselors and youth leaders can also be sexual predators, but there are usually more accountability measures in place on such a public outing than there are in a family's private home. However, I strongly recommend that you ask the youth leader how the facility is set up and what the plan is for sleeping arrangements. Confirm that there are segregated male and female sleeping quarters separated by physical and mental boundaries, such as walls and doors, rather than a one-room community sleeping arrangement. Ask what the consequences are for guys and girls pairing up and wandering off together unchaperoned. You might also want to forewarn your daughter that an older boy in the youth group may attempt to divert her attention away from God and the purpose of the retreat, and encourage her not to allow that to happen. If you feel she is not mature enough to maintain this boundary, you might consider postponing her involvement in such events until you feel confident of her ability to guard her heart and protect herself from inappropriate involvements.

PREVENTATIVE VERSUS REACTIVE MEDICINE

Remember, the best medicine is a good dose of prevention. By discussing well in advance your expectations for your daughter's relational future, you are preventing potential confusion and stress in your relationship and laying a strong foundation for even more character building as she matures. By raising the bar and setting high standards for her long before she begins thinking about calling boys or having a boyfriend, you're paving the way for her sexual and emotional propriety at every stage of her life.

encore performances

Children's children are a crown to the aged,
and parents are the pride of their children.

PROVERBS 17:6

Before we move on to book 2, I want to give you a few more ideas you can use with your daughter long after this book is collecting dust on the shelf. While it may take only a few weeks to read through this material with your daughter, you can do many other fun things in the coming years to keep these principles on the forefront of her mind.

Remember, sexuality education isn't a one-time lecture or even a series of conversations to get your daughter through puberty. It's a lifelong process of both parents *and* daughters learning, growing, maturing, struggling, resisting, and at times, unfortunately, failing. But it's also about learning from mistakes and pressing on to improve our character. I pray that this book will give your daughter a tremendous jump-start toward becoming the young woman God wants her to be, and that the following tips will provide you with excellent continuing-education opportunities as she blossoms into a young woman of sexual and emotional integrity.

If you aren't doing this already, one of the encore performances I encourage you to make is to...

DISCUSS A WIDE VARIETY OF TOPICS WITH HER

One reason some teens feel awkward discussing sexuality is that their parents don't typically discuss many deep issues openly and honestly with them. As children mature and gravitate toward their peers, it's easy to feel as if we're losing touch. It can be a challenge to find the time or opportunity to talk heart to heart about anything. Some teens tell me they have tried to talk to their parents, but that the mom or dad seemed distracted or disinterested. Stay in touch with your daughter by being willing to talk about the things most affecting her right now, such as her school, her friends, and her extracurricular activities. The more conversations you have about the everyday stuff, the more naturally deeper conversations will occur.

During these everyday discussions about the most common of topics, always be on the lookout for opportunities to...

HELP HER RECOGNIZE THE IMPORTANCE OF CHARACTER

Most young women have a short and shallow list of criteria for a potential boyfriend. When I ask younger girls what they want in a husband some day, *cute* and *rich* usually top the list. Our society has done our children a disservice by promoting physical appearance and financial status as the measuring sticks for desirability. However, as parents we can help our kids recognize more important things to look for such as the strong character traits of a godly spirit, a compassionate heart, a discerning mind, trustworthiness, tenderness, and respect for others. When you notice these traits in others (especially in your spouse), praise those characteristics in the presence of your daughter. I often say, "Erin, I love the way your dad is so patient with people and how everyone who knows him loves his tender heart. I hope you find a husband who respects other people and is so respected by others as well."

Usually, Erin grins and responds, "I hope I find a guy just like Daddy!"

Also encourage your daughter to discern the character of her friends. To help her do that, I suggest you...

TAKE AN INTEREST IN HER MALE AND FEMALE FRIENDS

Your daughter's friends need to know you and what values your family holds. You can do this by making your home a safe haven for teenagers where they feel comfortable hanging out in your presence. Although it may mean your family room is often wall-to-wall kids, it's worth the trouble. When our children would rather spend time with their friends in our own homes than go anywhere else, we don't have to wonder about who they are with and what they are doing.

In addition, you can constantly instill in your daughter a sense of healthy pride about making responsible decisions when you…

COMPLIMENT WISE CHOICES

Any time you catch her doing something right, whether it's feeding the family pets without being asked, reading her Bible on her own, or diligently working to complete a major homework assignment when she could have procrastinated, comment on it. Let her know you believe in her and that you also believe she'll do the right thing when she faces peer pressure and sexual temptations.

To further develop your confidence that she'll resist those temptations in the future…

TEACH HER THAT AFFECTIONATE BEHAVIOR IS A GIFT, NOT A REQUIREMENT

When it comes to relationships outside of your immediate family, your daughter needs to know she may show affection if it feels appropriate, and that she also has the right to refrain from it if she doesn't feel comfortable. For example, if an uncle, grandparent, or neighbor says to her, "Come give me a hug," but you can tell by the look on her face that she's thinking, *I really don't want to!* simply tell her, "If you don't want to hug right now, that's okay!" Then tell the person asking for affection, "If it's okay with you, she's not really in a hugging mood right now." By never insisting she hug or kiss someone when she prefers not to, you are teaching her that physical affection is a gift she can give when she desires to, not a requirement in relationships. This kind of confidence and ability to say no will equip her to say no to peer pressure, sexual abuse, and sexual temptation as she grows older.

You can also help set a high standard for your young daughter when you…

GIVE HER A SYMBOL THAT REFLECTS HER
COMMITMENT TO PURITY

When Erin was nine, I took her out on a mother-daughter date and presented her with a small box of Whitman's Sampler chocolates. I talked with her about how sexual intimacy was a sweet surprise she could look forward to, but that if she experienced it before marriage, it would feel as if she were giving her husband an already-opened box of chocolates on her honeymoon night. Since that conversation, she's kept the unopened box of chocolates on her bookshelf as her reminder that pure sex on her honeymoon night will be worth the wait and a wonderful gift to present to her husband.

Many parents buy their teenage daughters purity rings to wear on their wedding finger as a reminder of their commitment to virginity until marriage. Some of these young women present those same rings to their husbands at the altar on their wedding day. The more positive symbolism you can create in her mind, the more precious sexual purity will be to her.

Another effective way parents can equip their daughters to remain sexually pure, despite peer and societal pressure, is to…

ENCOURAGE HER TO JOURNAL ABOUT HER OWN
DREAMS AND GOALS

Many of the young women I counsel at Teen Mania Ministries confess they are overflowing with dreams for their futures. As parents, we can help our daughters guard their hearts against getting involved with the wrong guys at the wrong time by encouraging them to write their hopes and dreams (future educational pursuits, career goals, and hopes for a happy marriage and family) in a journal. As they put their innermost thoughts and feelings into words, it will help them resist the temptation to do things that would hinder the fulfillment of those dreams and goals.

If your daughter likes crafts, she can make a scrapbook journal. Encourage her to include her favorite pictures of herself, friends, and family and tokens from special events she wants to remember to tell her own family about someday. You might even ask if you can write a letter to your future son-in-law and/or grandchildren to tuck into her journal, expressing your hopes and dreams for your daughter and her future family, the things you enjoy most about her, and what your prayers for her are. How incredible it will be for your grown daughter to look back at those times when she was a young girl, full of hopes and dreams, and to see how God has brought certain ones to fruition. Her journal can also be a powerful tool she can use in helping her own daughter develop personal goals for her future.

We can also help our daughters think about the future when we...

Bring Her Along to Weddings

The white dress symbolizing purity...the rings symbolizing unbroken commitment...the unity candle symbolizing two united as one in Christ... Weddings are full of teachable moments! A few years ago our family attended an extraordinary wedding, not just because the bride looked so stunning or because the food was so great, but because the ceremony was rich with both Christian and Jewish wedding symbolism. Although I was embarrassed I had forgotten the invitation was for adults only, I was thankful I had accidentally brought my kids along because they witnessed an incredibly beautiful, God-honoring wedding ceremony that they still talk about today.

Here are some questions you can talk with your daughter about after the wedding:

- If the couple has saved sex until marriage, how do you think the bride felt walking down the aisle of the church all dressed in white?
- Do you think the groom felt she was worth the wait?
- If the couple had sex before the wedding day, what effect do you think it would have on how they felt at their wedding?
- Do you think their honeymoon would be less special to them if that were the case?
- How do you want to feel when you walk down the aisle in a white dress someday? How do you want your groom to feel?

We find the perfect time for yet another encore performance, as we...

CELEBRATE RITES OF PASSAGE

Remember when you celebrated her first word? haircut? lost tooth? You likely celebrated every step of your daughter's early development. But now that she's older, she has an even greater need for you to notice any occasion to celebrate her existence. Mom, celebrate every step toward adulthood and marriage with a private little party between the two of you. Take her out to her favorite restaurant the day you purchase her first bra. Plan a fun mother-daughter weekend to celebrate "Woman's Day" when she begins menstruating. Dad, plan a surprise party to celebrate a special birthday, such as her thirteenth or sixteenth. Such celebrations will not only strengthen your relationship, they will also help her revel in her femininity.

To further celebrate your daughter...

CREATE A JOURNAL ABOUT HER LIFE

My children love the celebration journals I have written for each of them. Every few months I write down all the wonderful things they are accomplishing, how they are maturing spiritually and physically, the things they did and said that made me laugh, and so on. They frequently ask, "Mom, what did you write about me five years ago?" What I suspect they are really saying is, "Remind me of how much you loved me back then and that you still love me now!" They know they'll get to take these journals with them when they move away from home so they can be reminded of the special years we spent together.

It's never too late to start such a journal. Begin writing to your daughter now as you are reading this book together or on her next birthday. When we celebrate our children throughout their lives, we are communicating our love in a truly wonderful way.

TAKING THE NEXT STEP

Now it's time to take the next step. It's time to set the stage for some fun, creative conversation that will prepare your daughter for victory in the sexual and emotional battles all human beings eventually face. I applaud you for coming along-side your princess in her journey through puberty. Your companionship, comfort, and encouragement will likely usher her through these years with grace, and with-out regrets.

If you are not a mother, but reading this book as the father, grandparent, youth worker, or other influential person in a special young woman's life, I com-mend you for your courage and desire to be an "askable" adult. In the upcoming chapters and the Creative Conversation sections, simply replace the word *Mom* with whatever word fits you best.

BOOK 2

for parents
and daughters

preparing the princess

Perhaps you're wondering, *Why are we reading this book together? Why can't I just read it on my own?* Before we get started, let's answer those questions. I also want to let you know, as the author of this book, why I am so excited that you and your mom (or dad, or other caregiver or caring adult) are holding this book in your hands. (By the way, I'll be using the word *mom,* but if you are reading this with someone other than your mom, just use whatever word fits best.) These are the reasons your mom wants to read this book with you:

- God loves you so much that He gave you a gift—not just any gift, but an incredibly special gift.
- Your mom loves you so much and wants the absolute best for you, so she wants to help you understand and enjoy this gift.
- Your mom and I want you to love God in return and to love yourself enough to guard and protect this special gift.

What gift are we talking about? The gift of your sexuality. Go ahead, now's a good time to gasp…or roll your eyes…and say, "Oh, Mom! Do we really have to talk about this? I already know everything!" More than likely your mom said the same thing when she was your age. But there's a lot more to sexuality than just knowing where babies come from. (Don't worry, if you don't know the whole scoop on where babies come from, we'll talk about that, too.)

Or maybe you know a few things but don't really want to know anything more. Maybe you feel like you are just not ready to talk about this. If so, guess what? You are at a perfect stage of life to begin talking about it with your parents.

Our goal is not to embarrass you or pry into your personal life or lecture you.

We simply want to tell you what we know about being a woman and to prepare you for some changes that will be taking place in your body and life in the near future. We want to tell you the things we *wish* our moms could have felt the freedom to share with us. We want to talk with you about your sexuality and about how you can guard this gift God has given you until it's time to unwrap it with your husband. Most of all, we want you to know you can talk about your feelings, questions, and fears with your mom or dad or a trustworthy adult. Believe me, even if you don't have any feelings or questions or fears yet, you will. It's just a matter of time. So we are going to address some of those feelings, answer those questions, and calm those fears before you ever have them.

We are going to start out our conversations by looking to God's Word, although probably not where you would expect. Rather than starting in Genesis with the creation story of Adam and Eve (that will come a little later), we're going to start in Psalm 45:11,13-15:

> The king is enthralled by your beauty;
>> honor him, for he is your lord....
> All glorious is the princess within her chamber;
>> her gown is interwoven with gold.
> In embroidered garments she is led to the king;
>> her virgin companions follow her
>> and are brought to you.
> They are led in with joy and gladness;
>> they enter the palace of the king.

In case you didn't catch what that verse really means to you, let me word it another way:

> You, my dear, are a princess
> and a stunningly beautiful creation of the King of the universe;
> and He is absolutely, positively head over heels in love with you.
> You have been richly adorned with spiritual beauty,
> and your role in life is to radiate God's magnificent glory to others.

Your mission is to live such a pure lifestyle
that your friends can't help but be influenced by you in a really good way.
As they try to imitate you, they will begin pursuing God
and a lifestyle of sexual purity as well.
Together, you girls are going to have such fun as you celebrate
God's goodness in your lives and grow in His grace.

Did you get that? *You* are a *princess* and *God* is your *King.* Pause a minute and let that sink in. Even say it out loud: "I am a princess and God is my King!" With this fact established, we will talk about the many things the King wants His princess to know about herself and her sexuality, even years before it's time for her to fully enjoy this gift.

As you read through this book together, you and your mom will engage in some creative and memorable exercises that will help you better understand the information in each chapter. These exercises will also equip you to offer wisdom to your friends about their own choices later on in life. All of these conversations and creative exercises are tried and true, as I have used them to talk with my own daughter for the past several years. They've helped my princess, Erin, prepare for the best life possible and allowed us to grow close to God and to each other as we continue to explore these topics together.

My prayer is that this book will do the same for you, Princess! So let's get started...

flattering curves ahead

God created man in his own image, in the image of God he created
him; male and female he created them.... God saw all that he had
made, and it was very good.

GENESIS 1:27,31

I remember how afraid I was to cross the Billy Goat Gruff's bridge on the kindergarten playground. I hated how the wooden slats moved when I walked on them
and how the chains rattled so loudly. I certainly didn't like that I could see through
those slats and chains all the way to the ground, which seemed like a long way
down to a five-year-old. Rather than crossing the bridge to go down the slide, I
usually turned around and went back down the stairs.

Crossing bridges can be scary. Sometimes we can choose not to go across and
stay safely on the same side. But there is a bridge every girl must cross in her lifetime, regardless of how scary that bridge may be. That bridge is called puberty.

Puberty (which comes from the Latin word *pubescere,* meaning to be covered
with hair) is the time in a girl's life when she crosses over from being a little girl to
becoming a young woman. Along with developing darker, thicker hair on your
pubic (bikini) area, legs, and armpits, you'll experience other exciting changes during this season. We'll talk about most of these before we're done with this book,
but for now we are going to talk about the most obvious changes—those that will
affect the size and shape of your body.

CROSSING THE BRIDGE

When I look back over my grade-school pictures during the time I was crossing
the bridge into puberty, I can see a striking difference from year to year. In just four
short years, from third grade to seventh grade, I evolved into a whole new person.

But the sad thing is, I didn't always like how that new person looked. Rather than growing *up* first, then *out,* I had my growth spurts in the opposite order. I grew out first, then up.

Between the ages of nine and ten, my face began filling out a little, especially under my chin, and my tummy had a similar little bulge. My chest, however, was still as flat as a board. Around this same time my older brother bestowed the nickname Walrus on me, which still makes me cringe with embarrassment.

However, between the ages of eleven and twelve, my body did a complete turnaround. I grew taller, my face became slimmer, my waist got trimmer, and the lumps and bulges around my face and tummy settled into much more flattering places, in particular my breasts and hips. I didn't see those flattering curves as gifts from God at the time, but I do now. The changes on the outside of my body were signaling major changes that were also going on *inside* my body, changes that would affect my life in a big way. We'll talk about those internal changes in the next chapter.

Maybe you'll cross the bridge of puberty in a similar way, spreading out first and then up. Or perhaps you'll travel across this bridge the way my best friend did. She had the opposite problem. She grew up long before she ever grew out. She had a hard time finding jeans small enough to stay on her hips but long enough to cover her ankles. People called her Giraffe, Bean Pole, and Zipper. Those nicknames hurt her feelings as badly as Walrus hurt mine. But toward the end of her journey across the puberty bridge, something wonderful happened. My friend grew flattering curves where there had never been any before, and this put an end to those nicknames. Just a few years earlier I had wished I could be taller and thinner, while she had wished she could be shorter and thicker. But then everything shaped up and neither of us had many complaints.

No matter where you are on the puberty bridge, whether you are currently growing out or up, know that your body *will* change. God's not done with you yet. Your body will continue taking its God-given shape, size, and form. You don't need to worry about making it happen. It will. As long as you are treating your body with respect by eating the right foods in the right amounts and exercising to maintain your metabolism and muscle strength, you will automatically form those flattering curves and develop the beautiful body of a young woman. A healthy body is the natural result of healthy choices.

However, when we make unhealthy choices about our bodies, we can encounter serious problems. As we cross from childhood to adulthood, girls can face some overwhelming temptations to do some foolish and harmful things, namely stuffing, starving, and flaunting our bodies. Let's look at each of these temptations.

STUFFING, STARVING, AND FLAUNTING

When I was growing up, my friends and I wanted the full-figure look. Some of us stuffed our bras with tissues so we could look as if we were developing breasts as quickly as our peers. We didn't know that many of our peers' "full" breasts were actually tissues too. If you've noticed that your friend's breasts are developing faster than yours, you may have experienced this temptation as well, or maybe you've even stuffed your bra before. There's nothing wrong with wanting fuller breasts, but do read on before you rush out to buy another box of tissues.

Because having a fuller figure is a trend of the past and "thin" is now "in," you are more than likely facing a different temptation. In order to look like some of the popular girls at school or the ones you see on magazine covers and in the movies, maybe you fantasize about shrinking your size and being much thinner so you can look more like Mandy Moore or Mary-Kate and Ashley Olsen. But wanting to look like someone else can drive a girl crazy. It can make you less satisfied with your own body, and even depressed and angry.[1]

Some girls become so obsessed with weight that they go to great lengths to become thinner, even if it means doing things that endanger their bodies and cause major health problems. Girls who starve themselves, take diet pills or laxatives, or throw up their food so as not to gain weight are far more concerned with short-term weight loss than with long-term health benefits. Before you put too much stock in a magic number on the scale, keep reading.

Other girls may face another temptation, one common to those who *do* like what they look like and are pleased with the shape their bodies have taken. If you sense that boys (particularly older boys), stare at your body or frequently notice how you look in your jeans and tight tees, you may be tempted to flaunt your body to get even more of their attention. Don't get me wrong; it's good to like your body. It's right to appreciate the strong, healthy, beautiful body God gave you and use it to serve Him. But it's wrong to use your body as a tool to turn a guy's head and feed your own ego. And while it may seem like a compliment that a guy is staring at you, scanning your body up and down, or making comments such as, "Hey, baby, here's my number! Call me!" it's not complimentary at all. Guys who treat girls in such a way are being disrespectful to them. (That's why such guys rarely say things like that to a girl in front of her mom or dad.) Before we get to the end of this book, you'll understand more about why such comments are disrespectful to you.

When we forget that true beauty comes from a heart that loves God, we assume that beauty comes from a body that looks a certain way. That's when we fall into the pitfalls of stuffing, starving, or flaunting. What's the best way you can avoid these traps? By accepting yourself as you are, because you are a beautiful child of God, a princess loved passionately by the King of the universe. Rather than adopting the world's twisted definition of beauty, adopt God's definition since He is the Creator of all things beautiful.

REDEFINING BEAUTY

So where does our society get its ideas about what makes a girl beautiful? Sharon Hersh, author of *"Mom, I Feel Fat!"* sat down with twenty-five middle-school-aged girls and asked them to describe the perfect girl. Their responses, in order of importance to them, were as follows:[2]

- thin
- blonde
- popular
- beautiful
- athletic
- has big breasts
- has a boyfriend
- confident
- straight white teeth (no braces!)
- has her own car
- doesn't have zits
- has her own phone

I agree with Sharon—the only one I know who fits that description is Barbie. It's amazing how a childhood toy can mold a young girl's ideas about where beauty comes from. Nineteen-year-old Kim echoed the heart's cry of many young women when she said: "As I grew up, the reflection in my mirror looked increasingly more like my mom than Barbie. I felt so betrayed by my own body because it didn't grow into the shape I thought it should be."

Like Kim, many girls grow up with unrealistic expectations about their bodies. It's not just Barbie dolls that create these false ideas of beauty. So do television celebrities, movie stars, magazine cover models, fashion designers, and many other aspects of today's pop culture.

But where does beauty really come from? Let's go back to the Bible to see what the Creator has to say about beauty.

> Charm is deceptive, and beauty is fleeting;
>> but a woman who fears [respects and serves] the LORD
>>> is to be praised. (Proverbs 31:30)

> Your beauty should not come from outward adornment, such as braided
> hair and the wearing of gold jewelry and fine clothes. Instead, it should
> be that of your inner self, the unfading beauty of a gentle and quiet spirit,
> which is of great worth in God's sight. For this is the way the holy women
> of the past who put their hope in God used to make themselves beautiful.
> (1 Peter 3:3-5)

Do these scriptures say we shouldn't style our hair or wear nice jewelry or clothes? Of course not. The Bible simply says that this kind of beauty fades and can't be depended upon. These verses are good reminders that physical beauty isn't going to last forever and that our primary focus shouldn't be on outward beauty. We need to adjust our definition of beauty to include not just what's on the outside, but what we look like on the inside, particularly in our minds and hearts. The beauty that comes from loving and serving God with a happy heart endures—even when our figures fall south and wrinkles adorn our faces. In this day of plastic surgery, eating disorders, and extreme makeovers, it's time for us to recognize that true beauty doesn't come from fresh makeup, the latest hairstyle, or how we look in our blue jeans. Rather, it radiates from the inside out, from a heart that delights in the Lord.

Think about it. You probably know someone who looks like she just stepped out of the hottest salon but has such a self-centered personality or rotten attitude that *beautiful* would never be one of the words you'd use to describe her. On the other hand, you probably know a girl who may not have modeling agents beating down her door, yet her sweet spirit makes her one of the most beautiful people you know.

Beauty is a royal gift for God's royal girls. As others take notice of our inner and outer beauty, we have an opportunity to turn their attention toward our Creator. Rather than using our beauty as a way of bringing glory to ourselves, we can reflect *God's* beauty for *His* glory. God wants others to see the beauty of Jesus in us so we can influence them to want to know more about Christ.

Your beauty is not "on hold" until your curves develop, or until you reach a perfect weight, or until guys begin noticing you. You can feel beautiful now by focusing on being the person God wants you to be rather than the celebrity you wish you looked like. The choice is yours. As you let your beauty radiate from the inside out, you'll feel much better about yourself, and those around you will not be able to keep from noticing as well.

Creative Conversation

What you will need:
- paper, pencils, and colored markers or crayons
- Barbie doll or magazine pictures of young, thin celebrities

First, draw pictures of an apple, a pear, and a banana. Then discuss the following questions:

1. What are the characteristics of each piece of fruit that make them easily recognizable? What is unique about each of their shapes?
2. What if the apple wanted to be shaped like the banana? Or the banana shaped more like the pear? Is it possible?

3. Which piece of fruit does your body resemble most right now? How do you feel about that?

Now, look at your Barbie or your magazine pictures of celebrities and discuss the following questions:

1. Have you ever wished you could look more like them? In what way(s)?

2. Does looking at Barbie or at these magazines make you unhappy with your own body? Why or why not?

3. Is it healthy for us to compare ourselves to others and wish to look more like them? Why or why not?

4. How can we avoid discontentment and low self-esteem and be happy with the bodies God gave us?

Close with a prayer, thanking God for creating us in His image and asking His help to accept yourself just the way you are, whether you are shaped more like an apple, a pear, or a banana!

your beautiful biological clock

There is a time for everything,
and a season for every activity under heaven.

ECCLESIASTES 3:1

When I was going through puberty, I had no idea that what was happening to my body would turn out to be the most wonderful blessing I could ever ask God for. I'm not referring to my flattering curves, fuller breasts, or rounded hips. I'm not talking about outward changes at all. I'm talking about the inward changes that were taking place at the same time. You see, as my body began taking a new (although sometimes awkward) shape, my biological clock was also taking shape and began ticking.

What's a biological clock, and why is it such a big deal? When people talk about a woman's biological clock, they are referring to the period of time in her life when her body has the ability to reproduce another life. A woman's biological clock will start to tick when her ovaries begin releasing one egg every month and her uterus begins developing a blood lining to nourish that egg if it becomes fertilized. Her biological clock will continue to tick for a certain window of time—typically about thirty years. Females can't give life to a baby until after they've experienced puberty and begun ovulating, and they can't give life to a baby after they've gone through menopause and stopped ovulating. (Don't worry—you'll understand what all of this means by the time we are done with this chapter!)

None of this meant much to me when I was your age and just crossing over that puberty bridge. But in my twenties, when my husband and I desperately wanted to have children of our own, it meant a lot. Nothing I've done has meant more to me than bringing my sweet daughter and wonderful son into the world.

Nothing brings me more joy than to watch them grow day by day into the young woman and young man God made them to be. I pray you'll get to experience this joy someday in your due season of life. The things you will learn in this book will certainly help you prepare for that day so that you have the healthiest biological clock possible.

In this chapter, we're going to discuss the parts of your body that make up your reproductive system. Then we'll cover menstruation, reproduction, and finally menopause. You may need to ask your mom to further clarify some of these words for you as you read, but that's okay! She's prepared for your questions, and if she doesn't know the answer, the two of you can research it together later.

But before we get into body basics, I want to make sure you understand one very important thing. *You* are a sexual being. Your mom is a sexual being. Every person you'll ever meet is a sexual being. Maybe you are thinking, *But I've never had sex! How can I be a sexual being?* You are a sexual being because your sexuality isn't defined by *what you do*. Your sexuality is *who you are*. For example, if you were to fill out a form at school and it said *Sex:* _____, would you write *never* in the blank? Of course not. You would write *female*. Our sexuality is primarily defined by whether we are male or female. We'll talk more about the meaning of sexuality later. For now, let's look more closely at the female reproductive system.

FEMALE BODY BASICS

Volumes of books have been written about how the human body functions sexually, so don't assume that this book contains everything there is to know. Sexuality is a topic we can continue to learn a great deal about throughout our lives, so if you have questions that aren't answered in this book, be sure to talk to your mom about them. As tempted as you may be to search the Internet for answers, I strongly discourage that idea because of all the not-so-good information you'll come across about sex. If asking your mom questions about your sexuality seems scary to you at this point, that will hopefully change as you work through this book.

You may already be familiar with the term *vagina*, which refers to the opening between a female's legs. This area is covered in pubic hair once a girl goes through puberty. But there are many other parts in the female reproductive system, which are described below, beginning with the innermost organs:

- *Ovaries.* Two almond-size organs that house thousands of female reproductive cells called *ova,* or *eggs.* A female is born with all the eggs she'll ever have, and when she goes through puberty, her ovaries begin releasing one egg each month. This process is called *ovulation.* If one sperm, which is the male's reproductive cell, attaches to this egg, the egg is fertilized and a baby begins to grow.

- *Fallopian tubes.* These two narrow tubes, which connect the ovaries to the uterus, are filled with tiny, hair-like structures called *cilia.* The purpose of cilia is to sweep the egg away from the ovary and the sperm away from the uterus, drawing them together so fertilization takes place.

- *Uterus.* Also called the *womb,* this is a baby's home as it is growing and developing for nine months. The uterus is shaped something like an upside-down pear. Each month, the lining of the uterus collects blood in anticipation of a fertilized egg's attaching itself and becoming a baby. Until it is born, the baby draws its nourishment from this blood. If no sperm fertilizes the egg, the blood lining gradually exits the body during the menstrual cycle, also called a *period,* which lasts from three to seven days.

- *Cervix.* The cervix is a round muscle separating the uterus from the vaginal canal. Its primary purpose is to contract, closing up and forming a mucous plug when a woman first becomes pregnant. This provides protection for the *amniotic sac,* the fluid-filled sac that surrounds the baby as it develops. When the baby is ready to be born, the cervix will begin opening, or dilating, and release the mucous plug. When the cervix measures ten centimeters in diameter (about the size of a tennis ball), it will allow passage of the baby's head and body.

- *Vaginal canal.* This elastic, muscular passageway extends from the vaginal opening to the uterus. It is approximately three to four inches long when fully developed. If a young woman uses tampons during her period, she inserts them into her vaginal canal. This canal is also called the *birth canal,* because during birth a baby exits the mother's body through this passage.

- *Hymen.* A thin layer of tissue located just inside the opening of the vaginal canal. This layer of tissue may be torn while doing certain activities, such as gymnastics or horseback riding, inserting a tampon, or during the first experience of sexual intercourse (we'll explain this in more detail in the next chapter). Some girls are born without a hymen.
- *Urethra.* This passageway is located in front of and totally separate from the vaginal canal and allows the passage of urine from the female body.
- *Labia.* Two different sets of skin folds that protect the vagina. The larger, outer folds are called the *labia majora,* and the more delicate, inner folds of skin are called the *labia minora.*
- *Clitoris.* A small, cylinder-shaped organ located toward the front of a young woman's vaginal area that is covered by a slight "hood" of tissue. When fully developed, the clitoris is about the size of an eraser on a pencil. Its sole function is to allow a woman to experience sexual pleasure since a concentration of nerve endings make this the most sexually sensitive part of her body.

Now let's talk about the function of some of these parts.

A Sure Sign of Womanhood

One of the first functions you'll become familiar with—if you haven't already—is *menstruation* or *having a period.* Some of the slang terms you may have heard for

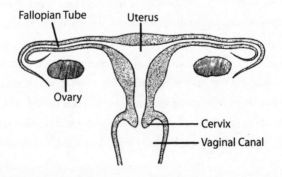

menstruation are "being on the rag" or "when Aunt Flo comes to visit." Such phrases are a girl's secret code that it's her time of the month to menstruate.

The onset of menstruation is marked by the flow of blood from the uterus, through the vaginal canal, to the outside of the body. This blood flow will last anywhere from three to seven days but averages five days and occurs approximately every twenty-eight days (or about once each month). Although it may feel like Niagara Falls at times, only about two to four tablespoons of blood exit the body during each menstrual cycle. This is a relatively small amount of blood in comparison to the body's blood supply.

When you begin your period, you may notice that your menstrual flow is irregular at times, producing heavy blood flow one month and extremely light blood flow the next. You may also bleed more often or less frequently than every twenty-eight days. This is normal. However, if your periods are extremely sporadic (you can never determine when or if they are going to come) even after you've been menstruating for a full year, you and your mom should talk to your doctor to see if there are any medical reasons why this may be so. There is no cause for alarm, but you should make your doctor aware of these things.

During this time of the month you will want to use one of the many feminine protection products available on the market. Maxi pads (for heavier blood flow) or mini pads (for lighter blood flow) attach to the lining of your underwear with an adhesive strip and collect the blood externally. Tampons are cotton cylinders that can be inserted into your vaginal canal by using a cardboard or plastic applicator. Tampons absorb the blood internally. A string is attached to the tampon for easy

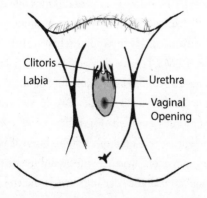

removal from the vaginal canal. Panty liners or maxi pads can also be used with tampons since leakage can occur when the tampon becomes saturated with blood. Before you use tampons for the first time, I recommend you read the product's enclosed instructions carefully and follow the directions about how often tampons should be changed. There can be health hazards to leaving tampons in your vaginal canal for too long.

Once your menstrual bleeding has stopped, you'll more than likely feel the need to clean your vaginal area to wash away blood residue and related odor. However, most medical doctors do not recommend the use of a douche, which is a container of fluid inserted into the vaginal canal to flush out the internal area. Good bacteria that fight off infections live inside your vaginal canal, and they are washed away when you use a douche. This, too, can be a health hazard. Instead of using a douche, I recommend you wash the external parts of your vaginal area, all around your labia minora and labia majora, with a product such as Summer's Eve Intimate Cleanser. It's just like liquid soap, only it's made for that especially delicate part of your body. This cleanser can also be used on a more regular basis to control body odor at other times during the month, not just after your menstrual flow has stopped.

A BURDEN OR A BLESSING?

During your period, you may experience mild headaches, backaches, breast tenderness, abdominal cramping, or bloating (slight swelling of the abdominal area). This is normal and no cause for concern. You may also feel like you are on an emotional roller coaster ride the few days before your period begins due to the fluctuation in your hormone levels (hormones are what your body produces to regulate many functions such as menstruation). These symptoms have actually been given a name, *premenstrual syndrome* or PMS, because they are so common among women.

However, if you have PMS, that's no excuse for you to act like a real witch to people, especially your family members who have to live with you during this monthly phase. Relationships can be damaged because of a woman's inability to control her emotions during this time of the month. So if you think you have PMS, talk with your mom about whether you should use one of the many over-the-counter medications to take the edge off some of the emotions, aches, pains, and crabbiness that can come along with periods. If you consistently experience severe depression or overwhelming anger just prior to or during your menstrual cycle, be sure to talk about this with your mom and your doctor as well.

While having your period may sound like a pain, I encourage you to recognize what's really going on behind the scenes. Your body is doing what God designed it to do so you can reproduce life someday. One of your ovaries is releasing an egg in the middle of each of your menstrual cycles. Your uterus is collecting blood throughout the month, and that blood is exiting your body because you are not pregnant. (When a woman becomes pregnant, she no longer has her period because the blood in her uterus is nourishing the baby. Once a woman has her baby, it usually takes a few months for her periods to resume again.)

What Should I Expect During Puberty?[1]

Ages Eight to Eleven
- Internal reproductive organs begin to grow.

Ages Nine to Fifteen
- Breasts increase in size.
- Pubic hair begins to grow.
- Vaginal lubrication and occasional discharge occurs.
- Sweat and oil glands are more active.
- Acne (pimples on your face) may occur.
- Internal and external reproductive organs continue to grow.
- Height increases.

Ages Ten to Sixteen
- Underarm hair appears.
- Menstruation occurs.

Ages Twelve to Nineteen
- Breasts near adult size and shape.
- Pubic hair grows thicker and darker and spreads to top of thighs.
- Menstrual cycle becomes more regular.
- Maximum height is reached.

The following time line illustrates a woman's monthly cycle and the miraculous activities taking place during this time.

Day 1	Day 2	Day 3	Day 4	Day 5	Day 6	Day 7	Day 8	Day 9	Day 10	Day 11	Day 12	Day 13	Day 14	Day 15	Day 16	Day 17	Day 18	Day 19	Day 20	Day 21	Day 22	Day 23	Day 24	Day 25	Day 26	Day 27	Day 28
B	B	B	B	B							O	O	O	O	O												

B = blood flow (days 1 through 5)

O = ovulation (sometime between days 12 and 16)

Days 6 through 28 = uterus collects blood for nourishment of possible pregnancy

Note that the menstruation cycle begins on the first day of blood flow (not the first day of the month, but the first day you begin bleeding). With an average twenty-eight-day menstrual cycle, ovulation (the release of an egg by one of your two ovaries) will more than likely occur approximately in the middle of this cycle, on or around day fourteen. A woman is most likely to become pregnant when she is ovulating.

Again, while this isn't information you need to know now, someday when you and your husband are ready to start a family, your understanding of this information could be vital. For now, you simply need to understand what will soon be happening in your body, if it hasn't happened already. Most girls begin ovulating and menstruating at approximately twelve years of age, but some start their periods as early as nine or ten years of age or as late as sixteen or seventeen. How old you are when you begin your period isn't a sign of your social maturity or your future ability to have babies.

If you've not started menstruating yet, be patient, but also be prepared. Carry a protective maxi pad in your purse, just in case you start while you are away from home. If your period catches you completely off guard and you have no protection, the school nurse can provide some for you or if all else fails, wrap a very long strand of toilet paper around the crotch of your panties until you can get something better. When you do start menstruating, or if you have started already, be sure to thank God that your beautiful biological clock is ticking!

LOOKING FAR DOWN THE ROAD

Your biological clock will likely operate throughout your teens, twenties, and thirties, and then begin to slow down and eventually stop somewhere in your forties or fifties. What do we mean by stop? Your ovaries will no longer release eggs, and your periods will stop. This time of life, called *menopause,* also comes complete with its own unique set of challenges, such as mood swings and hot flashes as body temperature fluctuates. This, too, will be a very special time in your life that you can be happy about. More than likely, you will have already had all the babies you want, and menopause means you won't have to fear unplanned pregnancy late in life. You will also not have to worry about having periods any longer.

NEVER STOP CELEBRATING

Regardless of the season of life we are in—whether we are going through puberty, in the midst of child-bearing years, or experiencing menopause, we have cause for celebration. A woman's body is beautiful both inside and out, and nothing short of an absolute miracle. What a joy to be created by God in such a wonderful way!

Creative Conversation

What you will need:
- fresh rosebud
- rose in full bloom

(If real roses are not available, you can use silk roses or draw them so you can visualize this exercise together.)

Discuss the following questions:

1. What is the most visible difference between a rosebud and a rose in full bloom?

2. What makes the rosebud uniquely beautiful?

3. What makes the full bloom uniquely beautiful?

Now take the bud and try to force it to bloom by grabbing each petal and spreading them out.

1. Is it possible to force the bud to bloom without permanently damaging it?

2. Is it possible for a young woman to force her body to blossom into maturity?

3. What is the only way for both a rosebud to bloom and a young woman to blossom into maturity?

Close with a prayer, asking God for patience as your body continues to develop and change throughout life. Be sure to thank Him that He makes all things beautiful in their own time.

sweet surprises

For this reason a man will leave his father and mother and be united
to his wife, and they will become one flesh.

GENESIS 2:24

You may have noticed that we've talked around a particular topic but not addressed it directly—eggs, sperm, fertilization, pregnancy. But how does an egg get fertilized? How does a woman get pregnant? How are babies actually made?

God has custom-tailored an incredibly wonderful gift for a husband and wife to enjoy together. This gift is by far one of the sweetest surprises you'll ever experience. What is this gift exactly? Sexual intimacy, which includes passionate hugging and kissing, caressing each other's body, and sexual intercourse, which is how babies are made. In order to help you understand the reproduction process more fully, let's discuss a few body basics of the male reproductive system.

A DIVINE DESIGN

As mentioned earlier, human sexuality is such a complex subject that it's not possible to fully explain it here. But this chapter will give you the information you need in order to understand the big picture of God's plan for sexual intimacy between husbands and wives.

Unlike the female, whose sex organs are located primarily within the body, the male has reproductive organs that are both inside and outside the pelvis. A male's primary reproductive organ is the *penis*. Here is an overview of the male reproductive system, beginning with the most internal organs:

- *Testicles.* These two egg-shaped organs produce the male reproductive cells or sperm. Slang terms that refer to these organs include *balls, nuts,* or *family jewels.* Maybe you've heard that it is very painful for a guy to get hit (or racked) in the testicles. It's true that these organs are very sensitive.

- *Epididymis.* Once the sperm are produced in the testicles, they travel to this mass of tiny tubes attached to the back of each testicle. Sperm remain in the epididymis approximately four to six weeks while they mature.
- *Vas Deferens.* A long tubelike structure that serves as a duct through which sperm travel from the epididymis to the ampulla.
- *Ampulla.* The widened portion at the end of the vas deferens that serves as a sperm storage area.
- *Seminal Vesicle.* This part of the body creates the whitish fluid called semen that sperm "swim" in. The addition of semen to sperm enables them to travel and reach their ultimate destination, the female's fallopian tubes where her egg awaits a sperm to fertilize it.
- *Prostate Gland.* This gland is located beneath the bladder (where urine is stored) and is responsible for making fluid that is added to the semen. It also causes the mild squeezing action (called *ejaculation*) that allows the sperm and semen to exit from the penis. The prostate gland also keeps semen and urine from mixing together, since the acid in urine would kill the sperm.
- *Urethra.* The internal tubelike structure through which both urine and semen exit the male penis.

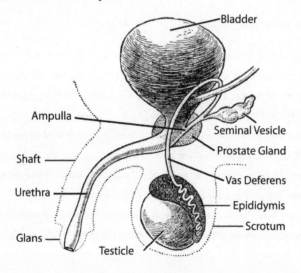

- *Glans.* The tip or the head of the penis, which, like the female's clitoris, is the most sexually sensitive part.

- *Shaft.* The long part of the penis, which is comprised of spongy tissue that fills up with blood when a male becomes sexually aroused. This process, called an *erection,* causes the penis to become very firm. Once the penis ejaculates semen, its shaft will return to its normal, soft state as the blood returns to other parts of the body.

- *Scrotum.* This pouchlike structure outside the pelvis is made from a thin layer of skin and muscular tissue that covers the testicles and epididymis. The scrotum not only houses the testicles, it also regulates the temperature of the sperm. If a guy's body is cold, the scrotum tightens and draws the testicles closer to his body so that they are kept warm. If he is hot, the scrotum relaxes to let the testicles hang further away from the body to remain cooler.

As you can see, both the male and female reproductive systems contain many intricate parts. God designed each to be finely tuned, expertly crafted, baby-making, pleasure-producing machines. Way to go, God! Continue reading as we dive a little deeper into the fascinating mystery of how God designed husbands and wives to fit together.

TWO BECOMING ONE FLESH

Let's go back to the Garden of Eden for a moment. If you recall, Adam was created first, and among all of God's creations there was no suitable helper for Adam. God loved Adam so much that He decided to custom-tailor a perfect helper for him, not just to help him with the work, but also to complete him in every way. In His awesome creativity, God sent Adam into a deep sleep, removed a rib from his side, and formed a similar creation that would be very pleasing to Adam. But she didn't look exactly like him. Her body was more delicate and beautiful to behold. She had flattering curves and smooth skin and moved gracefully. Scripture says Adam and Eve were "naked, and they felt no shame" (Genesis 2:25). Can you imagine how Adam loved to stare at his wife's naked, beautiful body? And Eve more than likely enjoyed the sight of Adam's strong, masculine body as well.

God commanded them to "be fruitful and increase in number" (Genesis 1:28). What did this mean? You guessed it! Have sex and make babies! God caused Adam to be sexually aroused at the sight of Eve's body, and Eve to be sexually aroused by the emotional connection she felt to Adam. These "automatic drives" caused them to want to obey this command. Adam and Eve loved each other, and so it was only natural for them to do exactly what God created husbands and wives to do—make love.

As mentioned earlier, lovemaking usually begins with hugging or caressing each other's bodies. Passionate kisses are a real "turn on" to both the male and female, and both usually become very sexually aroused once such kisses are exchanged. Their bodies draw naturally closer, and they desire to explore and excite one another sexually. The husband's penis fills with blood as he gets an erection. The wife's clitoris and labia receive additional blood flow as well, causing her vaginal canal to become more lubricated or wet. A husband and wife may spend some time touching each other's genitals (his penis and her clitoris). This is called *foreplay.* Eventually they may have *sexual intercourse,* meaning the husband will insert his firm penis into his wife's vaginal canal. The biblical phrase, "they will become one flesh" (Genesis 2:24), refers to this picture of the male and female bodies fitting together perfectly. In these precious moments of sexual intimacy, a husband and wife are joined together in the closest union possible. Within a few minutes the husband will feel so sexually aroused by being inside his wife's body that he will reach a peak of excitement. His penis will ejaculate his sperm-containing semen deep into her vaginal canal. The sperm will automatically begin swimming up through the uterus into the fallopian tubes in search of an egg to fertilize. This sweet, loving union is the process through which beautiful babies are made.

Sex feels very good to both the husband and the wife. The husband's pleasure is most intense at the moment he ejaculates. The wife may (or may not) experience an *orgasm* when she reaches her peak of sexual excitement. When a man ejaculates or a woman has an orgasm, it is as if a giant wave of pleasure washes over him or her. Immediately following their peak of excitement comes another wave of contentment as the couple relaxes in each other's arms, completely relieved of their sexual tensions.

You may be thinking, *Oh, I don't ever want to do that!* But believe me, you'll change your mind someday. The desire for sexual intimacy eventually becomes a part of every human being's life. God simply made us that way. He designed sexual intimacy to be enjoyed by husbands and wives within their marriage relationship. Your mom is going through this book with you in order to help you resist any temptation to disobey God's commands about saving sex for marriage, because she loves you and wants the best for you.

Sadly, not everyone does things according to God's plan. Some choose to pursue their own plans for sexual pleasure and miss out on discovering God's sweet surprises at the appropriate time. Let's look at some wrong beliefs that can cause a young woman to give in to the temptation to have sex before she is married.

Sweet Surprises or Bitter Mistakes?

I speak occasionally at a local maternity home, which is a place for unmarried pregnant girls to live and go to school. The first time I went there, I expected to see girls in their late teens or early twenties, but I was shocked to find out that some

What's the Big Deal About Teens Having Babies?[1]

- Teenage mothers are more likely to drop out of high school and live in poverty.
- More than 75 percent of all unmarried teen mothers began receiving welfare within five years of giving birth.
- Children of teen mothers have more health problems and developmental delays, and the infant death rate for children born to teen mothers is about 50 percent higher than for those born to women older than twenty.
- Children born to adolescent mothers are more likely to be poor, abused, or neglected, and less likely to receive proper health care and nutrition.
- Teenage fathers are more likely to engage in delinquent behaviors, complete fewer years of schooling, and earn less money than childless peers or fathers of children born to mothers over age twenty.

of these girls were only twelve or thirteen years of age. I've asked many of these young women what prompted them to have sex outside marriage. I think it would be helpful to you to hear some of their responses, along with the truths that these girls have learned the hard way:

- *I thought having sex would make me feel grown up.* Truth: Having sex doesn't make a girl a grownup any more than standing in a garage holding a flower vase makes her a Volkswagen Beetle. Any girl can go through the motions of having sexual intercourse, but it takes a real woman to control her sexual passions and patiently wait for her wedding day. Maturity isn't always displayed by what we do, but by what we choose *not* to do.

- *I didn't think having sex one time would hurt anything.* Truth: It only takes one sexual experience to get pregnant. To tell yourself you can have sex once but refrain from it in the future isn't very realistic. Once you become sexually active, it can be extremely difficult to stop. I'm not saying it can't be done, but I am saying it is much easier not to go there in the first place than to try to turn around once you've already traveled that path.

- *I didn't think I would get pregnant because I was using birth control.* Truth: Birth control methods aren't foolproof. Even when a couple is using birth control—such as a condom (a latex covering for a man's penis that keeps the sperm from going inside his partner's vagina) or birth control pills (designed to trick a woman's body into thinking she is already pregnant so she won't get pregnant again)—pregnancy can and does occur. Nor do most forms of birth control provide any protection from sexually trans-mitted diseases, some of which are life-threatening such as HIV/AIDS. Even condoms don't provide nearly the protection most people think they do because they often slip off, break, or the couple fails to use one every time they have sex.

- *I had sex because I thought I wanted to have a baby.* Truth: Girls who get pregnant on purpose usually want a baby because they want someone to love them, and they think the baby will. However, these girls are in for a rude awakening. Babies are very cute, but they are also very selfish. They require more time, attention, and energy than most young single mothers can give. If a girl just wants to feel loved, she should get a cocker spaniel, not a baby.

- *I felt I had to have sex for him to continue being my boyfriend.* Truth: While I hope you don't have a boyfriend for many years yet, when you do finally have one, please know you should ditch any guy who tells you sex is a requirement for the relationship. Chances are if he can't control himself with you, he can't control himself with other girls either, and that's not the kind of guy you want to be involved with. It's better to be single and sexually pure than with a boyfriend who expects you to compromise your standards for the sake of his selfish pleasures.

Of course, getting pregnant outside of marriage is only one of the many bitter consequences of premarital sex. Low self-esteem, depression, and a broken heart usually result as well. As a matter of fact, studies show that once a teenage girl engages in sexual intercourse outside of marriage, she becomes three times more likely to commit suicide than a girl who is a virgin.[2] Doing things according to God's perfect plan is the only guaranteed way of avoiding all of these harsh consequences and experiencing the indescribable joy and pleasure that sex within marriage can provide.

Consider this quote from Mike Mason's book *The Mystery of Marriage:*

What moment in a man's life can compare with that of the wedding night, when a beautiful woman takes off all her clothes and lies next to him in bed, and that woman is his wife? What can equal the surprise of finding out that the one thing above all others which mankind has been most [creative] in dragging through the dirt turns out in fact to be the most innocent thing in the world? Is there any other activity at all which an adult man and woman may engage in together (apart from worship) that is actually more… clean and pure, more natural and wholesome and unequivocally right than is the act of making love? For if worship is the deepest available form of communion with God…then surely sex is the deepest communion that is possible between human beings.[3]

Doesn't sex within marriage sound like it's worth the wait? As you look forward to living your life according to God's perfect plan—enjoying sexual intimacy only with your husband—you can anticipate the many sweet surprises such a wise lifestyle will bring.

Creative Conversation

What you will need:
- saltshaker (or packet of salt)
- sugar bowl (or packet of sugar)
- paper plate

Sprinkle some salt on one side of the plate and some sugar on the other side, creating identical piles of each. At first glance, these two look similar, right? Probably the only way to tell the difference is to taste them, so go ahead. Sample a few grains of each and note the difference. If you accidentally use salt instead of sugar in a homemade ice cream recipe or sprinkle sugar instead of salt on your french fries, you would recognize by the taste that you did something wrong, wouldn't you?

What has all this got to do with sexual activity? At first glance, a young woman may think sex outside of marriage is just as satisfying as sex inside of marriage. After all, sex is sex, right? Wrong. Multitudes of women, because of broken hearts, low-self esteem, unplanned pregnancies, or sexually transmitted diseases, will tell you that sex before marriage isn't as sweet as it may appear. In fact, giving in to sexual temptation may be one of the most bitter mistakes a person can make because it can have a lifelong impact.

But God designed sex to be a wonderfully sweet experience shared between a husband and a wife who feel no shame in each other's presence and are fully committed to each other for life. Don't be fooled by an impostor. Premarital sex is a cheap, bitter imitation of the real deal of married sex.

Discuss the following questions:
1. Why do many young people choose to be sexually active before marriage? List as many reasons as you can think of.

2. Why would a young person choose to save sex for marriage? List as many reasons as you can think of.

3. What do you think is the right choice for you? Why?

Close with a prayer, asking the Holy Spirit to help you save sexual activity until marriage so you and your husband can enjoy the sweetest relationship possible.

the rights of a princess

"For I know the plans I have for you," declares the LORD, "plans to prosper you and not to harm you, plans to give you hope and a future."

JEREMIAH 29:11

As a princess you are entitled to some special privileges. Maybe you envision the life of a princess as a life of leisure: sleeping in until noon, having maids and butlers do all your chores and cater to your every need, and getting anything you want without money being a concern. Even though your "princess" status may not come with such frivolous privileges, you are entitled to a special treatment of another kind. In this chapter, we'll be examining the royal rights that you, dear Princess, can claim as your own.

A Princess's Declaration of Rights

You have the right to own your own body.

You have the right to say no to anything.

You have the right to drive rather than be driven.

You have the right to be choosy.

You have the right to defend yourself and others.

You have the right to privacy.

You have the right to represent your generation well.

Let's take a look at each of these rights so you understand the special privileges you are entitled to.

You Have the Right to Own Your Own Body

No one has the right to touch your body without your permission. People can touch you in good ways (for example, a gentle hug or a pat on the back) and people can touch you in bad ways (for example, grabbing your bottom, touching your genitals, or trying to get you to touch theirs). Trust your judgment. If anyone tries to touch you in a sexual way, run away immediately—*no matter who that person is.* Tell your parents or another trusted adult, such as a teacher, coach, Sunday-school teacher, pastor, or counselor. Regardless of what the person may say, you are never to blame for someone else trying to touch you inappropriately. Such actions are considered *sexual abuse.*

Abuse can come from a variety of people—strangers, boyfriends, employers, coworkers, friends, or even relatives. Although the type of abuse varies, all abusers are selfish people who use others in ways they don't deserve to be treated as precious children of God. While sexual abuse is an absolute tragedy, the tragedy deepens if the abused person doesn't get help for coping with the abuse. When the wounds of abuse go untreated, the abused person often becomes an abuser of others. But it does not have to be this way. When a victim of sexual abuse talks with a responsible adult about what has happened or is happening, she can get help for stopping the abuse as well as for understanding what has happened so she will not abuse others.

While I don't want to scare you or make you paranoid, I want you to know that many girls under age eighteen are treated in sexually abusive ways. You can avoid being one of them by doing the following:

- Trust your judgment if you feel unsafe. Never hesitate to move away from someone who makes you nervous.
- Avoid being out alone after dark.
- Lock the doors when you are home alone. If you are home alone frequently, don't advertise that fact to others.
- If you go out with friends, stay in relatively public places where people could hear you if you screamed for help.

- Don't give a boy the impression you are interested in being sexual with him by flirting or responding to his flirting with you.
- If someone attempts to touch you in a sexual way, tell that person to stop immediately not just with words but also with actions. Pull away from that individual. Run away if you feel you are in danger.

YOU HAVE THE RIGHT TO SAY NO TO ANYTHING

Some girls walk into situations without stopping to think about whether it's smart or not. Games such as spin the bottle or seven minutes in heaven can seem like harmless child's play, but in reality they aren't. Think about it. In spin the bottle, you have to kiss whomever the bottle points to. Is that the way a princess discerns who she should kiss? By spinning a soda-pop bottle and just giving her precious kiss away to any dork that bottle lands on? I don't think so! In the game seven minutes in heaven, a boy and girl are sent into a dark closet with the expectation that he can do whatever he wants to her for seven minutes. Is that how a princess allows herself to be treated? Allowing a boy to use her for his pleasure for the entertainment of the crowd waiting outside the door? Absolutely not.

Regardless of what others try to get you to do, know that you are made in the image of God. He gave you a brain so you can decide what is right and what is wrong. If anyone ever tries to pressure you into doing something you know is wrong, doesn't seem appropriate to you, or that you just simply don't want to do, you have the right to say one little word that holds a lot of power—NO! (We'll talk more about the internal radar God gave you to discern right from wrong in chapter 6.)

YOU HAVE THE RIGHT TO DRIVE RATHER THAN BE DRIVEN

So what do you do if your friends want you to do something you don't want to do? That's when you have to learn to drive, Princess! Don't panic. I'm not talking about driving an actual car. I'm talking about driving your friends in a better direction than where they are trying to drive you. Let me give you a few example scenarios:

- Your friends want to call a boy and ask if he likes you. You don't like the idea. Rather than just going along and letting them make the call, you can drive instead of being driven by saying, "It doesn't really matter whether he likes me. I'm not old enough to have a boyfriend anyway. If he does like me, he'll let me know when he's ready. If he doesn't, I'd rather you not put him on the spot to say so. Let's go make a snack instead."

- You are spending the night at a friend's house, and she wants to go online after her parents have gone to bed. She says she wants to show you some pictures on the Internet that her parents would freak over if they ever found out. Instead of looking out of curiosity, you let her know, "I don't feel comfortable looking at things your parents wouldn't approve of. Let's listen to some music and play cards, okay?"

- Suppose a friend invites you to help in a car wash her church is doing to raise funds for the youth group. She suggests the two of you wear matching outfits—a bikini top and cutoff jean short-shorts. You tell her you don't have a bikini, so she offers you one of her extras. Instead of going along, you say, "I like the idea of matching outfits, but let's wear tank tops and shorts." If she insists on having her way, you respond with, "You wear what you want, but I'm going to wear something different."

You get the idea. Be your own person. Swim against the tide if the tide is flowing the wrong way. If you don't like how someone is trying to drive you in a wrong direction, or pressuring you to do something that makes you feel uncomfortable, then take control and steer clear of regret.

YOU HAVE THE RIGHT TO BE CHOOSY

A young woman usually sees being asked out by a guy as a sign she is datable or desirable. However, many girls don't give much consideration as to how datable or desirable *he* really is. They go out with anyone who asks so they'll feel better about themselves, even if it means spending time with a guy with a lot of problems and major character flaws. These girls sometimes think he just needs someone to love him and that their love can change him. However, the guy doesn't usually change. More often the girl does the changing—and not for the better.

In a few more years, when you start wanting guys to ask you out, know that dating is not about *being chosen* but about *choosing*. When the appropriate time comes, don't go out with a guy unless you believe he could make a good husband someday. Make sure you look for more in a boy than his just being cute or rich or popular. Physical appearance, financial status, or social standing don't measure how good a person really is. Instead, look for strong character traits. Is he a committed Christian whose actions and attitude reflect a sincere love for God? Is he respectful of others? Is he interested in who you are as a person rather than just in what you are willing to do in private? Is he trustworthy? Is he considerate?

You get the picture. Character counts. When it comes down to choosing a boyfriend someday, look for a young man of character.

YOU HAVE THE RIGHT TO DEFEND YOURSELF AND OTHERS

Don't *ever* tolerate someone's mistreating you or anyone else. If someone treats you poorly, remember that you ultimately teach people how to treat you. If you tolerate mistreatment, you are enabling that person to think it's okay to talk to you disrespectfully or to take advantage of you. Expect every person in your life to treat you like the young woman of God you truly are.

Also be willing to stand up for others if they are being mistreated. When I was in junior high, a girl in our school, Cheryl, had a crush on a much older guy named Thomas, who was downright mean to other people. Sometimes on the bus Thomas would be mean to Cheryl's friends, even punching them hard in the arms or thighs if they didn't do whatever he told them to do. He was a bully, but what made me the angriest was how Cheryl allowed Thomas to treat her friends. She'd just sit there and smile or laugh at them as Thomas was humiliating them in front of everyone. One day I was riding the bus home with Tonya, whom Cheryl claimed was one of her best friends. Yet when Thomas began picking on Tonya and even hit her, Cheryl did nothing but grin. I couldn't just sit there. Tonya was my friend too. I told the bus driver what Thomas was doing, and he made Thomas move to the front of the bus. Then I asked Cheryl, "How could you allow Tonya to be treated that way if she's your friend?" Thomas never messed with me, and he never messed with Tonya again.

Thomas and Cheryl got married after she graduated from high school, but sadly, he was an abusive husband who eventually left her to take care of three kids by herself. What a vivid reminder that you teach people how to treat you. If you tolerate abuse, it will continue and even grow worse. If you stand against it, it will eventually stop.

YOU HAVE THE RIGHT TO PRIVACY

Sometimes your friends think they have a right to be completely in your business. Games such as truth or dare are often attempts to pry into people's personal lives to see what kind of secrets they can squeeze out of them, including you. Maybe one friend thinks she should be allowed to read your diary. Perhaps another friend who spends the night thinks it's ridiculous if you want to go in the bathroom and close the door to change clothes by yourself. It's easy to feel as if you have no right to privacy at all.

But you have every right to privacy whenever you feel that need, regardless of what your friends expect. You don't have to let your friends read your diary nor do you have to confess what boys you've ever had a crush on or what secrets you've kept to yourself. You've probably already discovered that young girls often get a bad case of what I call "loose mouth disease." If you don't want certain things blabbed all over the school, I encourage you not to whisper them in a friend's ear, either. If you have something you really want to get off your chest or if you have a secret you want to confess, moms and dads are actually great for that. Parents are not interested in airing your dirty laundry in public or embarrassing you. They just want to be there for you when you need a listening ear.

Also know that you never have to undress in front of anyone if you don't want to. Maybe a few years ago you changed clothes in front of a friend without a second thought, but now that your body is beginning to develop (or slow to develop in comparison to your friend's) you may desire a little more privacy. If you prefer to go into a bathroom stall and close the door to change clothes, more power to you!

YOU HAVE THE RIGHT TO REPRESENT
YOUR GENERATION WELL

God is searching the earth, looking for a generation that seeks His face and wants to be in relationship with Him. What do you think God sees in your generation? More specifically, what does He see in you? How well do you represent your generation? No matter how you see your peers behaving or how casually they take their role as Christians, you have the right to represent your generation well when it comes to showing others what a Christian looks like.

You may not realize this, but God can use you to make a huge difference in the world. Some of the spiritual giants in the Bible were very young when God used them to do great things. For instance, David was a teenager when he confronted Goliath, a Philistine giant. God used David to kill Goliath and keep His people from becoming slaves to the Philistines. Daniel's friends Shadrach, Meshach, and Abednego refused to bow down to the king's idols and even allowed themselves to be thrown into the blazing furnace because they would rather die than betray their God. Because of their commitment and faith, God saved them from the fire. Esther was a young virgin when God exalted her as a queen. She approached the king on her people's behalf, but because the king had not called for her, she could have immediately been put to death. However, God gave her favor in the king's eyes and used her to save the Hebrew nation. And of course, we can't forget Mary, the virgin who was chosen to bring our Savior into the world. She was willing to bear the reputation of an unmarried pregnant teenager so she could be "the Lord's servant" (Luke 1:38).

You may think these are extreme examples and that God doesn't do miracles through young people like that any more. If so, you are wrong. For the past six years I've worked with an organization called Teen Mania Ministries that sends thousands of young people (some as young as eleven years of age) on mission trips to countries all over the world where they witness many miracles. God is using your generation in a mighty way to advance His kingdom and draw others to Himself. My thirteen-year-old daughter has already been on mission trips to Honduras, Costa Rica, and Panama, and hopes to go on many more. If you are interested in going on a mission trip, I encourage you to go to www.teenmania.org or call 1-800-299-TEEN for more information.

Of course, you don't have to go to another part of the globe for God to use you. You have a mission right there in your corner of the world. It's to love God with all of your heart, soul, mind, and strength and to love your neighbor as yourself (see Mark 12:29-31). If you do these two things as much and as often as you can—love God and love others by treating them with the same dignity and respect you're entitled to—then you are going to represent your generation well.

Remember, you are a child of God…a princess…a precious daughter of the King of the universe. Even if someone treats you less than royally or uses you for a purpose other than what God intended, *never forget who you really are.*

You deserve to be treated with dignity and respect. Period.

Also remember that others are worthy of the same respect. Live by the golden rule and treat others as you would have them treat you. Don't allow backstabbing, gossip, and abusive behaviors to destroy your life and your relationships. Draw a line in the sand. Make the choice to enjoy healthy relationships and to represent your generation well, regardless of how your friends may choose to behave. God has great things in store for you as you exercise each of these rights and enjoy life as His precious princess.

Creative Conversation

What you will need:

- one place setting of your nicest dishes (china, crystal, and silver if you have it)

Together, think of some of the craziest ways you could use a plate, glass, and fork—ways they were never intended to be used. For example, you could use a plate as a Frisbee, a glass to trap a firefly, or a fork as a gardening tool for your flower beds. Brainstorm as many other uses for these items as you can think of, and share your ideas aloud with each other.

Now let me ask you, does the mistreatment of these expensive items make them any less valuable? As long as they weren't broken or bent in the process, can they still be used for the valuable purposes for which they were created once they are washed up? Of course they can.

Now apply this analogy to young women. Although they may have been used or abused in ways God never intended, can they still fulfill the purposes for which they were created? Are they still beautiful and precious in God's sight? Are they still valuable human beings? Of course they are.

Discuss the following questions:

1. How do you imagine it would make a young woman feel to be sexually abused? What words can you think of that would describe what she may be thinking or feeling?

2. How might you respond to a friend who confided in you that someone had touched her in a sexually inappropriate way?

3. What are the best things a girl can do if she has experienced sexual abuse?

4. What are some ways you can avoid being sexually abused?

Close with a prayer, asking God to protect you and your friends from being mistreated by others. Also ask God to show you if there is someone who has been mistreated in the past and how you can best help that person avoid being abused further.

a princess's code of conduct

Children, obey your parents in the Lord, for this
is right.

EPHESIANS 6:1

Before you were even born, chances are your parents had big dreams for your life.
I know, because I've carried two children in my womb. During each nine months
my mind swirled constantly about what each of my kids was going to be like, what
each one's gifts and talents would be, what each would choose to do in life, and
how God might use each one. As a mother, I have made a commitment to be the
best parent I can be and to raise my children to be healthy, responsible adults who
want to honor God. In order to protect them from harm and to teach them how
to love God and others as well as themselves, my husband and I give our children
boundaries or codes of conduct we expect them to follow.

When you were just a toddler, your parents likely told you not to touch a hot
stove, stick your finger into an electrical outlet, or play with knives or matches.
Even if you didn't realize it at the time, they insisted you obey these rules in order
to keep you safe and healthy because they love you like crazy. Now that you are
becoming a young woman, the conduct they expect from you is more than likely
taking new directions, but the motive is still the same. Your parents love you and
want you to grow up safe and healthy.

In this chapter we are going to look at a suggested code of conduct, or principles and expectations, that your mom and dad may want to implement in order
to ensure that you keep safe and healthy, especially in your relationships with
others.

A Princess's Code of Conduct

A princess always respects parental authority.

*A princess behaves the same in her parents' absence
as she does in their presence.*

*A princess pursues friendships only with those both she
and her parents feel good about.*

A princess doesn't abuse her telephone privileges.

A princess surfs only parent-approved Internet Web sites.

A princess wears only clothes that look appropriate on her.

*A princess gets her parents' permission before inviting
someone into her home or getting into a car with someone.*

*A princess doesn't pursue a boyfriend or begin
going out with boys until her parents determine
that she is ready to do so.*

A PRINCESS ALWAYS RESPECTS PARENTAL AUTHORITY

When I was a little girl, I thought my parents knew everything. Whenever I had a question or didn't know how to do something, I always went to them. But when I became a "tweener" (in between being a child and a teenager), that changed. In my mind, my parents went from knowing everything to knowing nothing. I thought they didn't know about the world I was living in and that they couldn't understand the pressure I felt to have the right clothes and the right friends. I felt they didn't know what was cool or how to relate to me. (Of course, I never thought about the world they were living in with parenting, careers, house payments, and car repairs.) I thought I was a little too cool to relate much to them at all. Twenty-five years later, I am back to thinking my parents are pretty smart. Now I realize how dumb I was to think I knew more than they did.

When parents create guidelines for your behavior, they do so because they have the maturity and life experience to know what dangers lie ahead in your life. They've made their own mistakes, and they know what kinds of things led them to mess up. It's only natural, then, that your parents would want you to learn from their mistakes rather than make your own all the time. If you remember that they simply want to protect you out of love and concern for your well-being, it makes submitting to their authority easier.

The Bible has a lot to say about parental authority, such as "Honor your father and your mother" (Exodus 20:12) and "Children, obey your parents in everything, for this pleases the Lord." (Colossians 3:20). One of the smartest things a princess can do is respect her parents' desire for her to live according to their established guidelines.

A PRINCESS BEHAVES THE SAME IN HER PARENTS' ABSENCE AS SHE DOES IN THEIR PRESENCE

Do all things as if your parents were in the room with you and, chances are, you'll make your life a lot easier. Think about it. When kids get into trouble or make big mistakes that they regret later, it's usually because they were doing something their parents would not approve of.

This applies to whether you earnestly study for a test or decide to make a cheat sheet, whether you save your allowance to buy something or just steal it from the store, and how you treat your little brother or sister. It also applies to how you conduct yourself when you have a boyfriend someday. In other words, don't do anything when you are alone with a boy that you wouldn't want your parents to know about. The true test of your character isn't what you do at church or school or home when people are watching you. Your true character is revealed by what you do when you think no one is looking. So remember:

If you can do it in front of your parents, it's probably okay.
If you wouldn't do it in front of your parents,
it's probably not okay to do it in their absence, either.

A Princess Pursues Friendships Only with Those Both She and Her Parents Feel Good About

Some of the stupidest things I ever did weren't my idea at all. When I was twelve, I spent an afternoon with a friend at her house, but her parents weren't home. She recommended we walk down to the corner store and buy some cigarettes, but I knew my parents wouldn't approve. However, I wanted Tammy to think I was cool, so I went along with her plan. I soon proved to Tammy how "uncool" I really was when I began choking and coughing as I attempted to inhale. It was the first and last time I ever had a cigarette (they were nasty!). It was also the last time I ever went to Tammy's house.

When my mom picked me up that afternoon, the smell of smoke on my breath, clothes, and hair gave me away. I couldn't deny the evidence of my poor judgment. Mom was disappointed in me and announced that Tammy was a friend of the past. She said I could be nice to Tammy at school, but I was forbidden from calling her or spending time with her at all. At the time, I was crushed. Tammy and I had known each other since kindergarten. If I had only set a better example, stood up to Tammy, and said, "No, I don't smoke, and neither should you!" then maybe I could have positively impacted her life rather than having her negatively impacting mine.

Regardless of what could have been, I admire my mom for making the right call. Over the next six years, I watched Tammy go from cigarettes in the sixth grade to being a pregnant, drug-abusing alcoholic by the time she was old enough to graduate (which she never did).

Sometimes your parents see things in your friends that you fail to see from where you're standing. Know that their viewpoint is usually much more accurate than your own. Their maturity and life experience gives them wisdom and discernment. Your parents can choose to limit the time you spend with a friend until they get to know that friend better. They may prefer you not entertain a certain friendship at all because of a big difference in age, maturity level, or spiritual values. They can even forbid your spending time with a certain person or group of people. If that happens, let go of that unhealthy friendship to pursue one both you and your parents can feel good about.

A PRINCESS DOESN'T ABUSE HER TELEPHONE PRIVILEGES

While you may consider telephones to be one of life's absolute necessities, your parents may decide to put some limits on your telephone usage, especially if you love to talk or if you've abused their trust when it comes to acting appropriately on the telephone. Your parents may decide that some telephone calls should be made or received in a relatively public part of the house (such as the kitchen or living room) instead of in the privacy of your own room where you'll have no accountability. They may have rules about who you are allowed to call, who you are allowed to receive calls from, how long you are allowed to talk to certain people, and how late you can be on the telephone.

You may be rolling your eyes and thinking, *Good grief! It's just a phone call! It's not like I'm doing anything wrong!* Maybe not. But I have enough memories of things I said out of earshot of my parents to know that the telephone can be a huge stumbling block to a girl, especially if she is hungry for attention. I got into trouble when I was twelve because my older brother found out I had been calling his friends (who were six years older than I was) just to talk on the phone when no one was home. I thought calling them was fun, but they were annoyed and told on me.

For Christmas one year our family got a phone with an alarm clock and tape recorder built in. Just for fun, I pushed the record button one day while I was talking to a boy. Months later, I listened to that tape and was shocked at how "flirty" I sounded. No wonder that boy didn't talk to me much anymore. I probably scared him away.

I also remember playing some pretty mean tricks over the telephone. Not just prank calls or jokes, but some downright mean things, such as calling Robin to ask what she thinks about Kelly, casually forgetting to mention to Robin that Kelly was actually listening in on the other line. Telephones can become real friendship destroyers if they are used for backstabbing and gossip.

If your parents want to enforce some guidelines about the telephone, embrace them and abide by them. As you prove your trustworthiness when it comes to telephone usage, they'll probably give you more and more freedom later down the road.

A PRINCESS SURFS ONLY PARENT-APPROVED INTERNET WEB SITES

We didn't have Internet when I was your age, and I have to confess I am thankful. Why? Because as hungry as I was for attention and affection, there's no telling what kind of messes I would have gotten myself into if I'd had millions of strangers to connect with in chat rooms just a click away. Some girls have discovered the hard way that virtual relationships through the Internet can be incredibly dangerous. I frequently hear of yet another young woman who was enticed into the World Wide Web of romance, only to find herself stalked by a stranger. While I don't want to scare you needlessly, I do think you should know that some women are raped (forced to have sex with someone) or even killed by strange men they've met over the Internet and given too much information to (such as a phone number or home address).

Teens and Cybersex

I received an e-mail from thirteen-year-old Courtney: "I used my webcam to show a sixteen-year-old boy my body parts, and I saw his body parts. Does this mean I'm no longer a virgin?"

I explained that *virgin* means someone who has not had sexual intercourse, but that other things affect our purity mentally, emotionally, and spiritually. I encouraged Courtney to learn from her mistake, forgive herself, and make better choices, beginning with reading *Every Young Woman's Battle*.

Sending pictures, sexting, and sexy chatting is wrong even though you can't get pregnant or get diseases from it. It's about your internal purity and the huge impact it has on your future, safety, and relationships. Beyond that, cybersex-type activities have legal consequences. Many teens have faced legal charges because of what they've done on the Internet. If you're under eighteen, it's considered child porn to send sexual images, even if they're of yourself or a friend. So don't do it!

With those kinds of dangers lurking out there on the Internet, no wonder parents are concerned for their children's safety! Chances are, your parents may require that an adult be present in the room when you are surfing the Internet or checking e-mails. You may not be allowed to enter chat rooms or you may be restricted to surfing only a few parent-approved Web sites for homework or games. Whatever boundaries are established, know that they are not just put in place because your parents are control freaks. They more than likely wouldn't let you walk into a room by yourself to talk one on one with a group of strangers or look at sexually inappropriate pictures, so it makes sense that they don't want you logging in to chat rooms and Web sites that may contain pornography (pictures of people without clothes or in sexual situations). Consider yourself lucky that they care enough about you to create some boundaries when it comes to Internet usage. I encourage you to live by this rule wherever you go, whether you are using the Internet at your own house, a friend's house, or at a local library.

A Princess Wears Only Clothes That Look Appropriate on Her

Recently I was talking on a national radio show when a dad from Tennessee called in sounding desperate. He said, "My daughter has just turned thirteen, and now everything she leaves the house wearing seems to be either skintight, short-short, low-rise, or low-cut. I want to take her shopping for new clothes because I see that she's outgrowing a lot of the stuff she had before her body began to take shape." This dad went on to ask what kind of guidelines I suggest for selecting modest fashions (which we'll talk about in chapter 11).

While you may think this father sounds a little paranoid, I think he sounds like a dad who loves his daughter tremendously. You may have lots of clothes in your closet that don't lead you to ask, "Is this appropriate?" but as you continue growing and your body begins blossoming, those same clothes may begin to fit you a little differently. Never hesitate to ask your parents how something appears, and be willing to pass it on to a younger girl if you or your parents feel it reveals too much of your body. When you shop for new clothes, let your mom or dad be the judge about whether something looks appropriate on you.

A PRINCESS GETS HER PARENTS' PERMISSION BEFORE INVITING SOMEONE INTO HER HOME OR GETTING INTO A CAR WITH SOMEONE

Now that you are getting a little older, you may be given more and more responsibility to look out for yourself at times. You might be trusted to be alone for a little while if both your parents work or if they need to be out for some reason. This is a lot of freedom, and it takes a lot of maturity to handle it appropriately.

While it may be tempting to invite a girlfriend over without asking permission or let a friend in who comes by unannounced, it's never a good idea. Always call your parents to ask their permission, and if they say it's okay, your friend's parents also need to know you are home alone while their child is there. If you can't get in touch with either your parents or your friend's, wait to hang out until you have a green light from both sets of parents. I don't recommend that girls spend time alone in the house with guy friends at all, especially if their parents are unaware.

Also get your parents' permission before you go anywhere. Your family needs to know how to find you if they need to. Your parents need to know where you are going and who you will be with. If someone is driving you somewhere, understand that you are putting your life in that person's hands in more ways than one. Make sure your parents are aware of who you are with, who is driving, and what time you will be home. If you can't get in touch with your parents and find yourself stranded somewhere, call an adult neighbor, your pastor or youth pastor, a relative, or even the police. Every young woman must learn to make her safety a priority.

A PRINCESS DOESN'T PURSUE A BOYFRIEND OR BEGIN GOING OUT WITH BOYS UNTIL HER PARENTS DETERMINE THAT SHE IS READY TO DO SO

Imagine that your dad owns a vintage dream car—let's say it's a 1967 Ford Mustang convertible. He bought it sixteen years ago for a pretty hefty price, and it's taken him all this time and a lot of money to fix it up just the way he's always dreamed. It has a shiny, candy-apple-red paint job, new vinyl top, black leather seats, chrome wheels, with an incredible engine under the hood and fantastic hi-fi stereo speakers. It's a priceless treasure to him that he is so very proud (and protective) of. He keeps it locked up tight in the garage, but visits it often and enjoys taking it out for a spin around the neighborhood on occasion.

Now imagine some teenage boy he barely knows approaches him and says, "Hey, Mister! I've been watching you work on that car for years, and it is one hot rod! I just got my driver's license. Do you think I could take her for a spin?"

What do you think your dad would say? Right. *Not!*

Now imagine all the years your parents have invested in you, their precious daughter. So many of their hopes and dreams and prayers have been wrapped up in you, not to mention the thousands of dollars and many years they've invested in helping you become a terrific, well-educated, sensible young woman. What if in a few years some teenage boy approaches them and says, "You know, I've been watching your daughter for a while, and I think she's pretty cute. Do you mind if I take her out one night?" How do you think your parents will feel, especially if they don't know him or his family very well?

In case there's any question, you are *far* more valuable to your folks than any car. That's why they will likely want you to wait until you are older before you have a boyfriend or go out on dates. They want to know you are emotionally ready to face the challenges that dating and boyfriends will bring into your life.

We'll talk more about boys in chapter 13. For now, remember that your obedience regarding this and the other behaviors listed in the code of conduct go a long way in demonstrating your maturity.

How Will You Respond?

Over the course of the next several years, your life will be changing dramatically. As mentioned earlier, you'll be given more and more freedoms, and you'll likely earn more privileges. You'll have opportunities to prove your trustworthiness and good judgment.

As you experience these new freedoms and character tests, your parents may establish some additional rules to keep you on the right path as you mature into a young adult. If so, you have two choices: you can complain that they are being unfair and rebel against their authority (a very bad idea!), or you can thank God that your parents are so concerned with your character development and rise to meet the challenge (a very good idea!). By meeting their expectations for your behavior and living by this suggested code of conduct, you'll prove yourself to be a genuine princess who behaves royally and represents her King well!

Creative Conversation

What you will need:

- pencil

How long do you intend to live? A long time? Let's say you plan to live until you are ninety. Imagine your life of ninety years as a time line, similar to the ones you learned about in math class. Yours might look like this:

[| | | | | | | | | | | | | | | | | | |]
  0 5 10 15 20 25 30 35 40 45 50 55 60 65 70 75 80 85 90

Now put an X on the number that represents your current age.

Then put an X on the number that represents the age you would like to be by the time you leave home and become an independent young woman.

Now step back and look at the entire time line, noting how much of your life will be spent independent of parental authority in comparison to how long you are expected to submit to your parents' authority. Then do the following:

1. Even though it may seem like forever before you grow up and get to create your own code of conduct, how long is it compared to the rest of your life?

2. Together, brainstorm and list as many negative consequences as you can think of for not meeting your parents' expectations.

3. Now brainstorm and list as many positive things as you can think of that could come from obeying your parents' guidelines.

Close with a prayer, asking God to help you patiently abide by the guidelines established by your parents. Also ask that you would have wisdom when you are older to establish your own code of conduct for righteous living and healthy relationships.

your royal radar

But when the Friend comes, the Spirit of the Truth, he will take you
by the hand and guide you into all the truth there is. He won't draw
attention to himself, but will make sense out of what is about to happen and, indeed, out of all that I have done and said.

JOHN 16:13, MSG

I was recently flying from Dallas to Virginia Beach when out of the corner of my
eye I saw flashing lights outside my window. Looking up from the book I was reading, I peered out to see where those lights were coming from. My heart sank when
I saw them again. They were coming from the clouds below. We were flying
through a lightning storm in what suddenly felt like a huge aluminum lightning
rod. I continued to watch the brilliant lightning display, and my heart sank even
further when I saw more flashing lights. This time they were red, and it was obvious there was another plane not too far from us making its way through this same
storm. I couldn't help but wonder how the pilot could possibly maneuver through
the air without getting hit by lightning or crashing into another plane. Of
course, airplanes have topnotch navigation systems complete with built-in radar to
alert the pilot to any imminent danger. This pilot was no doubt carefully monitoring his radar.

Girls your age are in a similar situation. You are having to navigate through what
feels like some major storms—peer pressure and popularity contests, self-esteem
and body-image issues, and fluctuating hormone levels, just to name a few. In the
coming years, additional storms may develop.

You will need God's divine protection from such storms, but the outcome of
your journey is not entirely up to God. Some decisions and situations come under
your control. It's not that God won't be with you during these storms, but He has

given you free will to make your own decisions when you're flying through them. Of course, He gives you a divine guide to help you in making those decisions, kind of like built-in radar. That divine guide is called the Holy Spirit. Isaiah 30:21 tells us that at every turn, if we listen, we can hear a voice saying, "This is the way; walk in it." It's not usually an audible voice that you'll hear, but rather a Holy Spirit radar that says to your heart and mind, *WARNING, WARNING! This doesn't feel right!*

Maybe you've heard that kind of warning in your spirit before and chose to ignore it. Have you ever joined other girls to play a trick on someone while thinking, *Maybe I shouldn't do this?* Or cheat on a test while thinking, *This is not right.* Or maybe tell a lie to your parents, even though you could hear something inside of you saying, *You should tell the truth.* These examples show how easy it is to ignore your radar and make wrong choices. At times, doing the right thing may seem harder than doing the wrong thing, but doing the right thing is always worth the extra effort. It develops strong character, and it shows God that you can be obedient in little things now, leading Him to trust you with bigger responsibilities down the road.

In order to help you understand this important principle, let me give you some examples of young women who monitored their Holy Spirit radar and did the right thing.

- Trisha was bouncing a small rubber ball in her friend's parents' room. When it rolled under the bed, she tried to go after it. She reached underneath and felt a stack of magazines. When she pulled one out, she saw that it had a picture of a naked woman on the front. Her radar told her to put it back without looking, although her curiosity said, *No one will know! Just take a quick peek!* Fortunately, Trisha responded positively to her radar and guarded her mind against looking at pornography.

- When Renee went to her first varsity football game with her sixth-grade friends, some eighth-grade boys invited them to walk around. Since she knew the boys and they were in a public place, she went along with the gang. After they visited the concessions stand and ate some popcorn, the guys started complaining about how boring the game was. One suggested that they go underneath the bleachers and play some games of their own. He grabbed a plastic Dr Pepper bottle, poured out the soda, and said, "Who's up for a game of spin the bottle?" Renee's friends all chimed in, "Yeah! Let's do it! Come on!" But not Renee. Something inside her said, *This doesn't feel right. I don't think it sounds like a good idea to just give my kisses away to these guys!* She passed on the idea and joined some other friends sitting in the bleachers.

- When Katrina was in the seventh grade, she received a note in her locker from Ryan, asking her, "Will you go out with me?" A boy had never shown an interest in Katrina before, so she was excited. Ryan was the cutest, most popular boy in school, but he had just broken up with Ashley last week and with Leslie the week before. He seemed to be the kind of boy who just wanted to have a girlfriend all the time, and he usually spread rumors about them once he broke up with them. Part of Katrina wanted to tell Ryan yes so she could at least say she'd had a boyfriend. But her internal radar was warning her that she'd probably be dumped within a short amount of time, and that Ryan would just start bad rumors about her, too. She decided to guard her heart and told him, "I appreciate your interest in me, Ryan, but I'm not interested in being your girlfriend. Just your friend." When Ryan continued to press her on the issue by writing her notes and waiting for her after class to hound her about it in the hall-way, Katrina replied, "I'm willing to be friends with you, but not if you keep pushing me to be your girlfriend, okay?" Finally Ryan gave up, and Katrina had peace with her internal radar.

- Sarah had just started going to youth group at her church on Wednesday nights. While the youth pastor taught the lesson, some of her friends pre-tended to be taking notes, but they were really writing gossipy notes back and forth to one another. They tried to include Sarah, but something in her spirit reminded her that she wouldn't want people gossiping about her, so she refused to join in. The next week she told her friends she was inter-ested in the lesson and wanted to hear what the youth pastor was saying, so she sat with another friend up front rather than in the back with them.

Bravo Trisha, Renee, Katrina, and Sarah! And when you pay attention to your radar like these girls have learned to do, you'll be just as proud of yourself.

PAY ATTENTION
TO THE WARNINGS

Keep in mind that God put that radar within you to guide you. He sent the Holy Spirit to live in your heart and to enlighten your mind to know the difference between right and wrong, good and bad, and poor and wise choices. Let your common sense and your conscience be your guides. If things begin to seem inappropriate, be alert to your radar and resist doing things that make you uncomfortable or that you feel may be wrong. If you submit to your Holy Spirit radar and let Him be your guide, He will keep you safe.

But when you sense your radar telling you *WARNING, WARNING! This doesn't feel right!* yet you choose to ignore it, you're headed for trouble, because you can become desensitized to warning signs and eventually fail to notice them altogether. Then you might find yourself doing things you'd never dreamed you would do. Your desensitization can start with you simply ignoring internal warnings about getting involved with the wrong crowd, and then lead to more dangerous choices that might end in pregnancy or addiction to smoking, drinking, drugs, pornography, or sexual activity. If you respond to your radar when it first alerts you to danger, you'll avoid a lot of painful mistakes that can eventually ruin your life.

When your radar gets your attention, you may wonder what to do if you are with a girl or a guy friend or in a group of friends who are trying to get you to do something that goes against your conscience. Simply smile and say, "I'd prefer not to do that, okay?" You don't have to be offensive, just invite them to support your decision. If they continue to insist that you do something you don't feel comfortable doing, get offensive if necessary. Feel free to say something like, "Hey, I'm not going there, okay? And if *you* go there, I'm outta' here!" Let them know that if they can't respect you, they can't spend time with you. Remember, no one else can monitor and respond to your radar. That's your job.

Prepare to Soar

Just as an airplane's radar is designed to keep the aircraft and the people inside it safe, your internal radar is designed to keep your body, mind, heart, and spirit safe. If you learn to heed that radar and allow it to be your guide through life, you'll be able to soar to great heights, Princess!

Creative Conversation

What you will need:
- access to a four-door car

In this chapter we've discussed how a girl needs to pay attention to her radar in order to protect herself from dangerous temptations or inappropriate activities. To better visualize how important it is to guard yourself against temptation, go stand by a four-door car.

Mom, you are going to play the part of Temptation. To begin, simply stand outside of the car. Daughter, you are going to try to resist Temptation's lure by using the car as safe shelter. As soon as you get into the car, what does your radar tell you to do to keep Temptation from getting to you? Right. Lock the doors.

How many doors does your radar tell you to lock? One or two? Maybe three? Of course not! Your radar will more than likely tell you to guard all four doors, right? If there's even one door left unlocked, you're not safe, are you? The only way to be completely safe from an outside intruder is to pay attention to your radar and lock *all four* doors.

The same applies to life as well. You must be careful to pay attention to your radar's telling you to guard your body, mind, heart, and spirit if you hope to remain out of temptation's grasp.

Discuss the following questions:

1. How can you guard your mind from inappropriate thoughts? What are some examples of things your radar would tell you to avoid in order to remain mentally pure?

2. How can you guard your heart? What are some examples of things your radar would tell you to avoid to remain emotionally pure?

3. How can you guard your body? What are some examples of things your radar would advise you to avoid to remain physically pure?

4. How can you guard your spirit? What are some examples of things your radar would warn you to avoid to remain spiritually pure?

Close with a prayer, asking God to help you heed your radar and keep your body, mind, heart, and spirit free from danger and sin.

secrets to be shared

We're not keeping secrets, we're telling them; we're not hiding things,
we're bringing them out into the open.

MARK 4:22, MSG

Most girls have either had a secret or been entrusted with the secret of a close
friend. I remember whispering back and forth with friends on the school bus, on
the playground, in church, and at slumber parties, hand cupped over the listener's
ear to ensure privacy. I also remember making "pinkie promises" to keep those
secrets: "cross my heart, hope to die, stick a needle in my eye" if we ever told.

Keeping a secret seems to be a pretty harmless thing to do, unless it's the kind
of secret that *should* be shared. I had many such secrets when I was growing up,
and even though I didn't share them when I should have, I want to share them
with you now so you can avoid the mistakes I made in remaining silent.

As I entered puberty and blossomed physically, two uncles whom I loved and
trusted began flirting with me (talking to me in ways that made me feel like they
wanted to be my boyfriends instead of my uncles) and leading me into situations
that made me feel uncomfortable. Sometimes one would hide in my closet in my
room until I came in and closed my bedroom door. Then he would come out and
talk to me when no one else in the house knew we were alone together in my
room. Sometimes the other uncle would put his hand on my thigh when we were
driving somewhere, then wink at me and tell me how beautiful he thought I was.
He would slide his hand farther and farther up my thigh to see how far I would
let him go. Both uncles told me that our flirting game was to be "our little secret."
If only I had told my parents about what my uncles were doing, they could have
helped me see that as a child I wasn't responsible for my uncles' mistreatment of
me. But I kept the secret for many years.

Keeping that secret made it easier for me to keep other secrets I should have shared. When I was fourteen, I drifted into the wrong place with the wrong person at the wrong time. I went behind my parents' back in order to be alone in an apartment with an eighteen-year-old boy. When he insisted I have sex with him, I told him I didn't want to, but he wouldn't listen or just didn't care, and he forced himself on me. I should have told someone, but I didn't, because I was afraid I'd get in trouble for being with him in the first place. I kept this secret for years as well.

Had I told my parents how my uncles were behaving, I'm sure they would have protected me. Had I told them that an older boy had forced me to have sex with him, they could have helped me get counseling in order to sort out my feelings about the whole experience. But because my parents didn't know any of this until I was grown and gone from their home, I didn't see a counselor for the help I needed until I was married and had children of my own. As a result, I felt guilty and dirty for many years. Even though these two secrets were about things others had done to me, I soon began keeping secrets about things I was doing that I knew were wrong but didn't know how to stop. It was only when I began telling my secrets that I found the help and power to stop doing the things that made me feel dirty and ashamed.

Of course, I'm not the only girl who's ever suffered because she kept secrets that should have been shared.

WHITNEY'S CYBERSECRETS

After reading *Every Young Woman's Battle,* thirteen-year-old Whitney sent me the following e-mail:

> When I was eleven, I wanted to know more about sex, so my mom signed me up for a sexual purity class at our church. But I still didn't understand all I wanted to know. So over the years I have looked up on the Internet what sex means. I have never told my parents this because I feel they will not love me anymore. I saw things I knew I shouldn't be looking at, but I never told them. I have wanted to so many times, but I just can't. I can't

even ask them about sex because I'm afraid they may get upset or suspect something or make me go see a counselor. I also feel I am not a Christian anymore.

My heart goes out to Whitney and the many other young women who have guilty secrets they feel afraid or unable to talk about. As you think about whether Whitney is making the right choice in keeping this secret, consider these questions:

- How do you think Whitney's mother or youth pastor would respond to her asking questions about sexual issues?
- What do you think Whitney's mom would prefer she do to find answers to her questions instead of surfing the Internet for answers?
- What kind of answers do you think Whitney may have found on the Internet? Reliable ones? Biblically-based answers?
- Do you think she will be able to stop this behavior if she keeps her secret hidden? Why or why not?
- What would you do if you were Whitney's mom and Whitney came to you wanting help to stop looking at Internet pornography?
- What do you think Whitney should do? What would you do if you were in her shoes?

I hope that considering Whitney's dilemma will help you avoid a similar one of your own. If you have secretly been looking at pornographic Web sites or pictures, confess your secret to your mom, dad, or youth pastor and ask for help to stop.

That's what Allison and Emily did about their secret.

ALLISON AND EMILY'S SLEEPOVER SECRET

Thirteen-year-olds Allison and Emily have been friends for over three years, and they frequently spend the night at each other's houses. When they were ten, Emily suggested they play "husband and wife," getting on top of each other and pretending to do sexual things only married couples should do. Out of innocence, the girls played this game on occasion.

But now Allison and Emily are attending youth group at their church, and they've heard the youth pastor talk about how homosexuality (having sexual relations with someone of the same sex) is a sin. They begin to feel guilty for doing such things and worry they may be lesbians (women who have sex with other women rather than with men), which they realize would be wrong for Christians.

After weeks of worrying and feeling awkward around each other, the girls worked up the courage to tell each of their moms what they had done in the past. Even though they played out of innocence, they now knew it was a sin and asked God's forgiveness. Emily and Allison both wholeheartedly agreed that they shouldn't play that game anymore. They also promised each other that they'd never tell any of their other friends so neither of them would feel embarrassed about others' knowing what had happened.

If you have had a similar experience with a playmate and done sexual things you didn't know were inappropriate, you are not alone. Most kids have a similar experience and learn this lesson at some point in their lives. You do not need to struggle with guilt over it or wonder if there is something wrong with you.

Here are three things I want you to know if you can identify with Allison and Emily's story:

1. Young children often engage in innocent "child sexual play," frequently with someone of the same sex.

2. Having engaged in such activity doesn't mean you are homosexual. It just means you are human, with natural curiosities about your sexuality.

3. However, if you are reading this book, you are at an age of accountability. This means you are old enough to know the difference between what is appropriate and what is no longer appropriate, so you should no longer be sexual with anyone—male or female—until marriage.

I want to tell you about one more kind of secret that needs to be shared.

CRYSTAL'S BEDTIME RITUAL SECRET

Sometimes a girl discovers she doesn't need a partner to feel sexually stimulated, but that she can pleasure herself by touching her own vaginal area (called "masturbation"). At twenty-one years old, Crystal confessed she had been in the habit of masturbating herself to sleep most nights since she was a little girl. When she learned it was wrong, she tried to stop but was finding that very difficult.

> At first I masturbated because it felt good. As a teenager, I came to believe that masturbation would relieve my stress so I could relax and go to sleep. I had no idea I was creating a habit that would haunt me into my twenties. I wish I had told my mom about it and gotten some help for stopping when I was much younger. Years later, however, I have finally realized that God doesn't want me living in bondage to masturbation. After resisting the temptation over and over again, I can honestly say I know I don't have to give in to it any longer. God has shown me a way out.

Maybe you have touched your genital area at times simply because it felt good. Again, if so, you are not alone. This is a very common thing for young girls (and boys) to do. You don't need to struggle with guilt over it. However, I encourage you to stop, as masturbation can become a habit that can make it more difficult for you to resist sexual temptations as you grow older. If you find that you cannot stop, share this secret with your mom or dad. They understand what it's like to feel that desire and can help you overcome the temptation to continue giving in to it. Also pray about it, because God will give you the power to overcome anything that is not good for you. (By the way, I've known many girls who say they were never tempted to touch themselves sexually. If that's the case for you, rejoice and try not to give in to that temptation if it ever strikes in the future.)

One important lesson we can learn from these true stories is that we often do more harm than good by keeping secrets we feel guilty about. Like splinters, such secrets can fester and grow even more painful if we leave them buried and hidden, but we can heal much faster when we get the secret out into the open where it can no longer bother us. We can also get the wise counsel we need. Counseling may sound scary, but it's ultimately as healing as getting that splinter out. It hurts for a little while, but your heart feels so much better after the secrets are out and dealt with.

Rather than keeping secrets like the ones we've been talking about, it's much better to live an open-book life. What do I mean by an open-book life? I'm so glad you asked!

LIVE AN OPEN-BOOK LIFE

When you live an open-book life, you have no secrets, so you don't have to remember what lies you've told to cover things up. You don't have to worry about getting caught at anything, and you know that the people in your life love you for who you *really* are, not who they *think* you are.

I've prepared the chart below to show you the difference between living with

Consequences of Living a Secretive Life	Consequences of Living an Open-Book Life
You end up lying in order to keep secrets.	You don't need to lie because you have nothing to hide.
You are held hostage by your lies and can be blind to the truth.	The truth sets you free and brings understanding.
You live in fear of getting caught.	You live in freedom.
You remain ignorant of truth because you are afraid to ask questions.	You feel comfortable asking questions because you are hungry for truth.
You develop sinful cravings and bad habits.	You develop humility and strong character.
You worry that people wouldn't love you if they knew the truth.	You have confidence that people love you for who you really are.
You frequently worry that God is angry with you and won't forgive you.	You feel close to God and are able to joyfully obey His commandments.

secrets and living an open-book life. As you read these differences, ask yourself, "What kind of life do *I* want to live?"

If you are like me, living an open-book life sounds much more appealing than living a secretive life. If you agree, let me ask you…

DO YOU HAVE ANY SECRETS?

Even if you are harboring secrets from others, remember that you have no secrets from God. He knows everything. That thought shouldn't scare you, but give you comfort. He already knows everything about you and everything you've done, and He also loves you anyway. The Bible says in Job 36:5 (NLT), "God is mighty, yet he does not despise anyone! He is mighty in both power and understanding." He also doesn't want you to worry about what others would think if your secrets were out in the open. He wants you to live an open-book life. No secrets. No lies. No worries. Just peace and freedom.

Perhaps as you read this chapter, you've realized you are keeping some secrets you need to share. Is there anything in your life that has caused you to feel guilty, dirty, or ashamed? Are there things you have done by yourself or with someone else that worry you? Have you looked at or listened to things you know your parents wouldn't approve of? Have you said things or listened to someone else saying things you wouldn't want said in front of your mom or dad? Has anyone ever touched you or have you ever touched someone else in a private way? Do you have any secrets that need to be shared? Or questions you want to ask out of curiosity?

If so, I encourage you to talk with your parents about your secrets sooner (now) rather than later. They know you are only human. They've had their own experiences of making mistakes and then having to confess them. They are not as perfect as you may think, and they don't expect you to be perfect either. Just be honest with yourself and with them. They can handle the truth better than they can handle secretive behavior. They are here to help you or to get help for you if needed.

Remember, you and your parents are on the same team. Teammates don't keep secrets from one another, but confide in one another and work together toward a common goal. That goal is clear—freedom from secret sin, lies, and pain by living an open-book life. And the reward is tremendous—healthier, happier relationships with yourself, your family, and with God.

Creative Conversation

What you will need:

- pencil
- piece of paper

Draw one line down the middle of a piece of paper and another line across to divide it into four quarters. Title the left side of the paper "Productive" and the right side "Destructive." In the top box of the "Productive" side, list as many positive uses for fire as you can possibly think of. What are some of the wonderful benefits that fire brings into our lives?

Now on the other side, in the upper right box, list as many negatives as you can think of about fire. What are some bad or dangerous things about fire?

Notice that most of the secrets we've discussed in this chapter stemmed from natural sexual curiosities. Your sexual curiosities can be compared to fire. If you use those curiosities to ask questions of responsible adults, you can get answers and a greater understanding of God's gift of sexuality.

But your sexual curiosities can pose some potential dangers as well, especially if you try to satisfy them in unhealthy ways with secretive behaviors. In the lower left box, list as many good things about sexual curiosities as the two of you can think of (for instance, *curiosities tell us when we're ready to discover more about our sexuality, and they motivate us to seek the truth*). Then in the lower right box, list all the dangers you can think of (for instance, *sexual curiosities can lead us to seek information from unreliable or ungodly sources, and they can tempt us into doing things that aren't good for us*).

Once you've completed your lists, take a look at the big picture and discuss the following questions:

1. How do you feel about being curious about your sexuality?
2. What might make you hide your curiosity about sex?
3. What's one good way and one bad way to satisfy sexual curiosity?

4. Who are the people you can feel safe asking questions about sexuality?

5. Who are the people you should avoid asking or discussing sexual matters with?

6. What other sources of sexual information are not reliable and should be avoided?

7. Since God is the Creator of human beings and the Author of our sexuality, who knows how to best satisfy our curiosities? Is seeking God's answers to your questions about sex important to you? Why or why not?

8. How can you seek God's answers to questions about sexuality? (Hint: use the concordance in the back of your Bible to find passages where God addresses sexual issues.)

Close with a prayer, asking God to help you satisfy your sexual curiosities in healthy ways that honor Him. Ask Him to give you the courage to tell your parents about any secrets that should be shared. Also ask the Holy Spirit to help you keep your heart soft and splinter-free so you can live a completely open-book life.

the mind of a princess

> Do not conform any longer to the pattern of this world, but be transformed by the renewing of your mind. Then you will be able to test and approve what God's will is—his good, pleasing and perfect will.
>
> ROMANS 12:2

In the movie *Monsters, Inc.*, a large company makes its profits by bottling the energy created by children's screams. The idea is that the scarier their monster employees can be, the more screams they'll generate from the children they frighten, and the more energy they'll produce. However, one little girl in the movie is too innocent and naive about monsters to even know to be afraid of them. She doesn't scream in their presence; instead she squeals with delight and wants to play with them.

Of course, those cute little Disney monsters aren't really all that dangerous, so playing with them is no big deal. But that's not the case with some of the monsters lurking out there in the world—monsters which you may be too innocent and naive about to be afraid. These monsters are everywhere—in the stores where you shop, in the theater you go to, and even in your own home. Although they may seem harmless, they aren't.

What monsters am I talking about? Media monsters. You may not realize it, but numerous television shows, movies, musical artists, magazines, and Web sites can lead you down a dangerous path. How? By desensitizing your mind to harmful messages about sexuality.

TURNING UP THE VOLUME

You may be wondering, *What in the world does* desensitizing *mean?* It means you get so used to something that you stop noticing or realizing it. Let me give you an example of how we can become desensitized. Let's say my kids and I are riding in the car, listening to music. The volume is set on maybe 2 or 3. From the backseat, my son asks, "Mom, will you turn the radio up?" So I adjust the volume to maybe 4 or 5. But then we get out on the highway where big, loud trucks are passing us and drowning out the music, so I turn it up to 6 or 7. Then one of our favorite songs comes on, and my daughter says, "Mom, let's really crank it!" That means she wants me to turn it up to a head-banging (but not quite eardrum-piercing) level of 8 or even 9 if it doesn't make the car windows rattle. (We've never gotten brave enough to crank it to a 10 for fear of blowing out the speakers.) When we arrive at our destination, I turn off the engine and we get out of the car. But when we get back into the car and I turn on the key, the blaring radio almost blasts us out of our seats! Once we turn it back down and regain our composure, we are stunned to realize how loud the radio was. We had gradually been desensitized to its volume.

How does this compare with the desensitization that can occur with the media? Let's say a young woman listens to musical artists such as Britney Spears, Christina Aguilera, or Madonna every day, despite their messages that boys are simply toys for girls to play with rather than human beings to be respected. She tells herself, *Everybody listens to this kind of music—it's no big deal. (The volume is turned up slightly...)* Then she looks at teen magazines, sees glamorous celebrities wearing next to nothing and thinks, *Wow! If only I could only look that hot! (And the volume goes up...)* Then maybe she tries to look that hot by wearing something a little more revealing than normal. *(The volume goes up a little more...)* She's pleased with the attention she gets and by the heads she turns, but she's surprised when boys make suggestive comments to her or try to get her alone to kiss her. But she rarely sees a woman resist sexual advances in the soap operas, television sitcoms, and movies she watches, so she acts the part as she's seen it played in the media hundreds of times before. *(And the volume goes up even more...)* She allows herself to get swept off her feet as a passionate kiss turns into sexual activity. *(And the volume is blaring...)* Then one day she has her heart ripped to shreds as her boyfriend says, "I just want to be friends. There's this other girl..." or she discovers she's pregnant or has a sexually transmitted disease and wonders, *Whoa! How did this happen?*

Little by little this young woman had become desensitized to the media's destructive messages, and as a result she lost her ability to tell right from wrong. She could no longer make wise choices about her sexuality. When we listen to inappropriate songs and look at television shows and movies that don't portray sexuality as wholesome, sacred, and special, we too can become desensitized and make poor sexual choices.

How can you avoid becoming desensitized? By making wise choices now about the media monsters you entertain. We'll talk more about this in our Creative Conversation at the close of the chapter. For now, let's talk about what a princess can do to guard her mind.

TUNING OUT THE BAD STUFF

What are some practical ways you can tune out destructive messages in the media? Here are several ideas:

- Before you rent or go to a movie, ask your parents to check its rating. Any G-rated (for general audiences) movie is probably fine. If it's a PG movie (parental guidance suggested), watch it only with one of your parents or a responsible adult your parents approve of so they can answer your questions or comment about any inappropriate themes. If the movie is rated PG-13 (parental guidance is strongly suggested *and* viewers should be at least thirteen years of age), don't watch it. PG-13 movies contain sexual content, partial nudity, graphic violence, or foul language, none of which are appropriate material for the mind of a princess your age. Of course, if a movie is rated R (restricted audience), no one under seventeen is allowed without a parent. Steer clear of such movies.

- If you're watching a television show that talks or jokes about sex or portrays unmarried people being sexual with one another (for instance, going to bed together), either change the channel, turn off the television, or leave the room if you don't have control over what's being watched.

- If you're listening to music or a radio show that refers to sex in an inappropriate way, change the station or turn the radio off. If you're in someone else's car ask, "Do you mind if we change the station?" If they ask why, simply say, "This doesn't sound appropriate. Surely we can find something better."

- If you're at a friend's house, in a waiting room, or in a bookstore and you see teen magazines that glamorize anorexic celebrities who dress inappropriately and talk about their sex lives (such as *CosmoGirl, Teen People,* and *Young Miss*), resist the temptation to read those. Some great ones to get your hands on are Focus on the Family's *Brio* magazine and *Revolve,* a New Testament from Thomas Nelson Publishers in cool, girl-magazine form complete with articles and fun questionnaires.

- If you're surfing the Internet or checking e-mails and come across pictures of people without clothes on, exit the site or show your parents what you discovered. If you get inappropriate e-mails, pop-ups, or instant messages from strangers while you are online, tell your parents. They may need to get a filter for the computer to keep that kind of stuff far away. I also recommend that you not open e-mails from people you don't know. If you do, and there is a link that a stranger wants you to click on, DON'T! It could be an electronic virus that infects your computer or a pornographic Web site that infects your mind. Steer clear of chat rooms altogether because you never know who's in that room with you and what kind of information they are trying to get from their interactions with you.

When it comes to the thoughts we entertain, one of the best ways to tune out inappropriately messages is to tune in to something better.

TUNE IN TO THE GOOD STUFF

What kinds of thoughts should we entertain? What kinds of things can we meditate on and feel good about? If you look to the Bible to answer that question, you'll find it has a lot to say. Do you know which of Jesus's words are by far the most important for us to practice?

> "Love the Lord your God with all your heart and with all your soul and with all your mind." This is the first and greatest commandment. And the second is like it: "Love your neighbor as yourself." (Matthew 22:37-39)

This verse doesn't say you should sit around all day and meditate on nothing but God. He knows you have a life. He's the One who gave it to you, and He wants you to be the best student, daughter, sister, and friend possible. According to these verses, Jesus wants you to love God *more* than any of the other things in your life. We are to love God with as much strength and excitement as we possibly can. We show our love for God by focusing our thoughts and energies on things that are pleasing to Him. God wants us to do what Paul encouraged the people of Philippi to do:

> Whatever is true, whatever is noble, whatever is right, whatever is pure,
> whatever is lovely, whatever is admirable—if anything is excellent or praise-
> worthy—think about such things. (Philippians 4:8)

You don't have to read your Bible and pray twenty-four hours a day, seven days a week to feel as if you're keeping your mind focused on noble, praiseworthy things. If you need some practical suggestions on how you can fill your mind with good thoughts, take your pick from my top ten ideas of good things for girls to think about:

1. How much God must have loved you to send Jesus Christ to earth to be your personal Savior. Wow! Talk about passion!

2. What you want to be when you grow up and how you want to serve God with your life. As a doctor? missionary? teacher? writer?

3. What you can do to show your mom or dad how much you appreciate all they do for you. Brownie-point time!

4. How you can go the extra mile to learn even more about the subject at school that interests you most. Brownie-point time with your teacher!

5. How you might surprise your brother or sister by doing one of their chores for them. They'll think you're awesome for being so nice!

6. Making a coupon book for your best friend's birthday. What kind of coupons would she enjoy most? A personal manicure? A batch of her favorite cookies? An afternoon together playing your favorite games?

7. How you would spend an entire day (or week, or month) if you could go anywhere and do anything in the world you wanted to do. The sky is the limit!

8. How you would make your own movie, produce your own television show, create your own song, or write your own book. What would it be about? What are you most passionate about? Get creative!

9. What you would do if you inherited one million dollars? Who would you spend it on? Why?

10. Going on a mission trip to anywhere in the world. What country would you go to? What group of people would you help? Why?

If you focus your thoughts on any of these (or similar things), you'll be developing the mind of a true princess, and you'll be pleasing the King as well. Why? Because all of these things help you dream big—about God, about becoming all that you can be, and about serving others with your whole heart.

So keep guarding your mind and dreaming big, Princess. Allow your thoughts to run wild with the possibilities of how God may use *you* to express His lavish love to your family, your friends, and even those in the far corners of the world someday.

Creative Conversation

What you will need:

- pencil and paper

Sometimes we assume that the media choices we make are just fine because "everyone watches that or listens to that or reads that." But just because everyone's doing it, does that make it right? Rather than comparing our choices to what everyone else is doing, let's use a different measuring stick. First, on your piece of paper, list a few of your favorites in these categories:

- television shows
- movies
- songs
- magazines

Now make a list of the characters who appear in those favorite shows or movies, the musical artists who sing those songs, or the celebrities who are pictured in those magazines. Then discuss the following questions:

1. Do any of these people act flirty or inappropriate, either in real life or in the parts they play?
2. Are the clothes they wear modest, or do they try to flaunt their bodies for attention?
3. Is it common knowledge that these characters or celebrities are sexually active before marriage or unfaithful to their spouse?
4. Is sex something that is frequently discussed, joked about, or referred to in a disrespectful way in their scripts, songs, or articles?

Unfortunately, many girls subconsciously begin to look to celebrities and magazines far more than they look to the Bible for advice on life, fashion, and relationships. Hollywood glamorizes female pop stars who have what teens consider to be the right look, the right moves, and the right wardrobes. Many of these women set poor examples of biblical concepts such as modesty, sexual purity, and guarding your body, mind, heart, and spirit. Before you make an idol out of a pop star or television show or magazine, weigh their words against the Word of God. Don't just unscrew your head, put it under the couch, and let the television or radio fill you with worldly ideas about sexuality. Make wise choices about what you look at and listen to so you can keep those media monsters off your back and out of your life!

Questions for further discussion:

1. Mom, what were some of the shows you watched growing up that you now realize were bad influences? (For example, I regret learning so much about how teens "make out at Inspiration Point" from *Happy Days* and *Laverne and Shirley*.) What were some of the characters like on these shows? What did you learn from them? Do you think they influenced you to make choices you now regret? Or did you feel as if you were missing out on something if you weren't acting like them?
2. Daughter, who do you think are the most negative influences of your generation when it comes to sexual integrity? What television celebrities

or singers are setting bad examples? How do you think they affect girls
your age? What can *you* do to avoid being negatively affected by their
influence?

3. Both Mom and Daughter, what are some television shows, movies,
music, or magazines you can feel good about your family looking at
or listening to? Why do you think these would be good influences?

Close with a prayer, asking God to help you develop the mind of a true
princess—controlling your media choices before your media choices come to control you.

the heart of a princess

Blessed are the pure in heart, for they will see God.

MATTHEW 5:8

If you've ever ridden a roller coaster, you know it can be a fun but scary experience. One second you are riding high and your heart is in your throat. The next second you take a plunge and feel your heart sink into your stomach. You scream at the top of your lungs with both shock and delight. At times you may feel yourself start to cry out of sheer terror. And when the ride is over, you usually find yourself laughing hysterically, relieved that you lived through the experience.

The next several years of your life may feel a lot like those roller-coaster rides. At times your emotions may run high and you'll feel on top of the world. Other times you may feel as if you are sinking into a pit of despair. Sometimes you will have to laugh to keep from crying, and other times you may feel like throwing your face into a pillow and letting the tears flow. There may be times when you wonder if you'll ever get off the emotional roller coaster you're riding.

I assure you that as you approach adulthood, the ups and downs you experience during your puberty and teen years will eventually level out. In this chapter I want to tell you how you can keep your emotional roller coaster rides from feeling too out-of-control. Even though life always brings many ups and downs, you can do some things to guard your heart from getting your hopes up too high or getting hurt unnecessarily.

In Proverbs 4:23, God tells us, "Above all else, guard your heart, for it is the wellspring of life." In other words, protect and treasure your heart. Why is it so important to God that we learn to protect our hearts? The answer is in the word *wellspring*, which can also be interpreted as "source." The heart is the source of life. When God created us, He made our hearts central to our being—physically, spiritually, and emotionally. Physically, the heart is at the center of the circulatory system. It pumps oxygenated blood throughout the body. If the heart has trouble, the entire body is in danger of losing its life-giving flow of blood. Spiritually, the heart is the place that the Holy Spirit dwells when we invite Him into our lives (see Ephesians 3:16-17). Emotionally, the heart leaps for joy when we delight in something or someone. It also aches when we experience disappointment or loss. The heart is the core of all we are and experience in life, so when God says to guard it above all else, He is saying, "Protect the source of your life—the physical, spiritual, and emotional source of your well-being."

But preteen girls often give their hearts away rather than guard them. They sometimes get caught up in playing games with boys that can negatively affect their friendships and how they feel about themselves. Most girls fall into playing these games out of pure innocence at first, so if you recognize yourself in any of these stories or situations, don't panic. There's still time to learn to guard your heart from unrealistic hopes or from getting hurt by others. Let's look at the kinds of games I'm talking about.

THE GAMES GIRLS PLAY WITH BOYS

My daughter came home one day after she had just started sixth grade, feeling annoyed that a few girls in her class were playing a new game (at least it was new to Erin) called "I have a new boyfriend." These girls were doodling boys' names on their book covers, writing notes to boys during class, and going out of their way in the halls just to bump into the boy they had labeled as their boyfriend that week. She said, "Mom! Some girls change boyfriends almost as often as they change their underwear!"

Girls who frequently change boyfriends based on who floats their boat from one day to the next aren't preparing themselves for a committed marriage relationship someday. They are more likely training their hearts for divorce. They jump into relationships with boys they don't know very well (except that he's cute), and when the least little thing goes wrong, *Snap! I'm outta here! Next in line, please!* That's not a genuine relationship. That's a silly game. And the game goes both ways. Sometimes it's the boy who looks at the girl and says, "Nah! You're not good enough for me anymore! I'm going to move on to someone better." This can be a cruel, hurtful game; one that I hope you'll choose not to play.

Chances are, your parents don't want you to play that game either because they don't want to see you get your hopes incredibly high over certain guys only to have your heart broken time and time again. Every time a girl's heart gets broken, she feels a little less confident and a little more insecure. I don't know about your mom, but I remember getting burned at that game. I actually started playing incredibly young. I was only in kindergarten when I kissed Tom on the cheek during milk break and told him he was my boyfriend. I was elated when he went along with it for a little while, but then he told me a few days later that April was really his girlfriend, not me. *Ouch!* I was only six, but I vividly remember wondering, *Why is April better than me?* Even though April had been a playmate of mine on the playground, I suddenly didn't like her anymore. I was jealous.

Over the next several years, I remember targeting K.C., Davy, Jared, and Clay with my affections, yet none of them responded much, except K.C. told me he didn't like me as a girlfriend because I had too many freckles. *Ouch again!* I didn't realize that most boys that age think girls have cooties. I began to wonder what was wrong with me that I couldn't get a boyfriend. Then in fifth or sixth grade when boys did begin to notice me, my relationships didn't seem to last long. One week it was a note saying, "Will you go with me?" and the next week the note would say, "I quit you." With every breakup my heart and self-esteem sank a little lower.

Let's face it. Boys your age don't have a clue how to be a boyfriend or how to treat a girlfriend, so why go there and get your heart broken? While I encourage you to have friends who are boys, I hope you will define them as strictly that, saving the boyfriend label for years down the road. Wait until your parents will allow you to actually date or court a special young man who cares deeply for you and treats you with dignity and respect.

In the Meantime...

Everyone longs to feel loved and special, and there's nothing wrong with this desire. But sometimes looking for love from a boyfriend, especially too early in life, can ultimately do more harm than good. So I'm going to let you in on the secret to guarding your heart *and* receiving all the love and attention you need.

Between now and the season of your life when it *is* appropriate to have a boyfriend, do you want to know what the best training ground for a healthy, committed relationship in the future is? That training ground is right under your nose. It's actually your own house! By being connected to others in your own family such as your mom, dad, brothers, sisters, and grandparents, you get your "practice time" in for properly conducting loving relationships. There may be days when you don't want to spend time with your parents, and your brother or sister is getting on your nerves, but that's sometimes going to be the case when you have your own husband and kids someday too. You can't just say, "I quit you!" to the family you have now, nor can you snap your fingers and say, "Next in line!" when you're in a committed marriage someday.

We'll talk more in chapter 14 about how you can pursue stronger relationships with the people you live with. For now, Princess, know that your own family is where you get the best practice on becoming the best person, wife, and mother you can be someday.

Creative Conversation

What you will need:
- dark-colored piece of paper
- light-colored piece of paper
- scissors
- glue

Using the scissors, cut out two paper hearts, one from the dark paper and one from the light paper. Then glue the two of them together. While the glue is drying, read the following paragraph together.

While wanting to connect heart-to-heart with others is natural and appropriate, it's unwise to emotionally attach to one guy after another, assuming that each boy you think is cute should be your boyfriend. To understand why, imagine those two paper hearts, one dark and one light, bonded permanently together. But what if the day comes when one doesn't want to be bonded to the other anymore? What happens when one of those hearts says to the other, "I've had enough! I'm out of here!"?

Now attempt to pull the two hearts apart.

What happens? Dark fibers remain stuck to the light heart and light fibers still cling to the dark. The lesson is this: when you get emotionally attached to someone, you will always keep a part of that person, tucking those memories into your trunk of emotional baggage. You will eventually drag those memories into your marriage, where you may be tempted to compare your husband to one or all of your previous boyfriends. Also keep in mind that some parts of your heart, once given away, can never be given to someone else, such as first love, first kiss, and first sexual experience.

But that's not the only danger of attaching to a string of boys. Here's another example. Imagine a strip of clear packing tape. It's sticky, eager to bond with anything it touches. Once attached to a cardboard box, it won't come off without tearing the box and leaving paper residue on the tape. The piece of tape might still be sticky enough to bond to something else, but the more you attach and remove it from other things, the less sticky it becomes. Eventually, it loses its bonding ability altogether.

Something similar can happen with your heart. When you emotionally attach yourself over and over to different people, you can lose your emotional "stickiness." So if you continue to have one boyfriend after another after another, simply out of habit, you may lessen your ability to remain committed and faithful to one person for a lifetime.

Discuss the following questions:

1. Do you see that girls your age are beginning to fall into this pattern of having a different boyfriend every week or so? What do you think about it?

2. Do you think boys your age are really able to meet your emotional needs to feel loved and cherished? Why or why not?

3. What might you say to a friend who is going through relationships about as fast as she goes through a roll of toilet paper?

4. How can you avoid falling into this pattern?

5. How can Mom encourage you to guard your heart?

Close with a prayer, asking God to write His name on your heart and teach you how to guard it from unrealistic hopes and hurtful relationships.

the mouth of a princess

May the words of my mouth
and the meditation of my heart
be pleasing in your sight,
O LORD, my Rock and my Redeemer.

PSALM 19:14

One small part of my body got me into big trouble when I was in the sixth grade. My mouth. As I look back at some of the things I said to or about others, I can see I didn't understand how to be a Christian with my words. I would go to church on Sunday but talk trash with my friends, smart off to adults, and flirt with boys the rest of the week. I wasn't trying to be rude to people or talk ugly about others or even give guys the impression I was desperate for attention, but I succeeded in doing just that. And I suffered many negative consequences as a result.

I had no concept of loyalty to friends, and I talked about them when they weren't around to defend themselves. Talking bad about Stephanie behind her back to Michelle resulted in my losing Stephanie's friendship altogether, and Michelle no longer trusted me, either. Letting Denise's secret slip out at a slumber party about the boy she had a crush on got me yelled at big time, and another friendship bit the dust.

My mouth also got me in major trouble with my sixth-grade teacher, who was also a preacher and frequently worked on his sermons at his desk while giving us extra assignments to keep us busy. When I complained, "I wish you'd take us outside like the other sixth-grade teachers instead of working on your sermon!" in front of the whole class, I got sent to the principal's office and then to detention for two days.

Of course, the telephone posed a whole new set of troubles. I would have private telephone conversations with girlfriends and get up-to-date on all the dirty jokes going around or talk about what boys we liked and why. In seventh grade my frequent phone conversations with Michael became extremely inappropriate when he asked, "How far would you let me go if we were alone together right now?" I didn't think there was anything wrong with this conversation because we were just talking and not doing anything. I mistakenly assumed there was no sin in that, but if someone had been listening in on the other line, I think I would have died!

Backstabbing. Gossip. Mouthing off. Flirting. Inappropriate conversations. All of these are major temptations young girls face and offenses I'm not proud of committing. So how can you keep your lips from sinning? How can you avoid hurting other people's feelings and losing friendships? How can you steer clear of being disrespectful to adults and misleading guys with your words? You can't exactly live with a muzzle over your mouth, so you must learn to tame your tongue. But before we create a filter for our words, let's ask God what He thinks.

SEARCHING THE SCRIPTURES

What does the Bible have to say about the power of our words and how a princess is to use her mouth?

> For out of the overflow of the heart the mouth speaks. The good [woman] brings good things out of the good stored up in [her], and the evil [woman] brings evil things out of the evil stored up in [her]. But I tell you that [women] will have to give account on the day of judgment for every care-less word they have spoken. For by your words you will be [found inno-cent], and by your words you will be [found guilty]. (Matthew 12:34-37)

What will the words *you* choose reveal about your character and heart?

> But among you there must not be even a hint of sexual immorality, or of any kind of impurity, or of greed, because these are improper for God's holy people. Nor should there be obscenity, foolish talk or coarse joking, which are out of place, but rather thanksgiving. (Ephesians 5:3-4)

When you are talking with both your girlfriends and guy friends, can you consistently choose words that do not contain even "a hint of sexual immorality"?

> When we put bits into the mouths of horses to make them obey us, we can turn the whole animal. Or take ships as an example. Although they are so large and are driven by strong winds, they are steered by a very small rudder wherever the pilot wants to go. Likewise the tongue is a small part of the body, but it makes great boasts. Consider what a great forest is set on fire by a small spark. The tongue also is a fire, a world of evil among the parts of the body. It corrupts the whole person, sets the whole course of his life on fire. (James 3:3-6)

Did you catch that last part? The tongue "corrupts the whole person." That's why it's important to match your words with God's Word.

Here's one of my favorite verses, which promises that when we choose words that reflect the pure love of our Savior, we will be rewarded with His favor and friendship:

> [She] who loves a pure heart and whose speech is gracious
> will have the king for [her] friend. (Proverbs 22:11)

Your words to others and about others matter to God—both what you say and how you say it.

A FILTER FOR OUR WORDS

If you will commit these guidelines to heart and carefully guard the words that come out of your mouth, you can protect your friendships, earn the respect of adults, and be the kind of girl who is genuinely appreciated by her Christian brothers.

- *Treat others the way you want to be treated.* For example, let's say you hear something bad about your friend Tina. You know you wouldn't want someone saying something like that about you, nor do you want to betray Tina's friendship. Rather than spreading the rumor around, you assume it's not true and you don't repeat it. You might even ask the person spreading the rumor, "Does Tina know you're talking about her like that? Would she agree with what you're saying? If she found out what you've been saying, how would she feel?"

- *Never say anything about a friend that you wouldn't want her to know you said.* Unfortunately, girls can be pretty bad about repeating things a friend told them in confidence. Sometimes you might be tempted to tell others about a secret that a friend told you. (The one exception to this guideline is if a friend tells you something that falls in the "secrets to be shared" category—and then the only person you should tell is your mom.) Other times you might intentionally say something negative to make your friend look bad, thinking it will make you look better. However, the person you repeat those things to will usually judge you as an untrustworthy friend because you talk negatively about your friends behind their backs. So before you say something about someone else, stop and ask yourself, *Would I say this about her if she were standing beside me?* You could also ask, *Am I only going to make myself look bad by saying this negative thing about someone else?*

- *When talking to adults, keep in mind that God has placed them in authority over you and that you should show them respect.* If you do not agree with something an adult has done or said, and you feel the need to discuss the matter with that person, choose your words wisely and express your feelings using a very respectful tone. Maybe start out by calmly and respectfully saying something like, "Sir, may I ask you about…" or "Ma'am, can you help me understand why…"

- *Don't say anything to a boy that you wouldn't want your parents or another adult to hear.* Remember the princess's code of conduct? It applies to what you say as well as to what you do. Flirtatious words can get a girl into real trouble with boys. Like me, you may be tempted to tell yourself, *I'm not doing anything wrong. All I'm doing is talking to him.* However, the words you use can easily stir a guy up and cause him to be emotionally or even sexually aroused. If you are about to say something to a cute boy, pretend that your mom, dad, or teacher is standing right behind you. Even if the coast is clear and no adult is around, remember that God still hears every word you speak.

Of course, all of these guidelines are applicable not only to words that come out of your mouth but also to words written in notes and e-mails, exchanged in chat rooms, through instant messaging over the Internet, and through text messaging on cell phones. Sometimes using the Internet or cell phones can cause a girl to be much bolder than she might otherwise be. She might also be tempted to tell herself it's okay to use inappropriate words or communicate things that are inappropriate because she's not actually saying them out loud. However, if it's something you wouldn't say to a guy's face, you shouldn't say it in cyberspace or over cell phones either.

All of these guidelines can be boiled down to this: *If you can't say something kind, respectful, and appropriate, don't say anything at all.* And if you hear one of your friends saying words that shouldn't be coming out of a princess's mouth, don't let down your guard and chime in, thinking, *Well, if she says it, I can say it too.* Just respond by saying something nice about the person she's speaking badly about. Your friend will get the hint that you are not going down that road, and she'll have no ammunition to use against you in later conversations with others.

One final word on the mouth of a princess. You have the power to be an incredible blessing to everyone who knows you. How can you be that kind of person? By speaking nothing but kind words and blessings into other people's lives.

I had several friends in junior high school, but I distinctly remember Kathy and Leslie. Kathy was fun to be around because she had a quick wit and a sharp sense of humor, but she also had somewhat of a mean streak running through her. As long as she was making jokes about other people, I enjoyed her company. But when I became the next target of her twisted sense of humor, and she said some very funny but hurtful things about me at the lunch table, it made me question why I considered her my friend.

Leslie, on the other hand, was one of the nicest people you'd ever want to meet. She was always pleasant and sincere. I never heard her say anything bad about anyone, not even our teachers. She had a quiet way of slipping out of conversations she didn't want to be involved in without being offensive to anyone. She was the kind of friend I knew I could trust, not just with my secrets, but with my heart. When I was discouraged about school or feeling insecure about other relationships, Leslie was usually the person I turned to. She'd always have a word of encouragement for me and made me believe I could overcome anything and accomplish anything I set out to do. Her words were a source of inspiration to me during a very trying time in my life.

I don't know what happened to Kathy after we graduated high school. We drifted apart before we ever finished junior high. But Leslie and I still keep in touch to this day, almost twenty-five years later, and I still love and respect her dearly and cherish our friendship.

If you want to be a blessing to others and enjoy long-term, healthy relationships with your friends, you'll choose your words wisely and use your mouth to build others up, not tear them down.

Creative Conversation

What you will need:
- tube of toothpaste
- paper plate

Take turns wrapping your hand around the middle of the toothpaste tube and giving it a good squeeze, allowing the toothpaste to ooze out onto the paper plate.

Now each of you take turns trying to put the toothpaste *back* into the tube. Sound impossible? At least give it a try.

Once you've given it your best shot, discuss these questions:

1. How are our words like that toothpaste?
2. Once we say something out loud, how easy is it to "take it back"?
3. Have you ever said something you wish you had never said? What was it?
4. How did you feel after you said it? How do you think it made the person who heard you say it feel?
5. Have you done anything to try to make the situation right? What?
6. Is there anything more you can do? If so, what?
7. What lesson have you learned as a result? What will you do differently next time?

Close with a prayer, asking the Holy Spirit to help you carefully choose words that are fitting to a princess and a blessing and encouragement to others.

selecting a royal wardrobe

She is clothed with strength and dignity;

she can laugh at the days to come.

PROVERBS 31:25

It was the first day of junior high for my daughter, Erin, and I could sense her excitement and nervousness as we drove into the parking lot. As we approached the building, I couldn't help but notice how polished all the students looked, dressed in their brand-new school clothes. But then I caught a glimpse of a girl with the word *flirt* across her skintight T-shirt. I couldn't believe a sixth grader even owned such a shirt, not to mention that she was so proud of it that she wore it to school on the first day. What was she thinking? What was her mother thinking when she purchased it? What would her teachers' first impression of her be? What would her classmates, especially the boys, think about her character?

But a more important question is what do *you* think? Is this something you would wear? I know sometimes it's hard to determine what clothes are okay for a Christian girl to wear, because right now, fitting in seems so much more important than anything else. If you see your friends wearing certain clothes, you want to wear them too so you can blend in to the fashion scene. But when you see your friends wearing shirts that say things like *flirt* or *hottie* or *sexy,* you may not immediately recognize that those words are not appropriate—not just for a preteen girl but for any age woman.

I hope that by the time you get to the end of this chapter, you'll have a much clearer picture of how you want to dress and the messages you want to send to others about your character. But for now, let's consider what motivates the fashion choices of most preteen girls.

FASHION FACTORS TO CONSIDER

What are girls thinking as they shop for new clothes, or as they stand in front of their closets each morning asking the age-old question, "What am I going to wear today?" If the truth were told, one or more of the following concerns often motivates their choices:

- *Is this something my friends would wear? Will they laugh at me for wearing it?*
- *Does this look anything like I've seen music or television celebrities wearing?*
- *Will this get me noticed? Will it maybe make me more popular?*
- *Does this make me look older and more mature?*

There's certainly nothing wrong with wanting to fit in or look attractive, but let me challenge you to think a little more deeply when it comes to buying clothes and deciding what to wear each day. Consider these truths:

- *Just because a certain fashion is popular doesn't make it appropriate for a princess.* Spaghetti-strap tanks, extremely short shorts, miniskirts, and belly-revealing tops are a few examples of trendy fashions that may be popular, but aren't necessarily appropriate. Maybe your parents have allowed you to wear some of these things in the past because of your girlish body. But now that your body is changing, you'll soon (if you don't already) have a more grown-up body, and people will look at you in a different way. As you develop some of those flattering curves we talked about in the first chapter, you'll want to treat them with dignity and respect, covering them modestly. Some popular fashions make that very difficult to do.

- *Your clothes should be an expression of you, not everyone else.* Don't be afraid to be yourself! Buy and wear clothes that *you* like, not just what you see others wearing. Don't be afraid to be a trendsetter rather than a trend follower. If someone laughs at something you're wearing, don't hesitate to say, "Hey! I like this outfit, thank you very much!" or just laugh along with them rather than take it personally. And never laugh at what someone else wears. Instead, compliment their creativity or individuality. Everyone's taste in clothes is going to be slightly different. That's okay. It's what makes each of us unique.

- *Your clothes can set an example—good or bad—that your friends may follow.* Let's say twelve-year-old Angela wears spaghetti-strap tops. Her body isn't developed yet, so no one would consider her immodest. However, her eleven-year-old friend, Abby, is already developing and looks completely inappropriate in spaghetti-strap tops. When her mother says she doesn't think those tops are modest enough, Abby responds, "But Angela wears them!" Don't give other girls the impression that immodest fashions are okay, even if they look okay on you.

- *Your clothes can actually cause guys to stumble and fall into temptation.* If you wear skimpy clothes that reveal a lot of skin or tight clothes that reveal your developing curves, you are probably turning guys' heads and possibly even turning them on sexually.

    I discovered this the hard way. I was an early bloomer and developed breasts before most other girls. I didn't think much of it, but soon boys began noticing me. There was one boy, Christopher, who I had liked for years but he had never paid me any attention—except to run when he saw me coming. But one day that changed. Christopher saw me in the hallway when no one else was around. He came up to me and said, "Hey, wear that green- and white-striped sweater tomorrow, okay?"

    I wasn't sure why he wanted me to wear that sweater, but I was so thrilled that he actually talked to me that I didn't even question his motive. I wore it the next day and freaked out when I kept catching him looking at me throughout our sixth-period science class. The next day I again wore a sweater, thinking maybe Christopher had a thing for them. Or better yet, maybe he had a thing for *me* in sweaters. But he burst my bubble when he commented, "That one's not tight enough. I like it when you wear *tight* sweaters!" All of a sudden I realized that Christopher wasn't attracted to me because of my personality or because he thought I was pretty. He was attracted to my breasts. That was a lesson learned the hard way. Tighter shirts lead guys to see girls as just a collection of body parts. More modest clothes teach guys that you are a real person with a lot more to offer than just a bunch of flattering curves.

If you want guys to notice you because of who you are rather than just because of your body, check out what the Bible has to say about how we clothe ourselves.

SEARCHING THE SCRIPTURES

While Scripture isn't specific about how we are to dress, it does have some specific things to say about the "clothing" we should wear. Here are a few examples (with italics for emphasis):

> Let us behave decently, as in the daytime, not in orgies and drunkenness, not in sexual immorality and debauchery, not in dissension and jealousy. Rather, *clothe yourselves with the Lord Jesus Christ,* and do not think about how to gratify the desires of the sinful nature. (Romans 13:13-14)

> Therefore, as God's chosen people, holy and dearly loved, *clothe yourselves with compassion, kindness, humility, gentleness and patience....* And over all these virtues *put on love,* which binds them all together in perfect unity. (Colossians 3:12,14)

> All of you, *clothe yourselves with humility* toward one another, because,
> > "God opposes the proud
> > but gives grace to the humble." (1 Peter 5:5)

Notice that the Bible says nothing about spaghetti straps or miniskirts! Instead, God tells us to clothe ourselves with Jesus, humility, compassion, kindness, gentleness, patience, and love. Maybe you're thinking, *But I can't wear those to school!* Oh, but you can! Just not by themselves. You must also clothe yourself with actual clothes!

So, how can you translate all this scriptural stuff into practical terms? Read on.

CLEANING OUT
YOUR CLOSET

While only you (with the help of your parents) can ultimately decide whether each article of clothing is appropriate or inappropriate, I want to offer help for determining how others are going to be affected by your attire as you walk, bend, reach, and wiggle around throughout the day.

Use the following list of questions to evaluate each article of clothing in your closet. A yes may mean you need to clean that particular item out of your closet. If an article of clothing doesn't necessarily look immodest on you, be aware that this may change as you continue to develop larger breasts and hips. So continue to look at yourself in the mirror when you get dressed to make sure your clothes still fit appropriately. If the clothes look flattering to your figure, that's okay, but if they look like you are trying to flaunt your figure, it's probably time to hand them down to a younger, less developed princess.

- If someone is standing over you or if you are bending over, could they see down the shirt you're wearing?
- Do your shirts reveal any part of your belly or back if you do the "hallelujah test" (lift your hands above your head)?
- Do any of your tops have sexually suggestive slogans (such as "sexy" or "flirt")?
- Do any of your jeans ride your hips so low that your underwear (or the crack of your rear) can be seen from the back? What about when you sit down or bend over?
- Do you own any pants that have lettering or graphics across the seat to draw attention to your rear view?
- Do your skirts or shorts end above your thumbnail when your arms are at your sides?
- Back up to a full-length mirror and then bend over to touch your toes. Are your panties or buttocks on display in this position?
- Do any of your skirts ride excessively high above the knees when you're seated? In other words, could someone sitting or standing in front of you

catch a glimpse of your panties or upper thighs if you fail to keep your legs crossed?

- If you wear a bra, do you have any tops that are see-through or cut in such a way that your bra can be seen by others?

If the clothes you wear pass this test, you can be confident you are dressing modestly. Clothed in righteousness, modesty, and dignity, you'll be representing your character well, teaching others how to treat you, honoring your brothers and sisters in Christ, glorifying God, and dressing like a true princess!

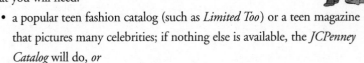

Creative Conversation

What you will need:

- a popular teen fashion catalog (such as *Limited Too*) or a teen magazine that pictures many celebrities; if nothing else is available, the *JCPenney Catalog* will do, *or*
- as a fun alternative, do this exercise on your next trip to the mall

As you flip through the pages of the catalog or walk the mall together, notice what the models are wearing. Also notice how the models pose in such clothes. For each outfit, consider the following questions:

1. Do you think these clothes would be appropriate for a preteen girl? a teenager? an adult woman? Why or why not?
2. What specifically makes them appropriate or inappropriate for each of these age groups?
3. What does the model look as if she is trying to communicate by wearing that outfit?
4. What do you think people interpret her outfit to say about her?
5. How would you personally feel if you were wearing those clothes to school? What about to church?
6. If certain styles are not allowed at school, is it okay to wear them to social gatherings or church where perhaps there is no stated dress code? Why or why not?

7. Think about your own clothes. What do you think they say to other people about you?

Close with a prayer, asking God to give you wisdom to dress in such a way that others see you as a stylish but modest girl with a lot more to offer than just a cute body.

being a friend
of influence

He who walks with the wise grows wise,
but a companion of fools suffers harm.

PROVERBS 13:20

It started when I was ten. I began floating from one "in crowd" to another, look-ing for a place to fit in. So I usually did whatever my friends did, even if it wasn't really my thing. When Kara and Amy tried out for cheerleader in the fourth grade, I did too. I actually had no desire to stand out on the sidelines of football games yelling and shaking pompoms, but I did for an entire season just to remain con-nected to my friends. However, I never mastered cartwheels or even the splits, so I retired from cheerleading the following year at the ripe old age of eleven. I didn't care that I wasn't cut out to be a cheerleader, but I was devastated that Kara and Amy soon began acting like they were too good to hang out with me anymore. I dreaded the daily bus ride home, because I knew the two of them would sit together and make up cheers and ignore me altogether. Fifth grade felt like it would drag on forever.

That's when Rachel took me under her wing. Rachel was one year older and acted like a cool big sister to me. She invited me to sit with her and her friends (mostly boys) in the back of the bus. There were other kids I could have sat with elsewhere, but those kids weren't "cool." Although I realize now they were good kids with level heads on their shoulders, at the time I thought they were too brainy or goody-goody to hang out with. I didn't realize I was treating them the same way Kara and Amy were treating me. So I took my place with Rachel and the older cool crowd.

In those backseats of Bus #19, I was introduced to games such as truth or dare and spin the bottle. It was fun as long as I got to be just a spectator, but I'll never forget the knot in my stomach when Rachel dared me to let Johnny kiss me. I assumed he would simply refuse, but when he didn't, I was on the spot. I had never had a boyfriend and felt absolutely no desire whatsoever to let any boy kiss me. But my desire to fit in drove me to disregard my disgust with the idea and pucker up. I later regretted giving my first kiss away on a childish whim in response to peer pressure, and to a guy I didn't even have a real relationship with.

I wish I could say I learned my lesson that day, but I continued to be negatively influenced by other friends over the years. In many ways I was strong. I never accepted invitations to parties where I knew there would be drinking or smoking or drugs. I knew those things were wrong, and my parents made it perfectly clear where they stood on those issues. But love and relationships were gray areas for me rather than clear-cut, black-and-white issues. I often got drawn into unhealthy boy-girl romances without realizing I could choose to swim against the tide of temptation rather than just go along with it.

So why am I telling you all this? Because I think I could have made better choices in life if someone had warned me about these common pitfalls of puberty. I was a pretty smart girl but had little common sense when it came to influencing, rather than being influenced by, my friends. But I hope you'll be different. I can't rewind the tape of my life, but I believe that with the right information you can make much better choices and therefore live without the regrets many other women and I have experienced. But before I share some tidbits about being a friend of influence, let's look at an example of true friendship.

JONATHAN AND DAVID

In the Bible, we read about the deep love and mutual commitment to friendship that David and Jonathan shared:

> After David had finished talking with Saul, Jonathan became one in spirit
> with David, and *he loved him as himself.* From that day Saul kept David

with him and did not let him return to his father's house. *And Jonathan made a covenant with David because he loved him as himself.* Jonathan took off the robe he was wearing and gave it to David, along with his tunic, and even his sword, his bow and his belt. (1 Samuel 18:1-4, emphasis added)

Most of us have had relationships in which we're wearing friendship bracelets one minute and stabbing each other in the back the next, but such was not the case with Jonathan and David. They were committed to truly loving each other and watching each other's backs. As a matter of fact, Jonathan betrayed Saul, his own father, for David's sake and went out to warn him of his father's plot to kill him. After Jonathan was killed in battle, David took Jonathan's crippled son, Mephibosheth, into the palace where he always ate at David's table. Jonathan's concern for David went deeper than his loyalty to his own father, and David's love for Jonathan continued long after his friend's death.

If you want to have a true friendship, such as the bond shared between Jonathan and David, you may have to extend yourself far beyond your comfort zone. What made Jonathan and David's friendship so special was that they loved each other as they loved themselves. They were as concerned with one another's welfare as they were about their own. If you truly love someone and are concerned about her well-being, you may have to speak the truth in love on occasion (and make sure you are speaking truth in *love* rather than in judgment—no one likes to feel judged). If you hear her saying things that aren't appropriate or see her doing things that you know aren't right, you may have to lovingly confront her.

In the coming years, you will more than likely see several of your friends making some big mistakes. Maybe they are not aware of the dangers of giving their hearts away too soon or fooling around with boys. If you love them as you love yourself, you will tell them the truth about their behavior, even if the truth is painful to hear. Proverbs 27:5-6 says:

> Better is open rebuke
>   than hidden love.

> Wounds from a friend can be trusted,
>> but an enemy multiplies kisses.

As you are watching your friends' backs, don't forget about watching out for your own as well. While you may have a friend who loves you enough to want the best for you, you can't always count on someone else's recognizing what you should and shouldn't do. Although you may need a little help from a friend now and then, for the most part you need to be able to recognize right from wrong for yourself.

Now let's talk more about what I wish I'd known about being a friend when I was your age.

RESISTING PEER PRESSURE AND BECOMING A FRIEND OF INFLUENCE

I wish someone had taught me the following principles about resisting peer pressure and being a friend of influence rather than being negatively influenced by others:

- *Drive rather than be driven.* You may recognize this from chapter 4, the chapter about a princess's Declaration of Rights, but I feel it's important enough to say again. You need to establish your own personal boundaries and rules for living rather than allowing others to make those kinds of decisions for you. If I had thought about it and sought God's direction first, I'm sure I would have never given that first or any other kiss away to someone I had no serious relationship with.

  Take control of your life. Consult with God and with your parents about important life matters, such as who you consider your friends to be, at what age you are ready to explore the possibility of a romantic relationship, how far is far enough to go in that relationship prior to marriage, and so on.

- *Popularity isn't all it's cracked up to be.* I know that every young girl desperately craves popularity—to be seen as cool and part of the "in crowd." Let me tell you a secret. Most of the people that you perceive to be popular probably don't even think they are! They are more than likely craving the same popularity as you. Popularity is a figment of imagination, and often seems just out of our reach. You can drive yourself crazy trying to get it, only to find that you've had it all along with some people and never stood a chance with others. A person who is viewed as popular by one person may be perceived as a total loser by another.

- *Just because something is popular doesn't mean it's right.* If your peers are doing something they shouldn't, they will try to convince you to join them so they can feel better about themselves. Think about it. If you were pursuing a boyfriend as a twelve-year-old and all your friends were chasing boys too, you'd probably feel okay. But if all of your friends were guarding their hearts from premature romances, you'd more than likely feel badly that you were chasing boys. That's why morality should be determined by God's standards, not the standards of your peers.

  This principle applies to other situations as well. For instance, just because several of your friends are abusing their bodies by starving themselves in order to lose weight, it's a foolish choice that can endanger your health and even your life. Don't ever allow others to influence you to make choices that are dangerous to your health.

- *There's a big difference between a peer and a friend.* A peer is someone in your age range, but a friend is someone who truly cares about you. You have many peers, but only a few care enough about you to help you make wise choices. Don't assume that just because someone is your peer that she is automatically your friend. Peers can't be chosen, but your friends can and should be handpicked by you. Choose friends who also have a strong faith in God and a deep desire to live with high moral standards. It doesn't matter what group they're in at school or how popular they are. What matters is that they share your love for Jesus and will be trustworthy companions and loyal friends.

- *What you tolerate you eventually imitate.* Sometimes people become friends with someone out of a desire to be included, but what happens if you discover that a friend doesn't hold similar values to yours? What if she does things you or your parents don't approve of? If you remain connected as close friends, you'll eventually become just like her. Choose your companions wisely. If you discover that your choice was not a wise one, and your friend resists your attempts to influence her for good, don't hesitate to move on to seek other, more like-minded friendships.

- *Reserve close friendships for people who truly want the best for you, just as you want the best for them.* Perhaps a friend of yours starts trying to tempt you into doing something you know isn't right. It's okay to care about that person and even try to help her, but know that she is not being a friend to you. Remember, a true friend wants what is best for you and won't try to get you to do things that can hurt you. You can care about this person and be nice to her, yet choose not to hang out with her anymore.

- *You can be a caring friend, but you can't be a savior.* I had a few friends when I was your age who started doing things that really concerned me. They flocked together during lunch, plotting how they could skip out on their last class so they could hang out together before taking the bus home. Sometimes they'd get on the bus smelling like smoke, so I figured out what they were up to. I talked to one girl I had known for a long time and told her I didn't think she was being very smart. I knew her parents would have a fit if they knew she and her friends were skipping classes to go smoke cigarettes. But she wasn't interested in what I had to say. She didn't consider it "loving" that I confronted her, but rather "annoying." She said I was a goody two-shoes.

    I share this story to make a point. If you try to speak the truth in love to a friend, and she won't listen, know that there is only so much you can do, such as pray for her. Sometimes you need to wash your hands of a friendship if you have done all you feel you can to help that person. Give her over to God; He knows what she needs and cares about her even more than you do.

Friendship is a gift from God, but we must be the kind of friend to others that we want to have ourselves: one that loves unconditionally and speaks truth into our lives so that we'll become all that God intends.

Creative Conversation

What you will need:

- pencil
- paper

Hundreds of newspapers carry the column called "Dear Abby." For years, people have written to Abby to ask her advice on what to do in difficult situations. In the coming years, many of your friends will experience difficult situations, especially in the area of sexual purity. They probably will never write to Abby. But they *will* very likely look to *you* for answers.

Are you ready to be a friend of influence? Do you think you can give others good advice when they're not sure about how to do the right thing? This creative conversation will give you good practice.

Pretend that Abby has gone on vacation and that she has asked you and your mom to fill in for her while she is away. Together, read the following sample letters asking for advice. Discuss for a few minutes what kind of advice you think would be wise in each situation. Then use the pencil and paper to write responses to each of these requests for help.

Dear Abby,

I'm twelve and most of my girlfriends have boyfriends, or at least someone who seems interested in them. I don't really feel the need to have a boyfriend yet, except that I just want to feel like one of the girls. Do you think I should find a boyfriend so I'll fit in better?

Boyfriendless

Dear Abby,

My friend who is eleven recently told me that when her brother's friend comes to their house, he forces her to kiss him and has even tried to put his hand up her shirt. She's afraid to tell her parents, but I'm afraid that if she doesn't, he'll keep on and maybe abuse her worse. What should I do?

Fearful Friend

Dear Abby,

My friends and I get together for slumber parties once in a while, but it seems like every time we do, whoever can't make it gets talked about behind their backs. It makes me afraid not to go for fear they'll talk bad about me when I'm not there, but then again I don't want to go because I feel bad afterward for joining in on the gossip and stabbing an absent friend in the back. Should I talk to my friends about how this makes me feel?

Backstabbing Buddy

Close with a prayer, asking God to help you live a life that sets a good example for your friends and to give you great wisdom about how to have a positive influence on your friends' lives.

toads or princes?

Love does not delight in evil but rejoices with the truth. It always protects, always trusts, always hopes, always perseveres.

1 Corinthians 13:6-7

Ask several elementary-age girls what they think about boys, and you'll probably get the same answer. "They have cooties!" But something strange begins to happen sometime around a girl's middle-school or junior-high school years. That boy who drove her crazy with his annoying habits a couple of years ago may soon drive her crazy in a completely different way—a romantic way.

So what happens when a boy begins to lose his cooties? That is when a princess must learn to discern whether he acts more like a toad or a prince and if he is worthy of her time and attention. In this chapter, we'll look at these issues:

- what to do when a boy acts inappropriately (like a toad)
- how to recognize when a boy acts respectfully (like a prince)
- the differences between boy friends and boyfriends
- why guy-girl age spreads are a concern
- what it means to "love him like a brother"

You may think of other issues or questions you want to discuss with your mom as we go through this chapter. I encourage you to write those down so you can talk about them during the Creative Conversation time. For now, let's get started with the first issue.

Knowing a Toad When You See One

What do you think would happen if a commoner entered a royal palace, walked up to the king's daughter, slapped her on her rear end, and said, "Hey, Sweet Thing! Why don't you come and hang out with me at my pad for a while?" She would likely shrink back in horror, thinking, *Eeeww! He must be referring to his lily pad because he's acting like a toad!* The king would waste no time tossing the commoner out of the palace, demanding that he never return. No princess should ever be treated so disrespectfully.

You are a princess too, and you deserve respect and proper treatment from everyone, including boys. Sometimes young men don't show such respect. If you act as if you enjoy their disrespectful comments or gestures, thinking it's exciting that they're flirting or paying attention to you, you're teaching them that you do not expect royal treatment. You're teaching them that it's okay to act like a toad around you. They'll never give you the respect you deserve if you don't require it from them right from the start. Remember, *you teach people how to treat you.*

There are many forms of toadlike behavior, such as inappropriate remarks, written comments, or physical acts. An inappropriate verbal remark may come from the cute older boy who says, "Hey, babe! Why don't you call me?" Or a guy can make a rude sexual comment such as, "Oooh, you sure are looking good in those jeans!" or "Can I have some of that?" Written examples include notes with sexual questions or comments or e-mails with sexually graphic jokes or pictures. Physical examples include pinching, grabbing, or rubbing your private parts (such as your rear end or breasts), blocking your path to get your attention as you're walking somewhere, and trying to hug or kiss you without your permission. Non-verbal examples include staring at your body parts, licking their lips, or making sexual gestures with their hands, for instance grabbing their crotches to catch your eye.

So what should you do if a boy behaves this way toward you? Here's a suggested step-by-step line of defense against toadlike behavior:

- The first time a boy talks or behaves inappropriately to you, *ignore him!* Chances are he's just trying to get your attention. If he doesn't succeed in getting that attention, you're making it less fun for him. Your ignoring him will embarrass him much more than if you were to respond at all.

- If he continues to talk or behave inappropriately even after you've made it clear by ignoring him that you're not going to play his game, it's time to speak up to let him know how you feel. Avoid making a big scene that gets him the attention he wants. Simply say in a quiet voice, "I don't appreciate the way you are talking. If you can't speak respectfully to me, then please don't speak to me at all." He may make fun of you for acting like you're too good for him, but he's just trying to ease his own discomfort by making you uncomfortable. Don't let him get to you.

- Feel free to involve an adult at any time. If you have ignored him and given him fair warning that you'd like him to leave you alone and he's still acting like a toad, it's definitely time to bring in an adult. Tell your teacher or principal, and definitely tell your parents. They can coach you about what else you should do, and they may choose to talk directly with the boy and/or his parents if necessary. If that's the case, don't feel badly for him. He needs to know that his behavior is inappropriate so he can learn to treat girls with the respect they deserve, and how better to do that than to call attention to his toadlike behavior toward you?

RECOGNIZING A PRINCE WHEN YOU SEE ONE

It's the theme of many movies and television shows; the pretty young girl ignores the nice guy who's crazy about her and would do anything to protect her, but she goes gaga over the rude dude who just wants to take advantage of her. Although it will be a few years before you begin dating, I want to give you some advice for down the road: *A princess should fall for a prince, not a toad.*

How can you know the difference? We've just talked about how a toad treats girls disrespectfully. A prince does the opposite. A prince is in awe of a princess and wouldn't dream of doing or saying anything to offend her. He keeps his hands to himself or reaches out to give the princess a helping hand, but never attempts to touch or grab her in private places for his own pleasure. He talks about things that are appropriate to speak of in public and that wouldn't offend or hurt other people's feelings. He understands that the princess belongs to the King, so he treats her the way her Father would want her to be treated, with dignity and respect. In this way, he honors the princess, the King, and himself.

If it is your desire and God's plan that you should marry some day, I pray you will ignore the toads and hold out for a prince who treats you as the princess you truly are.

BOY FRIENDS VERSUS BOYFRIENDS

Many young girls have no desire to deal with romantic relationships so early in life, and sometimes I am asked, "Can a girl just have boy friends? Is it okay if she doesn't want a boyfriend?" You bet that's okay, and probably more desirable at your age since it's going to be several years before you can date anyway.

During this season of life, however, you may have a boy friend who suddenly begins acting more like a boyfriend (in the romantic sense). He may begin talking to you more and more or waiting for you in certain places where he knows you'll eventually show up. He may tease you or even try to get you to do things that "just friends" don't normally do, such as hold hands, kiss, or leave the crowd to go be alone together. If that happens, remember the nature of friendship. Friends talk with each other, laugh together, look out for each other, and so on, but true friends don't go out of their way to turn each other's head or turn each other on sexually. Friends care about protecting each other's bodies, minds, hearts, and spirits and will avoid behaving inappropriately toward each other.

A DANGEROUS COMBINATION

Maybe you've thought that boys your age seem clueless as to how to be friends with a girl. Perhaps you have even become friends with an older boy because he seems more mature and willing to pay attention to you. While it's probably okay to have some friends that are not your exact same age, I recommend that you stick to friends (both guy and girl friends) who are in the same grade level or in either one grade above or one grade below you until you are closer to finishing high school. Why? Because during these preteen and teenage years, boys aren't just developing *socially,* they are also developing *sexually.* They may be more willing to pay attention to you, but it may be because they have selfish motives and find that younger girls make easier targets for sexual activity.

This was the case for me. Remember how I allowed myself to be put in the wrong place at the wrong time with the wrong person? He was eighteen and I was only fourteen. I wouldn't have felt as powerless over him had he been fourteen or fifteen himself. I would have had more courage to stand up to his toadlike behavior if we had been on the same social level.

Perhaps you're thinking, *Oh, but I'm close friends with a much older guy, and he would never do anything like that!* Guess what? I thought the same thing about Wayne, the guy who sexually abused me. I completely trusted him, and that's why I felt safe being alone with him in the first place. Sometimes we don't discover a person's true character until it's too late to protect ourselves. The best protection is simply not to allow yourself to grow too close to a much older boy. Develop friendships with boys your own age rather than trying to fit in with the older crowd. Then you'll feel more in control of the relationship and less vulnerable to temptation to do something inappropriate.

LOVE HIM LIKE A BROTHER

The Bible encourages us to love other people as if they are our brothers and sisters, because they really are our brothers and sisters in Christ (see Romans 12:10). But what does it mean to love a guy like a brother? How can a girl put that into practice?

Imagine if someone was messing with your little brother (if you don't have a little brother, pretend you do for a moment). What would you do? Chances are, regardless of how well the two of you do or don't get along, you're going to feel somewhat protective when it's someone besides you giving him a hard time. You're going to want to step in and let that person know you don't appreciate her treating your little brother that way.

Or imagine you have an older brother, and a girl at school is dressing immodestly and flirting with him big time. You know she goes from one boyfriend to the next, and you're afraid she's got your brother in mind as her next romantic target. How do you feel? Protective? Do you want to make sure he doesn't get his heart ripped out and stomped on by this girl? You bet.

Well, if you can imagine loving your brother enough to protect him from being teased, tormented, or tempted into an inappropriate, unhealthy relationship, imagine feeling that way toward *every* boy on the planet. Imagine not wanting to see any of your brothers in Christ stumble and fall into a situation where they're going to be hurt, used, or taken advantage of. If that's how you feel, not only are you going to want to protect them from others, but you're also going to try to avoid hurting, using, or taking advantage of them yourself.

Even if you grow to like a boy as more than just a friend or a brother and hope to have him as a boyfriend someday, don't act like a female toad and start chasing him, teasing him, or flirting with him. Continue acting just as a princess would, with honor, dignity, respect, and appreciation for the prince God made him to be.

THE GOLDEN RULE

As you learn to recognize when a boy is acting like a toad and when he's acting like a prince, you'll have a much clearer view of what kind of mate you'd like to have someday. Just remember that if you want a boy to treat you like a princess, you have to treat him like a prince. The golden rule says, "Do to others as you would have them do to you" (Luke 6:31). If you respect boys as friends and love them like brothers, they'll learn to love you like a sister and give you the royal treatment you deserve as well.

Creative Conversation

What you will need:

- pencil
- New Testament

First, read 1 Corinthians 13:1-13 together to find out what true love looks like.

Below are ten statements that a young man may communicate to you at some point in your friendship or future dating relationship. He may make these statements verbally (he actually says them in so many words) or nonverbally (he says them with his body language, but without using any words). You must be able to tell the difference between when a guy is being unloving and inappropriate toward you and when a guy is acting lovingly toward you.

Once you've read 1 Corinthians 13, you're ready for the test. Read each of the following statements, and then answer either *loving* if his words are a sign that he is treating you with respect and kindness, or *unloving* if he is being selfish and disrespectful toward you.

_____ 1. I want what *feels* best to me.

_____ 2. I want what *is* best for you.

_____ 3. Who cares if your parents think I'm too old for you? I think you're hot. Why not sneak out tonight and meet me somewhere?

_____ 4. I'm willing to wait until we are older to start going out with each other.

_____ 5. I'll love you *if* you let me touch you.

_____ 6. I love you, so I refuse to pressure you into doing something you don't want to.

_____ 7. If it feels good, we should do it.

_____ 8. If it feels that good, it's worth waiting for.

_____ 9. Our parents don't have to know what we do when we're alone.

_____ 10. I wouldn't want to do anything our parents wouldn't approve of.

Close with a prayer, asking God to help you know when a guy is acting lovingly toward you and when he is acting unlovingly toward you so you can know the difference between a prince and a toad.

Answers: 1. Unloving 2. Loving 3. Unloving 4. Loving 5. Unloving 6. Loving 7. Unloving 8. Loving 9. Unloving 10. Loving

sandcastles and glass houses

Everyone who hears these words of mine and does not put them into
practice is like a foolish [woman] who built [her] house on sand. The
rain came down, the streams rose, and the winds blew and beat
against that house, and it fell with a great crash.

MATTHEW 7:26-27

Have you ever spent a great deal of time and effort making a sandcastle, only to
watch it crumble in a matter of seconds or be completely washed away by a wave
that came far onto the shore? Building the castle can be fun, but watching your
creation come to ruin can be a disheartening experience.

I sat in my beach chair on Galveston Island, watching my children learn this
lesson the hard way. Repeatedly they filled and dumped their buckets of damp
sand in just the right places, carved doorways and windows using their shovels and
spoons, dug out surrounding moats, and built bridges. But the consistency of the
sand was such that if it got either too wet or too dry, the towers and pillars and
bridges would collapse.

In contrast, I couldn't help but notice a beautiful beach house just yards
behind us. It was three stories high and from the beachfront appeared to be built
almost entirely out of glass. I could just imagine the magnificent ocean views from
each of the rooms. Surely they were breathtaking.

As we basked in the sun and my children played the day away, building their
castle, it occurred to me that they were using the same material to mold their little
sandcastles that was used to build the magnificent beachfront house. You may not
know this, but glass is sometimes made of silica, or silicon dioxide, which is found

in sand. Sand is transformed into glass when it's heated to a very high temperature and melts.

Why all this talk of sand and sandcastles, glass and glass houses? It's the best way I know to explain that you need to prioritize your relationships. The friendships you're forming at this point in your life are kind of like sandcastles. You can have lots of fun building them, but it doesn't take much for a friendship between two preteens to come to ruin. Why? Because you're still building your social skills, and so are your friends, and it may take several practice runs before you get the hang of nurturing a rock-solid friendship that withstands the wind and waves of life.

I've had the same best friend for the past sixteen years, but we didn't meet until I was twenty-one years old. Between the fourth grade and my junior year of college, I probably had between twenty and thirty good friends, but I've only kept in touch occasionally with three of them over the past twenty years. Most of our friendships we enjoy as teenagers will eventually fall by the wayside, much like all sandcastles do.

There are, however, some relationships that I wish I could go back and invest more time and energy in as I was growing up. Why? Because they were much stronger than sandcastles. They were more like that glass house that withstands the storms of life and the tests of time. Who are the people that have remained a fixed part of my life? My mom, dad, and brother.

What makes family relationships much stronger than most of our friendships? It's kind of like what turns that sand into glass. These relationships have withstood a lot of heat! Our family experienced life together and weathered many tragedies and triumphs. We laughed together when one of us did something silly or when we gathered to watch our favorite television show. We cried together when my sister died and when my grandmother was diagnosed with Alzheimer's disease. We prayed together when my dad was laid off from his job and when he had to have his eye removed because of cancer. We've cheered each other on as we have pursued our own dreams and accomplished lofty personal goals. Even though living with your parents and siblings may seem like a burden or a bore to you now, there will probably come a day when you wish you had gotten to know them more and grown closer to them while you had the chance. Don't throw all of your efforts into building sandcastle friendships. Invest time developing some glass-house relationships with your family members as well.

In chapter 9 I said that the best practice for being in a committed relationship—marriage—is living in a family. Does it surprise you that I didn't say dating is the place where you get to practice what it means to be married? If so, think about this. Dating is spending a few hours per week looking your best and being on your best behavior, but marriage isn't like that at all. Marriage is living with someone, seeing all that person's best and worst characteristics, learning to tolerate annoying behaviors, working cooperatively to manage a household, and so on. Marriage is great, but it requires relational *work,* much like the relational work you have to do now living with your own family.

So what are some practical ways to build stronger glass-house relationships with the family God has given you? I recommend you begin by learning to speak their love languages.

LEARN THEIR LOVE LANGUAGE

In his book *The Five Love Languages,* Gary Chapman explains that people interpret love in five unique ways:

1. *Acts of Service*—going out of your way to do something nice for someone, such as make them a snack, clean that person's room, or run an errand
2. *Gifts*—giving someone a special card or a token of love or appreciation
3. *Quality Time*—carving time out of your day to focus attention on connecting emotionally with someone
4. *Words of Affirmation*—verbalizing how much someone means to you or paying someone a sincere compliment
5. *Physical Touch*—giving someone a pat on the back, a hug, a neck massage, a kiss on the cheek, or a similar physical expression of affection

One good way to discover each of your family members' love languages is to simply ask them. It would make great dinner or drive-time conversation for you to ask each family member, "What would mean more to you, for someone to do something nice for you, give you a gift, spend time with you, compliment you, or give you a hug?"

Once you learn what love languages each of your family members speaks, try these ideas to help you strengthen your relationships with your mom, dad, sisters, or brothers:

Acts of Service

- Surprise your brother or sister by making his or her bed.
- Offer to help your mom set the table or jump in and start folding the laundry without being asked.
- Get out a bucket, liquid detergent, a sponge, and the water hose and wash your dad's car one warm Saturday afternoon.

Gifts

- Cut some flowers from the yard to put on the dinner table for everyone to enjoy.
- Pick out everyone's favorite snack next time you go grocery shopping with one of your parents.
- Tuck a sweet, decorated note into everyone's purses, briefcases, or backpacks that says something like, *Guess who loves you!*

Quality Time

- Go watch your sibling's soccer game or ballet practice just to show your support.
- Ask if anyone wants to take a walk through the neighborhood with you after dinner.
- Ask a family member to go out on a "date night" with you once a month or so and plan a fun evening the two of you will enjoy together.

Words of Affirmation

- Compliment your family members when you see them all dressed up. Better yet, tell them how beautiful they are when they're not fixed up at all.

- Let people know how much you appreciate the things they do around the house and the ways they help you, such as writing down a phone message or taking you to school.
- Ask about other people's days and congratulate them on little victories, such as completing a major project or making a good grade on a test.

Physical Touch
- Never stop hugging your mom and dad and brothers and sisters. Everyone needs hugs!
- Give your little brother or sister a frequent pat on the back or a gentle shoulder squeeze.
- Offer to give free back massages or foot rubs at the end of a long day. Using the person's favorite fragranced lotion makes it an even more delightful experience for you both.

As you continue to grow older, you will naturally feel the need to experience more and more independence and freedom. But know that you can gain independence and freedom without losing the love you have for your family members. Enjoying your mom, dad, and siblings now will not only allow you to feel closer to them throughout your lifetime, but will also prepare you to more fully enjoy your own husband and children someday.

Creative Conversation

What you will need:
- eight to ten rocks for each of you
- Old Testament

Read the following passages and note their similarities:
- Genesis 28:10-22
- Genesis 31:36-54
- Genesis 35:9-15

Each time a significant event occurred in Jacob's life, he commemorated it with a stone pillar as a spiritual marker. Think back to the significant experiences you have had as a family—experiences that brought great joy, pain, fear, or feelings of victory. For each significant experience, pick up a rock and claim how God has used this experience to draw your family closer together. Then take all the rocks you labeled and find a special place, such as a corner of the yard or a flower garden, to establish a permanent place for them. Each time you see them, be reminded of God's love and mercy for your family and the loving relationships you want to continue cultivating with your mom, dad, and siblings.

Close with a prayer, asking God to help you maximize the years you have to enjoy living with your family and to show you how to create lots of loving memories together.

whiter than snow white

Surely you desire truth in the inner parts;
you teach me wisdom in the inmost place.
Cleanse me with hyssop, and I will be clean;
wash me, and I will be whiter than snow.

PSALM 51:6-7

I was ten when my Sunday-school teacher, Mrs. Joyce, taught a lesson I would never forget. Using a flannelgraph illustration, she created a vivid picture of a dream she had when she was a young girl, a dream she believed God gave her. In her dream Mrs. Joyce, stained black from head to toe with sin, stumbled up the hill to Calvary and bowed down at Jesus's feet as He hung dying on the cross. With her head held low because of all the bad things she had done in her life, she felt a drop of Jesus's blood land on top of her head. At that moment, the black stain of her sin vanished, and she miraculously turned bright white, radiating the purity and holiness of her Savior. Her sadness turned into overwhelming joy, and she was never the same again. Whenever her "whiteness" began to grow a little gray from other sin, she would imagine going back to the cross and praying, "Lord, make me clean. Wash my sin away again." She always knew that Jesus honored her request and that there was nothing she could do to make God refuse to cleanse her over and over again.

Why did Mrs. Joyce's Sunday-school lesson make such an impact on me? Because over the years, I also felt as if I had become stained black with sin. I had done some things that made me feel dirty and guilty. I felt shame over doing things I knew I shouldn't have and not doing the things I knew I should have. Even after

I asked God to forgive my sins, I later found myself feeling a little gray and needing to be washed in His blood again. I've come to understand that God never denies such a request, because He loves washing us white as snow.

We've talked about a lot of things in this book. We've talked about how to dress, how to talk, and how to avoid acting in ways that can get you into inappropriate situations with boys. We've talked about body image, what kind of media to expose yourself to, and how to protect God's gift of your sexuality. But we haven't talked about what happens if you fail in one of these areas. We've not talked about what to do if you feel the "blackness" of sin staining your conscience. Is it really possible that you can be totally forgiven? Is it really possible to be washed white as snow like Mrs. Joyce was in her dream? You bet. Princess, you can be even whiter than Snow White because of the blood Jesus shed just for you, for the forgiveness of your sin.

THE BIG IMPACT OF THE BIG PICTURE

Maybe you're not aware of what Christ did for you on the cross. Or perhaps you know what He did but are not sure how it affects you. So let's talk about what the Bible teaches and how it can impact your life.

When God created Adam and Eve, He wanted them to live in perfect unity with Him and enjoy close fellowship with Him. Because our Creator God is holy (meaning perfectly righteous), He cannot be in the presence of sin. Adam and Eve's rebellious bite of that forbidden fruit resulted in the first sin, and it broke God's heart to send them out of His paradise (where only sinless people can live) and into the world (where sin exists). We refer to this as the "fall of man," as it caused all humans to be born with the same sinful nature.

The Bible tells us we all sin and fall short of the glory of God (see Romans 3:23). In other words, none of us is perfect or holy enough to be in God's presence. But because He loves us so much, God desires for us to be in fellowship with Him, so He made a huge sacrifice to pay the price to rid us of our sin. In the Old Testament days (before Jesus was born) it was God's law that a perfect animal, often a lamb without any birth defect or blemish, had to be killed so its blood would get rid of the people's sin in God's eyes, or "atone" for it. But even when animals were sacrificed, people's hearts were still far away from God. It wasn't easy to obey all of God's laws, and most people just wanted to do their own thing, even if it meant sinning against God.

However, God had a plan to remedy all of that. First, He performed this awesome miracle. He sent His Son, Jesus, to earth as a human being, to be born through a woman who had never had sex with any man—a virgin. Jesus loved, respected, and obeyed His parents and God. He never committed any sin. The Bible says He was tempted to sin like everyone else but never gave in to that temptation (see Hebrews 4:15). He was the Lamb of God, without spot or blemish, sent into the world as a final sacrifice to get rid of our sin, once and for all, so that no additional sacrifices would be needed. Just as it was prophesied throughout the Old Testament, Jesus was crucified on a cross, but then He rose from the grave to prove He had victory over sin and death. He paid the penalty for our sin so we could enjoy fellowship with God once again and live for eternity in heaven with Him.

Jesus's blood is powerful enough to atone for all the sins any of us would ever commit. When He hung on the cross, He was paying for every person's sin for all time. He not only died for the sins you have already committed, but He also died for the ones you have yet to commit. It doesn't matter whether sin is in the past, present, or future—Jesus got rid of it all. Even if you had been the only person on the earth, Jesus still would have died just for you, because He loves you that much. Not only did God bridge the gap between our sinfulness and His holiness so we could be with Him in heaven, but He also sent the Holy Spirit to live with us, inside our hearts, where we can enjoy fellowship with Him any time we want. It's the Holy Spirit who helps us want to avoid sin and live a life of obedience to God.

Receiving the Ultimate Gift

Jesus Christ wants to be your personal Savior, to forgive your sins, wash you white as snow, and guarantee a place in heaven for you. He wants the Holy Spirit to live inside your heart to guide you into becoming more and more holy, to help you make wise decisions, and to show you how to live a fruitful (productive) life. But in order for you to enjoy these gifts, you must first *receive* them.

Think about this: Suppose I give my daughter a gift. It's in a small box. I place it on her desk in her room one day during her final year of high school. She sees the present and thinks, *Oh, that's nice. Mom gave me a gift.* But she doesn't open it. She goes off to work. She's trying to save her money for college, so she's holding down two part-time jobs and working as many hours as she can because she knows that getting into college and staying there for four years until she finishes her degree is going to be very expensive. Between tuition, books, rent, utilities, and food, she's overwhelmed at how much money she is going to need, so she works harder and harder and longer and longer hours. She doesn't have time to stop and open a gift. She's too busy trying to earn her way to college.

But if she would just stop to open the box, she would see a check for enough money to cover all four years of school and living expenses. She doesn't have to work to earn it. It's been given to her as a gift. But until she realizes its value and receives the gift, she's going to keep knocking herself out and falling short of her goal.

This is exactly what many people do with God's gift of salvation. They've probably heard the news that Jesus died so they can go to heaven, but they don't realize its value and don't open the gift. They think that if they're going to get into heaven, they need to work hard to be good and do all the things they should to gain God's favor. But they're overlooking the fact that we don't have to work to earn it. As a matter of fact, there's nothing any of us can do that's good enough to get us into heaven. The only ticket into heaven is the acceptance of Jesus's gift. The only way to holiness is to receive the Holy Spirit into your heart to guide you. It's not hard. All you have to do is acknowledge:

> Lord, I am a sinner. I am stained black with sin that I can't get rid of. But I know that the blood that Jesus already shed for me on the cross is enough to make me as white as snow. I receive the wonderful gift you've given me—the gift of forgiveness and eternal salvation. I want to live in heaven with you someday and fellowship with you forever. I want the Holy Spirit to live inside my heart

so that I can enjoy fellowship with you even now. Thank you for loving me, and I trust that you will teach me how to love you more. In Jesus's name, amen.

LESSONS FROM MY BATTLEFIELD

Before we close this chapter, I want to pass on to you a few lessons that I hope will stick with you like Mrs. Joyce's lesson stuck with me. These three important principles can serve you well and give you overwhelming comfort, peace, and security as you continue to grow in your relationship with the Lord.

1. *What Jesus did for you on the cross is enough.* You don't need an additional miracle to set you free from sin. When I was twelve, I did something terrible. I stole my grandmother's necklace. I didn't know until after I took it that it was a special gift to her from my grandfather. But by the time my mother figured out what I had done and confronted me with it, I had already lost the necklace. I apologized to everyone and went with my mom to buy my grandmother a new necklace, but I knew there was no way it would ever have the special significance that the one I stole had. I think I must have asked forgiveness from God at least ten times, but I never felt a peace about the situation until after I was an adult. While growing up, I beat myself up frequently over doing such a bad thing, and I never felt worthy of my grandparents' or my parents' love.

   Underlying all of my self-pity was the belief that Jesus's blood wasn't enough to remove my stain. I thought I needed some special miracle to set me free, and until I got that miracle, I felt I had to beat myself up as a way of paying the price for my own sin. But I can't pay a price high enough to cover sin. Neither can you. You must believe that what Christ did for you on the cross is enough! The price is paid and the gift of forgiveness has been given. You must simply confess your sin and receive the gift.

2. *God gives not only mercy but also grace. Therefore, forgiveness is not a permission slip to sin.* When you experience a moment of weakness and want to do something you know is wrong, don't fall into the "God will

forgive me anyway" trap. Instead rest in the safety net of Philippians 4:13, "I can do everything through [Christ] who gives me strength." God promises in 2 Corinthians 12:9 to give you all the grace you need to avoid sinning and live a righteous life.

3. *Conviction is from God, but condemnation is from Satan.* Conviction says, "Hey, this isn't right. You know you shouldn't do this. You don't have to do this. There's a better way!" Why does God convict you after you have done something wrong? Because He loves you too much to leave you in sin. He wants nothing but the best for you, and He knows that living in righteousness will bring much greater joy and fulfillment than living in sin. On the other hand, condemnation says, "You are such a loser. You've done it again—messed up royally. You know you'll never be able to do things right. You'll never be a good person. Just accept the fact that you are bad and there's no hope for you." Why does Satan say such things? Because he is the father of lies (see John 8:44) and comes to steal, kill, and destroy people's peace and self-esteem (see John 10:10). He wants you to think there's no way God could love you enough to forgive you after all you've done. But remember, one drop of Jesus's blood is all it takes to make you whiter than Snow White, and that blood has already been shed for you. Receive the gift and tell Satan to hit the road with his lies and condemnation.

MORE THAN ENOUGH

The Bible promises, "Therefore, there is now no condemnation for those who are in Christ Jesus, because through Christ Jesus the law of the Spirit of life set me free from the law of sin and death" (Romans 8:1-2). What does that mean? It means that because you have Jesus Christ as your personal Savior, you aren't a slave to sin. Sin has no power over you, because temptation never becomes sin without your permission. You can make the choice to turn and go the other direction. However, when we do fail to do the right thing, thank God that the blood Jesus has already shed is more than enough to restore us to a right relationship with Him.

Creative Conversation

What you will need:

- chalkboard, chalk, and eraser, *or*
- dry-erase board, marker, and eraser, *or*
- paper, pencil, and eraser

Write down as many different sins as you can think of. Some good examples might be lying, cheating, and stealing. Also review the Ten Commandments (see Exodus 20:1-17) for some other ideas.

About each one ask yourself, "Is Jesus's blood powerful enough to wipe away this sin?" If you answer yes, then erase each sin as you answer this question. If you answer no, leave that sin written down. Once you've completed the list, discuss your answers to the following questions:

1. Did you have any sins that were not erased? If so, what were they, and what makes you think these are exceptions to God's forgiveness? If not, then you are right—there's nothing God won't forgive when we come to Him with repentant hearts!

2. How does it feel to know that Jesus can remove each of your sins?

3. What difference would it make in people's lives if they understood that the price Jesus paid is more than enough to purchase eternal salvation and freedom from sin?

4. What difference can it make in your life to know there's nothing you've ever done in the past nor anything you could ever do in the future that Jesus's blood can't erase?

5. Rather than use Jesus's blood as a license to sin whenever we want (because we know we'll be forgiven anyway), how should we respond to God's incredible mercy?

Close with a prayer, thanking Jesus for His willingness to pay such a high price to purchase your forgiveness and eternal salvation. Ask Him to help you keep your heart as white as snow so you can enjoy close fellowship with Him.

the priorities of a princess

> For you created my inmost being;
>
> you knit me together in my mother's womb.
>
> I praise you because I am fearfully and wonderfully made;
>
> your works are wonderful,
>
> I know that full well....
>
> All the days ordained for me
>
> were written in your book
>
> before one of them came to be.
>
> PSALM 139:13-14,16

As we drove down a shady, tree-lined country road several years ago, I noticed my daughter (nine years old at the time) staring silently out the window. "Whatcha thinking, honey?" I asked.

She didn't say anything right away, and I sensed she was wrestling with the right words to say. Finally she spoke her mind. "Mom, I've been thinking. I don't think I want to wait until I get out of high school before I start dating."

My heart sank. What was she thinking? Surely not that she was ready to start dating *now!* We had talked a few times about what Erin wanted to do with her life, and previously she said it was ridiculous for girls her age to have boyfriends. But what now? Had all of that changed? I swallowed the lump in my throat and responded, "Well, sweetie, why don't we talk about it? What are you thinking?"

"I think God wants me to do something special with my life, Mom, and I don't want to wait until I get out of high school to start dating... I want to wait until I get out of *college* first!"

Now that may have been easy for her to say when she was nine, and Erin may very well change her mind about all of this before she graduates college. But I am incredibly proud of her for having lofty goals and for thinking about God's purpose for her life rather than letting herself be consumed with simply wanting to get married—as if that were the only goal a girl should have. While there's nothing wrong with wanting to be married, your first priority should be discovering what God wants you to do with your life so that if you choose to marry, you can select a husband who is willing to help you achieve those goals.

What about you, Princess? Do you sense that God has a special purpose for your life? Do you realize that when He created you in your mother's womb, He wove certain things into the fibers of your being? He gave you a certain personality and temperament, special gifts and talents, and a unique way of thinking and doing things so you could accomplish certain tasks He created you to do in the time you spend here on earth.

THE TRUE PURPOSE OF A PRINCESS

Maybe you've never thought about what your God-given purpose might be. Most girls your age haven't. More than likely, many of your friends think their purpose in life is to look as cute as possible, buy the latest fashions, hang out with the right friends, find a boyfriend, get married someday, and live happily ever after. Most of us have had those kinds of ideas since we played with our Barbie dolls. On every trip to Toys "R" Us we asked for new clothes for Barbie, other doll friends for Barbie, and a Ken doll so Barbie could have a boyfriend. Then we bought the wedding dress and tuxedo for Barbie and Ken, and for our birthday or Christmas we asked for the dream car and dream house to complete our collection of all the right stuff for Barbie. We often grow up with the same expectation that life is all about us—our friends, our boyfriends, our weddings, and the stuff we can buy to make our lives complete.

But God didn't design us just so we could accumulate the right clothes, the right friends, boyfriends, cars, and houses. He had a much greater purpose in mind when He made you, Princess! He made you to work alongside the King to advance His kingdom!

But what does advancing a kingdom other than your own look like? Do you remember how Mia Thermopolis discovered she was a genuine princess and an heir to the throne of Genovia in the movie *The Princess Diaries*? Early in the movie, her only dream in life was to have the cutest boy in school take notice of her and to experience her first kiss. Her dream eventually came true, but it turned out to be more of a nightmare. But her grandmother, the Queen of Genovia, helped her catch the vision that she was, in fact, a true princess. As a princess, Mia needed to fulfill the purpose for which she was created. Because she loved and trusted her grandmother, she respectfully submitted to accepting her royal role. Although it was a difficult decision to make, Mia put the best interests of others before her own selfish interests. She left her comfort zone, her school, and her friends to take her rightful place as the Princess of Genovia. All of a sudden, the things she used to stress about and the dreams she once had for her own life seemed tiny compared to the thrilling adventure that awaited her.

In *The Princess Diaries 2*, we see some of that adventure unfold, and Mia demonstrates her heart for others in a big way. Rather than soak up all the attention as Princess of Genovia while riding on a carriage in a royal parade through town, Mia stops the carriage in the middle of the parade. She hops off and walks over to a group of shabby-looking orphaned girls and tells them that they, too, are princesses. She takes them by the hand and brings them out into the streets to become a part of the royal parade and creates a grand memory they'll never forget. Her heart for the people of Genovia grows bigger and bigger as she learns the ropes and begins serving her country with love and compassion.

This, Princess, is your purpose as well. Jesus Christ, the King of all creation, wants you to know you aren't just *any* girl. You are *His* girl. And the first priority of a princess is to find out what the King would like her to focus her time and attention on. How would He like her to serve the people of His kingdom?

We've mentioned it before, but it's worthy of repeating—when Jesus was asked what our first priorities should be, He responded, "Love the Lord your God with all your heart and with all your soul and with all your mind" and "Love your neighbor as yourself" (Matthew 22:37,39). In other words, Jesus said the most important thing in life is for us to love God first, then love others as much as we love ourselves.

PUTTING PRIORITIES INTO PRACTICE

What does loving God first look like? How can we show love to others? How can we demonstrate the love we are to have for ourselves? Here are a few examples of loving expressions to spur you in that direction:

We Can Show Our Love for God By...
- reading our Bibles
- praying to Him
- telling others about Him
- memorizing Scripture
- singing worship songs
- taking care of the earth
- attending church
- obeying Him
- giving tithes and offerings

We Can Show Our Love for Others By...
- giving a friendly smile
- paying a compliment
- telling them about God
- volunteering to help
- avoiding gossip
- praying for their needs
- offering a hug or handshake
- forgiving them
- going on a mission trip

We Can Love Ourselves By...
- being a good student
- eating healthy foods
- learning more about God

- enjoying hobbies
- getting plenty of sleep
- forgiving ourselves
- maintaining personal hygiene
- exercising
- planning for the future

I've learned that the way to discover true fulfillment in life is by doing these exact three things: loving God first, loving others, and loving myself. Make those three relationships your priorities, and you'll enjoy true love, peace, hope, and joy, Princess!

FINAL WORDS OF WISDOM

As you continue to blossom into the young woman God created you to be, you can expect great happiness and joy, but also expect many challenges. You may have days when your emotional roller coaster takes a huge dip and you feel really down. You may be tempted to become a couch potato and even watch things on television you know you probably shouldn't. You might think about escaping into the World Wide Web for answers to your questions about life instead of turning to responsible adults for answers. Some days your girlfriends may act rude toward you because they're having a bad day. There might even be times when you're tempted to think having a boyfriend or being more popular would solve all your problems. (Not!)

When these things happen, remember *who* you are and *whose* you are. You are a princess who belongs to the King of all creation! You've been given many royal gifts from God. You know how to exercise your royal rights to protect yourself from people who don't have your best interest in mind. You know how to make royal choices to guard your own body, mind, heart, and spirit from things that might tempt you to sin. You recognize media monsters and now have the tools to keep them far away. You choose your companions wisely and value strong relationships with your friends and family. You've been given built-in radar to guide your steps, and you can be washed whiter than snow if you ever fail to stay on the right path.

Finally, with Jesus as your number one priority, you have a fantastic future ahead of you as you become the wonderful young woman God created you to be.

What more could a princess ask for?

Creative Conversation

What you will need:
- Bible
- baby picture of your daughter

Together, read Psalm 139:13-14,16, then discuss the following questions:

1. Mom, what were some of the dreams you had for your daughter when she was in your womb? Do you remember some of the prayers you prayed? How did God answer them?

2. Daughter, what do you think it means to be "fearfully and wonderfully made"? Look at your baby picture. Would you describe yourself as being made this way? Why or why not?

3. Do you believe God really ordains all our days before we are ever born? Does He really have special things that He creates us to accomplish for Him while we are here on earth? Why do you believe the way you do?

Now read Jeremiah 29:11, then discuss the following questions:

1. Mom, based on how God knit your daughter together with her unique personality, gifts, and talents, what do you think God's plans for her life may include?

2. Daughter, do you agree with Mom's ideas? What are the desires God has placed in your heart for your future? What do you dream your future will be like? How do you envision serving God and others with your life?

3. What are some things you can begin doing right now to work toward becoming that kind of person? How can your parents help? What kind of direction do you need from God?

Close with a prayer, asking God to help you make loving Jesus, others, and yourself your top priorities so you can make royal choices and live happily ever after.

BOOK 1

Chapter 1

1. D. Kirby, L. Peterson, and J. G. Brown, "A Joint Parent-Child Sex Education Program," *Child Welfare* 61, no. 2 (1982): 105-14.

2. M. L. Bundy and P. N. White, "Parents as Sexuality Educators: A Parent Training Program," *Journal of Counseling and Development* 68, no. 3 (1990): 321-23.

3. Advocates for Youth: Parents' Sex Ed Center, Washington, DC, www.advocatesforyouth.org/parents/.

4. Bundy and White, "Parents as Sexuality Educators," 321-23.

5. J. M. Benshoff and S. J. Alexander, "The Family Communication Project: Fostering Parent-Child Communication About Sexuality," *Elementary School Guidance and Counseling* 27, no. 4 (1993): 288-300.

6. Tina S. Miracle, Andrew W. Miracle, and Roy F. Baumeister, *Human Sexuality: Meeting Your Basic Needs* (Upper Saddle River, NJ: Prentice Hall, 2003), 263.

7. S. Singh and J. E. Darroch, "Trends in Sexual Activity Among Adolescent American Women: 1982–1995," *Family Planning Perspectives* 31, no. 5 (1999): 211-19.

8. Miracle, Miracle, and Baumeister, *Human Sexuality,* 271.

9. Miracle, Miracle, and Baumeister, *Human Sexuality,* 271.

10. Miracle, Miracle, and Baumeister, *Human Sexuality,* 272.

11. Centers for Disease Control and Prevention (CDC), *HIV Prevention Strategic Plan Through 2005,* January 2001.

12. N. L. R. Anderson and others, "Evaluating the Outcomes of Parent-Child Family Life Education." *Scholarly Inquiry for Nursing Practice: An International Journal* 13, no. 3 (1999): 211-34.

13. Kirby, Peterson, and Brown, "Joint Parent-Child," 105-14.

14. National Campaign to Prevent Teen Pregnancy, With One Voice, 2002: America's Adults and Teens Sound Off About Teen Pregnancy, Annual Survey, quoted in SIECUS (Sexuality Information and Education Council of the United States), "Shop Talk," January 17, 2003, www.siecus.org/pubs/shop/volume7/shpv70052.html.

15. Susan M. Blake and others. "Effects of a Parent-Child Communications Intervention on Young Adolescents' Risk for Early Onset of Sexual Intercourse." Family Planning Perspectives 33, no. 2 (2001): 52-61.

Chapter 2

1. J. M. Benshoff and S. J. Alexander, "The Family Communication Project: Fostering Parent-Child Communication About Sexuality," Elementary School Guidance and Counseling 27, no. 4 (1993): 288-300.

2. Tina S. Miracle, Andrew W. Miracle, and Roy F. Baumeister, Human Sexuality: Meeting Your Basic Needs (Upper Saddle River, NJ: Prentice Hall, 2003), 266.

3. Randolph S. Charlton, ed., Treating Sexual Disorders (San Francisco: Jossey-Bass, 1997), 5.

Chapter 3

1. Mary Pipher, Reviving Ophelia: Saving the Selves of Adolescent Girls (New York: Ballantine, 1995) 19-20.

2. Sharon A. Hersh, "Mom, I Hate My Life!": Becoming Your Daughter's Ally Through the Emotional Ups and Downs of Adolescence (Colorado Springs: Shaw, 2004), 43-44.

3. Dr. James Dobson, Preparing for Adolescence: How to Survive the Coming Years of Change (Ventura, California, 93003: Gospel Light/Regal Books, copyright 1999), 85-86. Used by permission.

4. Jane Meredith Adams, "Mommy, Am I Fat?" WebMD with AOL Health, http://aolsvc.health.webmd.aol.com/content/article/11/1739_50367.

5. Adams, "Am I Fat?" http://aolsvc.health.webmd.aol.com/content/article/11/1739_50367.

6. Margery D. Rosen, "Is Your Child Headed for an Eating Disorder?" Child (August 2000), 62.

7. Rosen, "Eating Disorder," 62.

8. Rosen, "Eating Disorder," 62.

9. Grace J. Craig, *Human Development* (Upper Saddle River, NJ: Prentice Hall, 1999), 286.

10. Jose Cano, interview by author (Teen Mania Ministries, P.O. Box 2000, Garden Valley, Texas, 75771, 1-800-299-TEEN).

11. Karen Conterio and Wendy Lader, *Bodily Harm: The Breakthrough Healing Program for Self-Injurers* (New York: Hyperion, 1999), 21-22.

12. Excerpted from pages 3-4, *What Kids Need to Succeed: Proven, Practical Ways to Raise Good Kids (Revised, Expanded, Updated Edition)* by Peter L. Benson, PhD, Judy Galbraith, MA, and Pamela Espeland, © 1998. Used with permission of Free Spirit Publishing Inc., Minneapolis, Minnesota, 1-866-703-7322, www.freespirit.com. All rights reserved.

13. Dr. Sylvia Rimm, *See Jane Win: The Rimm Report on How 1000 Girls Became Successful Women* (Philadelphia: Running Press, 2001), 16-29.

Chapter 5

1. Josh McDowell, address to the Association of Christian Counselors' World Conference, Dallas, Texas, October 1997.

2. Richard Wesley, "My Daughters, My Heart," *Essence* 23, no. 2 (1992): 77.

3. Monique Robinson, *Longing for Daddy: Healing from the Pain of an Absent or Emotionally Distant Father* (Colorado Springs: WaterBrook, 2004), 117.

4. Robert S. McGee, *Father Hunger* (Ann Arbor, MI: Vine, 1993), 213-14.

5. Linda Neilsen, "Your Father, Why Bother?" *Fathering Magazine,* 2004, www.fathermag.com/405/father-daughter/.

6. Joe Kelly, "The Father Factor," *The MentorGirl Voice,* January 2003.

Chapter 6

1. Gary Chapman and Ross Campbell, *The Five Love Languages of Children* (Chicago: Northfield, 1997), 101-3.

2. Rhonda Kelly, "Communication Between Men and Women in the Context of the Christian Community," Council on Biblical Manhood and Womanhood. Reprinted from *Faith and Mission,* Fall 1996.

3. Deborah Tannen, *You Just Don't Understand: Women and Men in Conversation* (New York: Perennial Currents, 2001), quoted in Rhonda Kelly, "Communication Between Men and Women."

4. Chap Clark and Dee Clark, *Daughters and Dads: Building a Lasting Relationship* (Colorado Springs: NavPress, 1998) 76-77.

5. John Hicks, "Developing Deeper Friendships Through the Art of Asking Questions" (Faith Encounter Inc., 1997), www.faithencounter.org/ deeper-friend.htm.

6. Robert Wolgemuth, *She Calls Me Daddy: Seven Things Every Man Needs to Know About Building a Complete Daughter* (Wheaton, IL: Tyndale, 1996) 59.

Chapter 8

1. The Kaiser Family Foundation, *Sex on TV: Content and Context,* 5 February 2001, found at www.nationalcoalition.org/cablechoice/mediastats.html.

2. Kaiser Family Foundation, Program for the Study of Entertainment Media and Health, *TV Sex Is Getting "Safer,"* 4 February 2003, http://www.kff.org/entmedia/20030204a-index.cfm.

3. "New Look at TV Sex and Violence," *National Catholic Register,* April 2000, 16-22.

4. "More TV Sex," *USA Today,* 30 March 2000, 1D.

5. American Academy of Pediatrics, "Sexuality, Contraception, and the Media," *Pediatrics* 107, no. 1 (2001): 191-94.

6. Karen S. Peterson, "Study: Teens Who Hurry Love Less Likely to Use Birth Control," *USA Today,* D6, www.usatoday.com/news/health/2004-01-12-birth-control-usat_x.htm.

7. Melissa Daly, "Let's Talk About Sex," *Seventeen,* July 2003, 112.

8. Lisa Collier Cool, "The Secret Sex Lives of Kids," *Ladies' Home Journal,* March 2001, 156, www.lhj.com/lhj/printableStory.jhtml?storyid=/ templatedata/lhj/story/data/15093.xml.

9. Cool, "Secret Sex Lives," 156.

10. Linda Marsa, "Pregnant Pause," *Seventeen,* 2001, 178.

11. Joyce Howard Price, "Teens Want to Wait for Sex," *Washington Times,* 17 December 2003, Nation/Politics section, www.washingtontimes.com/ national/20031216-102509-9120r.htm.

12. Mireya Navarro, "Experts in Sex Field Say Conservatives Interfere with Health and Research," *New York Times,* 11 July 2004, www.mnaids project.org/publicpolicy/news/ExpertsinSexFieldSayConservatives InterfereWithHealthandResearch.htm.

13. Tom Buford, *Your Children and Pornography: A Guide for Parents* (Madison, TN: Tommera, 2001), 5, www.nationalcoalition.org/cablechoice/

mediastats.html. Entire book is available for download at
www.firesofdarkness.com/Moms/YourChildrenDownload.pdf.

14. Andrea Rock, "Stalkers Online," *Ladies' Home Journal,* March 2000, 60.

Chapter 10

1. Survey of 1,000 teens by The National Center on Addiction and Substance
   Abuse at Columbia University, reported by CNN.com, "Study Finds Older
   Boys Are a Bad Influence," 2004, http://www.brudirect
   .com/DailyInfo/News/y2k/Aug2004/210804.htm.

Book 2

Chapter 1

1. In one study, after viewing fashion magazines full of thin models, female
   students were less satisfied with their own bodies, more depressed, and
   angrier. Leora Pinhas and others, "The effects of the ideal of female beauty
   on mood and body satisfaction," *International Journal of Eating Disorder* 25
   (1999): 223-25.
2. Sharon A. Hersh, *"Mom, I Feel Fat!" Becoming Your Daughter's Ally in Developing a Healthy Body Image* (Colorado Springs: Shaw, 2001), 111.

Chapter 2

1. Adapted from J. M Reinisch, *The Kinsey Institute New Report on Sex: What
   You Must Know to Be Sexually Literate* (New York: St. Martin's Press, 1991),
   quoted in Tina S. Miracle, Andrew W. Miracle, and Roy
   F. Baumeister, *Human Sexuality: Meeting Your Basic Needs* (Upper Saddle
   River, NJ: Prentice Hall, 2003), 268.

Chapter 3

1. Adapted from Tina S. Miracle, Andrew W. Miracle, and Roy F. Baumeister,
   Human Sexuality: Meeting Your Basic Needs (Upper Saddle River, NJ: Prentice Hall, 2003), 268.
2. Ed Vitagliano, "Study Finds Teen Sex, Suicide Are Linked, *AFA Journal*
   (October 2003), http://headlines.agapepress.org/archive/10/afa/ 62003e.asp.
3. Mike Mason, *The Mystery of Marriage: Meditations on the Miracle* (Portland:
   Multnomah, 1985), 121.